Retreat
FROM
safety

JOAN CLAYBROOK

AND THE STAFF OF

Public Citizen

Retreat
FROM
safety

Reagan's Attack on America's Health

PANTHEON BOOKS   NEW YORK

Copyright © 1984 by Public Citizen

All rights reserved under International and Pan-American Copyright
Conventions. Published in the United States by Pantheon Books, a division of Random House, Inc., New York, and simultaneously in Canada
by Random House of Canada Limited, Toronto.

Library of Congress Cataloging in Publication Data

Claybrook, Joan, 1937–
  Retreat from safety.

  1. Public health—United States. 2. Safety regulations—United States.
  3. United States—Politics and government—1981–   . 4. Reagan,
Ronald. I. Public Citizen, inc. II. Title.
RA445.C53 1984   363'.0973   83-24926
ISBN 0-394-72244-2 (pbk.)

Manufactured in the United States of America

Design: Robert Bull

First Edition

CONTENTS

ACKNOWLEDGMENTS

The authors of the individual chapters are as follows: "Infant Formula," Katherine A. Meyer; "Food and Nutrition," John S. Shepard and Sophy Burnham; "Drugs," William B. Schultz; "Product Safety," Joan Claybrook and Sophy Burnham; "The Health and Safety of Workers," Joan Claybrook and David Bollier; "Environmental Protection," Christopher Harvie and John S. Shepard; "Transportation Safety," Joan Claybrook and David Bollier; and "Energy," Michael Totten.

This book was a collaborative effort. Many people contributed ideas and editing suggestions. Phyllis McCarthy reviewed and checked all the chapters, prepared many of the notes, and guided the book to publication. In addition to the authors, Lori Abrams, Mimi Brody, Barbara Freeze, Allen Greenberg, Janet Hathaway, Joan Levin, Jan Pilarski, David Vladeck, and Sidney M. Wolfe, all of Public Citizen, reviewed the book for accuracy and presentation.

Carl and Irene Auvil, Natalie Marra, and Anne Strainchamps prepared research materials.

Among the knowledgeable individuals from other organizations who generously reviewed the book for technical content and clarity are Richard Ayers, Natural Resources Defense Council

(NRDC); Carolyn Brickey, Food Research and Action Center; David Doniger, NRDC; Fran Dubrowski, NRDC; Carol Foreman, Women's Policy Studies; Clarence Ditlow, Center for Auto Safety; Robert Greenstein, Center on Budget and Policy Priorities; David Hawkins, NRDC; Maureen Hinkle, Audubon Society; Carolyn Isper, Save EPA; Michael Jacobsen, Center for Science in the Public Interest; David Lennett, Environmental Defense Fund; Ralph Nader, Center for Study of Responsive Law; David Pittle, Consumers Union; Lois Roisman, Council on Foundations; Anthony Roisman, Trial Lawyers for Public Justice; Margaret Seminario, AFL-CIO; Philip Simon, Center for Study of Responsive Law; Thomas Smith, Public Voice; and Steve Wodka, Frederick Baron and Associates.

We are also grateful to the people who helped in the production and typing of the book: Barklie Eliot, Meryl Maneker, Judie Pasquini, Gloria Hestor, and Linda Keenan.

Also deserving of acknowledgment are numerous federal civil servants who wished to remain anonymous but still believe the government exists to serve the people.

INTRODUCTION

One hundred thousand US workers are exposed at their jobs to significant doses of ethylene dibromide (EDB), an insidious chemical fumigant used to protect fresh fruits and grains. Thousands of food products are exposed to EDB on their way to market, and recent investigation has found significant residues on food products. EDB can cause birth defects and is highly carcinogenic. It can also cause acute symptoms, often leading to death, as in the case of Robert Harris and James Harris, whose exposure on the job to EDB caused dizziness, numbness, and death in less than seventy-two hours. While the dangers of EDB are well known, President Reagan's Occupational Safety and Health Administration (OSHA) and Environmental Protection Agency (EPA) delayed even proposing EDP exposure limits for workers or residue limits for food products until they were publicly criticized by Congress and the press, and pressured by manufacturers—whose food products started being removed from supermarket shelves by concerned state officials in winter 1983–1984.

Commercially made infant formula contains many ingredients that are essential to the health and development of newborn babies. Without vitamin B-6, for example, infants suffer convulsions; without chloride, learning disabilities result; without thia-

mine, brain damage can occur. Some vitamin deficiencies can be
fatal. Mrs. Robert Bishop's son was fed Neo-Mull Soy formula for
the first fifteen months of his life. Because of a vitamin deficiency
in the formula, the child started to have difficulty running and
within six months was almost completely paralyzed. To prevent
tragedies like this, Congress passed a law and ordered the Food
and Drug Administration (FDA) to issue quality-control regulations for infant formula. While the Reagan White House delayed
eighteen months debating whether to issue the regulations, three
million cans of defective formula were sold to unsuspecting parents and consumed by thousands of infants.

Many Americans are trying to eat less salt because it is a
major cause of high blood pressure and heart disease. But unbe-
knownst to most people, canned soups and vegetables and processed meats contain huge amounts of salt, or sodium. Despite the
clear desire by consumers for sodium labeling on foods, the FDA
has refused to issue regulations that would help consumers make
healthier choices at the supermarket.

In 1981, the FDA announced it was instituting a "fast-track"
approval process for new drugs. One of the drugs approved under
this process, in April 1982, was a new arthritis drug, Oraflex, which
its manufacturer, Eli Lilly, heavily promoted with press coverage
and through mailings. Shortly thereafter, ominous reports began
to surface. A forty-seven-year-old American woman died with
liver damage that her doctor believed was caused by Oraflex. She
had been taking no other drugs and had no illness other than
arthritis when she started taking the drug. In June 1982, Public
Citizen discovered that Lilly's drug was associated with twelve
deaths in England, where it had been on the market for two years.
Even as the evidence mounted, the FDA refused to withdraw its
approval for Oraflex. It remained on the market in the United
States until more deaths were disclosed and the British decided to
ban it. Only then did Lilly decide to take Oraflex off the market.
The same month that the Oraflex scandal broke, Vice-President
Bush said, "I do want to stress that no one wants to expose American drug consumers to increased risk. Safety standards will not be
compromised. We wouldn't permit that."

Acid rain is formed from the emissions of coal-burning industries. It is carried by wind and later deposited on terrain hundreds of miles away, killing massive numbers of trees and plants and suffocating lakes. In the United States, emissions from the coal-burning plants in the Ohio Valley have destroyed millions of acres of trees and ruined hundreds of lakes from Wisconsin to Maine and Canada. William Ruckelshaus, President Reagan's second EPA administrator, made control of acid rain a top environmental priority and pledged to formulate a plan for action by September 1983. The White House Office of Management and Budget overruled Ruckelshaus, and the program is now on the back burner.

Every day, the Reagan White House makes decisions of critical importance to the health and safety of the American public. These are but a few examples. They illustrate the failure of the Reagan government to diligently implement and enforce statutes enacted by Congress to address the documented hazards of our technological society—dangerous drugs, polluted air and water, toxic chemicals, unsafe car design and engineering, and countless other known, significant risks.

Rather than bolster the federal health and safety regulatory agencies in their work to protect the public, the Reagan administration, animated by profound ignorance and rigid ideology, has inflicted severe damage on these unique institutions of our society. The agencies no longer respond to the needs of unorganized victims of technological hazards. Instead, they service the business executives and stockholders who are responsible for the hazards—a radical shift that can be traced to January 20, 1981, the day Ronald Reagan assumed the presidency from Jimmy Carter. This book concerns the basic power struggle between different segments of society over property rights and human values, and the role the Reagan administration has played in influencing the outcome beginning with that day in 1981. It is about the government's failure to carry out its responsibility under the law to strike a humane balance between the economic right of a business to act in its own self-interest and the public's right to be protected against unnecessary harm.

Who should pay for cleaning up polluted air? What level of

safety do we want for food and drugs? Who should bear the risk of exposure to dangerous chemicals? During the past fifteen years, Congress has heard the opposing points of view on these issues and decided to enact statutes to control the antisocial behavior of business enterprises and to preserve the quality of American life. Since 1966, four new regulatory agencies have been created to limit the complex hazards of our industrial society:

- the National Highway Traffic Safety Administration (1966);
- the Occupational Safety and Health Administration (1970);
- the Environmental Protection Agency (1970); and
- the Consumer Product Safety Commission (1972).

These agencies joined two existing agencies, the Food and Drug Administration and the US Department of Agriculture's Food Safety and Inspection Service (meat and poultry inspection), programs originally established in 1906. Finally, the Department of Energy, created in 1975, administers a variety of energy conservation and production programs of great importance to consumers.

Each of these regulatory agencies and their statutes were established after weeks and sometimes months of congressional hearings that documented corporate abuses which endangered the lives and health of Americans. The laws sought to remedy problems that consumers, acting individually through their marketplace decisions, could not influence in a meaningful way. Congress understood, too, that consumers were ill-equipped to protect themselves from enormously complex technologies whose risks are sometimes unclear even to their manufacturers. Moreover, many of the dangers, such as asbestos, toxic chemicals, food additives, or dirty air, are invisible and do not extract their penalties for a decade or more.

This "new" type of federal regulation, often known as "social regulation," differs from the traditional "economic" regulation of such industries as broadcasting, transportation (rates and routes), or financial investment. This economic, or "cartel," regulation that many businesses favor seeks to limit competition in the marketplace, regulate business access to the market and the rates charged, as well as perform other "referee" functions. The health, safety, and environmental agencies, however, were meant to act as *advocates* for consumer health and safety concerns whose importance to society cannot be measured in dollars. The chief goal of these agencies is not to stabilize markets but to *alter* market behavior, where necessary, to minimize its antisocial side effects.

Without government regulation, a manufacturer regulates the quality, content, design, and performance of products to suit *its* needs—and discloses only that information which serves its private ends. When the federal government regulates on behalf of health and safety, however, a measure of public responsibility is established for all manufacturers. This societal standard essentially governs the behavior of companies—in designing and producing a product, managing workplace safety and health, or disposing of industrial waste and pollution. Contrary to the rhetoric of the Chamber of Commerce, the question is not whether there is too much regulation in the marketplace, but rather *who* is doing the regulating—the manufacturer or the government?

Manufacturing companies and trade associations have usually resisted these regulatory laws because they prefer their own private regulation of our lives—an invisible, indirect, less accountable regulation controlled only by crude and often ineffectual marketplace forces. Occasionally, victims of private regulation pursue an after-the-fact liability lawsuit to recover damages. But by that point most victories are too little, too late.

Despite its obvious benefits to consumers, government regulation has been tarred by business groups as inefficient, often unnecessary and inept, and always irritating. Industry claims government regulations add burdensome new costs to the other fixed costs of doing business. Of course, industry rarely counts the benefits of regulation, for these accrue to the customer or the community. Nor do regulated industries like to acknowledge how they have often become more streamlined, efficient, and innovative as a result of the process and product changes stimulated by regulation.

Scapegoating aside, regulation is not motivated by spite or for frivolous reasons. By enacting health and safety regulatory statutes, Congress declares that business enterprises, in the course of daily profit-making activities, have intruded upon citizens' property rights in a way that conflicts with our social and moral values. The laws are enacted to prevent innocent victims from suffering harm by reducing the imbalance of power between the perpetrators of technological harm and the consumers affected by it. Thus, it is now unacceptable for children's sleepwear to be flammable, for drugs to be unsafe, and for meat to be contaminated or adulterated. The very enactment of these laws is a rejection of the mythical "free market" model and a finding that business is incapable of regulating itself in these areas to protect the public health and safety. The public understands and accepts this governmental role. Public opinion polls show that most Americans continue to overwhelmingly endorse the actions of the health and safety regulatory agencies.

The Reagan administration, in servicing its "constituents" (as former EPA official Rita Lavelle called the regulated companies), has abolished existing health and safety standards in wholesale lots and has virtually halted the development of new standards. Reagan's deregulation has been a rampage that has brushed aside rational, scientific arguments and scorned due process and democratic participation. The three-year war against regulation, waged from the inner sanctums of the White House and its Office of Management and Budget, has seriously altered the quality of America's air and water; the crashworthiness of new cars; the cleanliness of foods; the cancer risks of workplaces; the development of safe, efficient energy alternatives; and more. Virtually every American is affected in major or minor ways by Reagan's deregulation.

The federal regulatory process is governed, under the Administrative Procedures Act, by concepts of fairness and openness. Under the Act, an agency must publish in the *Federal Register* (a daily government publication widely available in public libraries) its proposal to issue, amend, or revoke a regulation. The notice must explain the proposed regulation in detail, describe the reasons for the proposal, and cite the legal authority under which it is being issued. The public must be given a meaningful opportunity to participate by submitting comments or testifying at public hearings. The agency's final decision must also be published in the *Federal Register* and must be supported by the public record developed by the agency and public comments.

The Reagan administration has often ignored these fundamental principles. In some cases, the public has not been informed of agency decisions. In others, the agency has conducted secret proceedings before inviting public comment. In still others, the rule-making record does not support the final decision. And the White House has been deeply involved behind the scenes in subverting the process.

The farsighted checks and balances built into the US Constitution nearly two hundred years ago have helped stop some parts of the Reagan deregulatory agenda. The courts particularly have not been receptive or deferential to the politicalization of the regulatory process. The Supreme Court and the federal courts of appeal have struck down numerous regulatory actions of the Reagan administration. In April 1981, the Occupational Safety and Health Administration (OSHA) tried to withdraw a pending challenge to the cotton dust standard that is designed to protect textile workers from the crippling lung disease byssinosis on the pretext of preparing a cost/benefit analysis. But the move was rebuffed. The Court upheld the standard and refused to permit a cost/benefit analysis, indicating its implementation is "part of the cost of doing business." In June 1983, the Supreme Court overruled the rescission of the automatic restraint standard for cars (requiring air bags or automatic belts) as an "arbitrary and capricious" decision.

In 1983, a federal appeals court chastised OSHA for failing to protect hospital workers from a cancer-causing sterilant, ethylene oxide (the agency was ordered to issue a permanent standard within a year). To avoid a lawsuit challenging its failure to adequately control benzene, another carcinogen, OSHA promised to initiate an expedited rule-making. Federal appeals courts struck down the EPA's attempt to reduce pollution requirements in various regions of the country and prohibited EPA from suspending regulations controlling toxic discharges into municipal sewer systems. The federal appeals court also forced EPA to reimpose hazardous waste incinerator controls that the agency had arbitrarily suspended without the required public notice, and in 1983, a federal district court overturned the Treasury Department's repeal of requirements for labeling ingredients in alcoholic beverages. The court said the revocation was "ill-considered and superficially explained." Thus, although numerous decisions to deregulate or to not issue standards have not been challenged in the courts during the Reagan term, and some others have been upheld, it is clear that the courts have been skeptical of the ideological drive to eliminate or drastically weaken health and safety standards.

Congress, too, has resisted supporting the Reagan campaign against regulation. Despite considerable administration pressure, none of the health and safety laws have been significantly altered. In the environmental area, this is particularly important because the clean air and clean water statutes are written with great specificity and include deadlines that agencies must meet. A massive battle to amend the Clean Air Act in 1981 and 1982 failed to make any headway because of the raw determination of Rep. Henry Waxman (D-Calif.), the chairman of the Health Subcommittee in the House of Representatives, and Sen. Robert Stafford (R-Vt.), chairman of the Public Works Committee in the Senate. Vigorous attempts to cut back the pesticide laws have also failed. In fact, nine out of ten major environmental statutes currently up for renewal are awaiting action by Congress. Amendments to weaken the Delaney Clause, which bans cancer-causing additives in foods, have been stalled in Congress for two years. In short, it is unlikely that the administration will succeed in making wholesale revisions in health and safety laws, as business lobbyists had initially hoped.

If Congress and the courts disapproved of much of Reagan's deregulatory agenda, and could occasionally thwart its advance, there is much that the Reagan deregulators have accomplished on their own, administratively. This is indeed where they have focused their efforts. Their chief tools in this area have been budget cuts, staff reductions, and enormous enforcement cutbacks. While condemning crime in the streets and welfare cheaters, Reagan has drastically cut funds and activities to enforce the law against companies who violate health and safety standards or fail to recall defective products. Enforcement activities have been cut more than 50 percent in most of these agencies, and information about regular offenders, which used to be publicized, is no longer available. Rep. Albert Gore, Jr. (D-Tenn.) described the result: "They just decided not to enforce the law. This sets up a conflict between those who would obey the law and those who would violate it, and gives the advantage to the violators." The irony has apparently been lost on presidential counselor Edwin Meese, honored as "Crimefighter of the Year" by the Conservative Free Congress and Education Foundation, and on Attorney General William French Smith, who has called for tougher criminal laws and enforcement—for individuals, not corporations.

Several administration officials have been at the vanguard of the deregulatory campaigns. The most visible is Vice-President George Bush, who headed up the Task Force on Regulatory Relief that was formed in March 1981. Working closely with Bush and the task force have been Office of Management and Budget (OMB) director David Stockman; Christopher DeMuth, head of the OMB Office of Information and Regulatory Affairs; and James Tozzi, his assistant, who resigned in 1983 in order to represent private clients. The task force and OMB collaborated closely in identifying "burdensome" regulations, soliciting industry's views, and intimidating agencies to "suspend" or eliminate certain regulations.

Not long after the task force was formed, White House staff boasted about its role of servicing industry interests. C. Boyden Gray, who represented a number of America's large industries in private practice and now is legal counsel to Vice-President George Bush, told the members of the US Chamber of Commerce that his office welcomed the opportunity to intervene on their behalf:

> If you go to the agency first, don't be too pessimistic if they can't solve the problem there. If they don't, that's what the Task Force is for. Two weeks ago [a group] showed up and I asked if they had a problem. They said they did, and we made a couple of phone calls and straightened it out, alerted the top people at the agency that there was a little hanky-panky going on at the bottom of the agency, and it was cleared up very rapidly—so the system does work if you use it as a sort of an appeal. You can act as a double check on the agency that you might encounter problems with.

But the heady destruction of government programs during Reagan's first two years was slowed considerably by congressional investigations in late 1982 that revealed a series of scandals at the

EPA. The revelations essentially marked the end of Reagan's most brazen regulatory rollbacks, and immediately cast suspicion on the decisions of other agencies. The press became more alert to the alarming scope and consequences of the deregulatory mayhem. The public became more sensitized as well, with daily headlines and lead stories on the evening television news about cover-ups and conflicts of interest. Reagan was forced to dismiss his appointees at EPA and persuaded William Ruckelshaus, with his reputation as Mr. Clean, to give EPA integrity again. Five months after Anne Burford had resigned as EPA administrator, the Bush task force quietly closed its doors. The vice-president did not even attend the final press conference. One high-level White House aide commented, "Deregulation doesn't have the same priority for us it used to have. The political dividends aren't very high."

As public opinion, Congress, and the courts caught up with Reagan's antigovernment cowboys, a period of normalization began. The dismissal of personnel stopped, the indiscriminate attacks on entire programs subsided, and a few relatively minor safety and environmental standards actually began to be issued by some agencies. But Reagan's top regulatory czars continued to pursue procedural, backdoor strategies to deregulate, keeping most of them away from the media spotlight. Rep. John Dingell (D-Mich.), the combative chairman of the House Energy and Commerce Committee, described the president's attitude toward Congress: "You go ahead and write the substance [of a given federal program], and I'll write the procedure and I'll shaft you every time."

While many of the administration's deregulatory strategies, therefore, came to rest on procedure, their intent was highly substantive. The administration's plan has three primary components. First, all decisions about regulation are centralized in the White House and the OMB, which has based many of these decisions on political considerations. This has required a tight web of secrecy to shield OMB's questionable off-the-record contacts with regulated industries and its strong-arm pressures against agencies. Second, the scientific framework for regulatory decisions has been largely discarded and highly discretionary tools—chiefly cost/benefit analysis, weaker cancer guidelines, and "voluntary" regulation—have been substituted. In the guise of more rigorous analyses, the deregulators actually subverted the government's scientific and research capabilities and conducted slipshod regulatory analyses. Third, the Reagan deregulators systematically undercut public access to government information and to the regulatory process itself.

Centralizing and Politicizing Regulation

This has been the centerpiece of the Reagan deregulatory battle plan. Without consulting Congress, Reagan made OMB the clearance center for all regulatory decisions, within three weeks of taking office, by issuing Executive Order 12291. The order sets up new procedures shifting authority over major regulations from cabinet secretaries to the OMB. The executive order also authorizes the OMB to require sweeping analyses of proposed regulations, to review existing programs, and to postpone and eliminate regulations. The significance of these changes was noted by Representative Gore, a vocal critic of the Reagan regulators: "The critical question is, who makes the decision on the substance of a regulation? Is it made in the agency where the procedural safeguards are present, or is it made in OMB, outside those procedural safeguards?"

The answer is now quite clear. By dint of its historical authority to set the president's budget agency by agency, and its responsibility to control paperwork and approve government requests for industry data, the OMB is now in total control—of agency budgets, agency information, and agency regulatory decisions. This enormous power has been harnessed by the Reagan OMB (Stockman, DeMuth, Tozzi) and the White House itself (Reagan, Bush). Empowered as no other White House office ever has been, Reagan's OMB set about working behind the scenes, in concert with regulated industries, to eliminate government safety and environmental standards, often with only passing regard for the agencies' statutory obligations.

It is revealing that most of the initial standards targeted by the administration for elimination or amendment came from lists supplied by the regulated industries. On April 6, 1981, for example, Vice-President Bush announced thirty-four "Actions to

Help the US Auto Industry"—a list adapted from a longer shopping list prepared by Ford, General Motors, and Chrysler. The thirty-four "actions" dealt with existing standards and proposals of the National Highway Traffic Safety Administration (NHTSA) and the Environmental Protection Agency (EPA) to reduce auto deaths and injuries and to curb auto emissions. Consumer and environmental organizations were never consulted for their comments.

In June 1981, a legal specialist of the Congressional Research Service challenged the constitutionality and legality of Reagan's Executive Order 12291. In a major report, Morton Rosenberg argued that the executive order is illegal because it "totally displaces" the "discretionary authority of agency decision-makers," in violation of congressional statutes, and centralizes that authority in another agency, the OMB. To protect against legal challenges and enlarge OMB's legal authority, Reagan lobbyists pressed to enact a deceptively titled "regulatory reform" bill that would institutionalize the procedural changes included in the executive order. The bill centralizes power in the White House, excludes the public from the regulatory process, and bypasses the fairness requirements of the Administrative Procedures Act. The bill would also make the independent regulatory commissions, such as the Consumer Product Safety Commission and the Federal Trade Commission, conform to the political control of the OMB for the first time in history. Although the bill passed the Senate unanimously in 1981, it was stopped in the House by the opposition of a number of Democratic committee chairmen who oversee the various regulatory programs. It now has minimal chances for enactment by the end of Reagan's term.

The executive order not only provided the administration with the ostensible legal rationale for seizing power that formerly belonged to regulatory agencies, it ushered in a new era of regulatory subversion in which regulated industries and sympathetic government officials could broker deals and violate the law without any public record of the transactions. The examples abound:

- On behalf of the tire industry, the OMB pressed the National Highway Traffic Safety Administration

(NHTSA) to eliminate a treadwear rating system of great value to consumers.

- EPA's former chief of staff, John E. Daniel, testified before Congress "that the OMB stalled, tried to reverse, or altered EPA regulations on water quality, uranium mill tailings, and air quality standards." OMB also leaked proposed regulations to the regulated industry so it could bring tremendous pressure on EPA.

- OMB blocked the Occupational Safety and Health Administration's proposed regulations for the labeling of chemicals in the workplace. After six months, OSHA administrator Thorne Auchter was so angry that he asked beer magnate Joseph Coors, a key Reagan political supporter, to intervene with the vice-president to allow issuance of the proposed regulation. Auchter wanted a weaker federal regulation to preempt tougher state labeling laws.

- In 1982, the FDA and HHS secretary Richard Schweicker wanted to require aspirin makers to label their product with warnings about Reye's syndrome, a disease causing convulsions and sometimes death in children who take aspirin when they have chicken pox or the flu. But OMB official James Tozzi intervened on behalf of aspirin manufacturers and stopped the FDA from informing the public.

- When EPA's Anne Burford issued a regulation for high-level radioactive wastes over the objections of OMB, EPA's chief of staff John Daniel testified that he received a call from an OMB official warning "There was a price to pay for doing what we had done and we hadn't begun to pay."

- On November 7, 1983, Christopher DeMuth sent EPA administrator Ruckelshaus a letter chastizing him for interpreting the Toxic Substances Control Act too narrowly and for making "excessively conservative decisions" about potential risks of toxic substances. Several EPA proposals, including one on acid rain, had been stopped by OMB. DeMuth complained that the agency "can and should be more willing" to tolerate some risk in new chemicals "without imposing either controls or testing requirements. Presumably, some risks should be regarded as reasonable."

The pattern of OMB intervention was blasted by Representative Gore: "I think it was no accident that only thirty days after a secret meeting between OMB and the Chemical Manufacturers Association, the hazardous waste disposal regulations were ordered by OMB to be reviewed . . . that shortly after a secret meeting between the Air Transport Association and the OMB, air carrier certification rules were designated for review by OMB . . . that shortly after a secret meeting between OMB and the American Mining Congress, the Interior Department's rule on extraction of coal was postponed indefinitely."

Few of the Reagan deregulatory initiatives could have been secured without a protective veil of secrecy to hide procedural improprieties. That is why, once OMB had established itself as the point of access for regulatory decisions, its top officials became extraordinarily secretive about its reviews of agency regulations. They refused to disclose to the public or press which regulations they were reviewing, which ones they insisted be changed, or to document their *ex parte* (private, off-the-record) contacts with regulated industries for inclusion in the agency dockets. "One is impressed with the total lack of supporting documentation," complained Representative Dingell in 1981, "evidencing the reasons why a particular regulation was found to be inconsistent with the executive order [i.e., why it should not be issued]."

All this violates the underlying premises of the Administrative Procedures Act of 1946, which requires public access to the regulatory process and disclosure of information. Thirty-five significant instances of disregard for the law's requirements were documented in October 1983 by Robert Nelson of the Democracy Project. Nelson concluded that "secret and preferential influence is now characteristic of Reagan's regulatory process."

Slipshod Science and Analytic Hoaxes

The engine for much of the regulatory process is the scientific and economic research conducted by agencies. Research must identify and verify hazards, design test instruments for safety standards, justify new regulatory proposals, help industries determine how to comply with regulations, and design and adapt regulatory programs to be cost-effective. Yet the Reagan administration has undercut the scientific, technical resources of the regulatory agencies and has substituted such analytic hoaxes as cost/benefit analysis and "voluntarism." Currently being formulated are new cancer guidelines that would discount animal studies and require human epidemiological evidence—i.e., people actually killed, maimed, or diseased in significant numbers—before any action could be taken.

The anti-intellectual bias of the Reagan deregulators is most apparent in its budget and staffing cutbacks. Environmental research; energy conservation research; cancer research; research at the Centers for Disease Control; research in auto safety, drug safety, toxic chemicals; and consumer product safety—all have been drastically cut. At the NHTSA, the experimental safety vehicle program and the fuel economy research program, both critical for setting future safety and fuel economy standards, were eliminated completely. At the time, they constituted more than one-quarter of the agency's motor vehicle safety research. The knowledge developed in these regulatory agency research programs is critical to making effective decisions. It is the intellectual bank account for the nation. Not conducting this research inhibits citizen participation in government, hinders press and congressional understanding of government activities and inactivity, quashes academic research, and discourages business innovation. To drastically cut government funding for health and safety research is to destroy the seed coin for informed policies that can anticipate emerging hazards and the technologies to control them.

Similarly, these health and safety agencies have lost highly skilled technical staff whose expertise is vital to the functioning of the regulatory programs. Most agencies have lost over 30 percent of both their budgets and staff. The vibrant, idealistic younger staff has been discarded through reductions-in-force while the experienced senior staff has been lost through early retirements, transfers, and resignations. Ethical scientists have quit rather than promote or sustain programs they believe to be scientifically incorrect. OSHA scientist Peter Infante was fired (and later reinstated under pressure) for asserting that there is strong evidence that formaldehyde can cause cancer in animals. The brain drain will continue as President Reagan implements his latest proposal to severely cut back on the number of middle-management personnel. And future agency administrators will find it even more difficult to attract capable staff and get them hired through the Civil Service maze. Even outside experts have been discounted. Rather than engage in open, spirited debate, President Reagan has stacked advisory committees with ideological clones and dismissed dissenters. An EPA research bill was vetoed because it required the advisory committee to have diverse representation.

Even the government's Merit Systems Protection Board, which protects the rights of federal employees, has protested. (Two of the three board members are Reagan appointees.) In a recent report, the board speculated whether the government could stand the strain of severe personnel cuts. "Does the merit system have a point of 'metal fatigue,' a point at which critical elements in the alloy of its human capital fail and the 'framework of continuity' collapses?"

Besides cutting budget and staff, the OMB has exploited its control of government paperwork to restrict the flow of industry data to regulators. In 1980, without the specific authorization of law, the OMB initiated a new Information Collection Budget to limit the amount of information that agencies can request from regulated industries. Fifteen months before an agency can send a request for information to companies it regulates, it must estimate how long it will take them to respond in succeeding fiscal years. But realistically, no agency can know that far in advance what requests it will need to make, how many questions will be asked, or how long a company might take to answer the questionnaires. This Orwellian scheme, intended to minimize the paperwork of regulated businesses, has the effect of greatly restricting the flow of information to federal decision makers.

The result of the concurrent reductions in research budgets, talented and experienced agency staff, and agency information gathering capability is that the government has far less information than the regulated industry with which to make key regulatory decisions. It also encourages companies commenting on detailed proposals to withhold critical data because if it is not submitted voluntarily, the information budget and research funding limitations might prevent the agency from ever getting it. This is hardly the way to address complex, highly technical issues such as controlling cotton dust in the workplace or diesel emissions from motor vehicles. What inevitably occurs then are decisions based on whim, simplistic preference and intuition, or simply raw, crude data supplied by regulated industries without any critical analysis by an independent-minded government. And in many cases, the absence of knowledge and information prevents any decision from being made at all.

The subtle hypocrisy of the Reagan deregulators is that while slashing research and information programs, they insist (through Executive Order 12291) that agencies perform complex cost/benefit analyses of proposed regulations. Also, before a regulation can be promulgated, the benefits must be shown to exceed the costs, and the lowest cost alternative must be selected, even if it is not among the most beneficial. Although cost/benefit analysis is officially enshrined as an objective, neutral tool for evaluating regulations, its actual use is highly selective and biased. For example, it is not used to evaluate the need for tax expenditures, Pentagon appropriations, business subsidies, or other programs *favored* by business; it applies primarily to health, safety, environmental, and a few other regulatory programs. Moreover, the OMB summary worksheets do not even have space for listing the benefits of regulatory programs. The focus of the OMB review is on the alleged cost savings to industry based on information supplied primarily by the beneficiary industry. While benefit data is admittedly hard to acquire, and even more resistant to quantification (how much is your life worth?), cost/benefit analysis degenerates into a crude hoax when the benefit side of the equation is ignored. Cost/benefit analysis is, as a 1981 House committee report noted, "simply too primitive a tool."

Despite its boasts about pioneering a more rigorous, analytic approach to regulation, the Reagan administration has in fact moved willy-nilly to deregulate without having the faintest idea of the actual cost to the public. The Reagan White House has promoted the thesis that voluntary action by industry works and that modifying the behavior of the general public—for example, asking them to voluntarily wear safety belts—will reduce death and trauma without new product designs or installation of engineering controls. But the administration has not published any evaluations demonstrating that the health and safety standards they attack either do not work or are less effective than nonregulatory approaches. The serious analyses that have been made outside the White House confirm the time-tested notion that preventive remedies are far cheaper than treatment after harm has already occurred. "The main prevention program of the Reagan administration," commented Dr. Sidney Wolfe, director of Public Citizen's Health Research Group, "is one designed to prevent industry from paying the cost of doing business."

What makes the OMB's claims to scientific rigor so ludicrous is its own technical inexperience. "OMB has no technical knowledge," said OSHA deputy director of safety standards Thomas Seymour. "They get their slant from contacts in industry." Although the OMB successfully established itself as the clearinghouse for most regulatory programs, its staff has virtually no scientific expertise to analyze complex decisions dealing with toxic wastes, food additives, air pollution, unsafe drugs, defective consumer products, or automotive design and engineering. The OMB staff is comprised chiefly of economists and budget analysts predisposed to quantify benefit information, even though the benefits of life and health and clean air cannot really be quantified. In 1982, the General Accounting Office, the investigatory arm of Congress, confirmed that the Reagan regulatory analyses are inconsistent and inadequately documented; in addition, OMB's comments are rarely in writing, making it impossible to determine what role OMB plays. It also noted that even when effective analyses are made they could be ignored because Reagan's OMB reserves the right to waive the requirement for a "regulatory impact" analysis.

The slipshod science and bogus analysis conducted by many OMB officials and regulatory agencies reaches its culmination in gross misstatements about the success of the deregulatory program. "In contrast to the charges we have heard," said Christopher DeMuth in October 1983, "the air and water is getting cleaner. Occupational accident rates have been dramatically down. The highway safety rate in the last three years has been dramatically improved." Claims such as these are highly suspect not only because data-collection systems are no longer as reliable, but because as has been documented in the case of workplace and automobile deaths, the Reagan recession has led to drastic reductions in employment and much less discretionary driving by vulnerable populations that in turn has led to the declines in death and injury.

It is this kind of dishonesty that helped catapult Murray Weidenbaum's famous calculation—that regulation is costing American business more than $100 billion a year—into the limelight. Weidenbaum, a St. Louis economist tapped by Reagan to head his Council of Economic Advisors in 1981, arrived at this figure by multiplying the budgets of regulatory agencies by a factor of twenty—a crude estimate of the ratio of the cost of industry compliance to the agencies' budgets, based on studies Weidenbaum made in the early 1970s. Weidenbaum has promoted the $100 billion figure, and it has been widely quoted, but, in fact, it is merely so much hot air.

In the name of improved scientific rigor, the Reagan regulators are cooperating with the White House Office of Science and Technology Policy to develop new scientific standards for deciding whether to regulate cancer-causing substances. The only trouble is, these new guidelines represent a retreat from the scientific principles that have traditionally governed cancer regulation. For example, scientists generally agree that laboratory tests on animals are useful in predicting human cancer risk, that it is scientifically valid and necessary to test high doses on animals, and that there is no safe level of exposure to carcinogens. Each of these principles, which logically demand a strict level of carcinogen regulation, are being challenged. If weaker cancer guidelines gain respectability, regulators could reject animal data and insist that human fatalities occur before taking action to protect against exposure to carcinogens. Of course, by the time cancers are discovered in humans, decades later, it is too late.

Suppressing Information and Restricting Citizen Access to Government

The third major strategy used by the Reagan administration to cripple health and safety programs involves the suppression of information. The preceding section described how information gathering and collection has been crippled; the companion goal is to withhold government information that already exists. The federal government generates and distributes authoritative research, statistics, technical analyses, and consumer publications about the scores of technological hazards we face. The regulatory agencies are the fountainhead for reams of valuable information, commissioned in the public interest and funded by public taxes.

"A nation that is afraid to let its people judge truth and falsehood in an open market," said President John F. Kennedy, "is a nation that is afraid of its people." For the Reagan government, this seems to be the case. Mindful that some information can be embarrassing or explosive, or might undermine its policies, it has systematically tried to restrict public access to information about the government or supplied by the government. Consumer publications have been one of the first casualties. Overall, at least two thousand different publications are no longer available. These include "The Car Book," a comparative guide to car crashworthiness requested by more than 1.5 million consumers, and an OSHA publication on cotton dust for textile workers, which was later reprinted after its cover was changed and the text toned down.

When publications have survived the budget cutters, they remain available only at higher prices. USDA's "Dietary Guidelines," which had been distributed free to seven million Americans, is now sold for $2.25. Subscription rates for many periodicals have been drastically raised, including such basic documents as the *Federal Register*.

Despite its professed belief in "an informed marketplace," the Reagan administration has eliminated many consumer labeling proposals. New cars will not have crash ratings on their windshields, as once proposed; ten classes of prescription drugs will not be sold with "patient package inserts," leaflets that warn consumers about the risks and side effects of the drugs; companies making alcoholic beverages will not have to disclose the contents of their products on their labels; meat processors will not have to disclose whether their meat products contain a lower quality and potentially harmful "mechanically deboned" meat; the Department of Energy has refused to require energy efficiency labels for appliances. The list goes on and on.

Still other consumer information programs, such as the USDA's Nutrition Education and Training program, which educated children and school food managers about food nutrition, have been slashed. OSHA's New Directions program, which helped educate workers about workplace dangers, has been severely cut back.

Many government facilities that dispense information—libraries, information catalogs, film collections, and more—have been restricted by budget and staff cutbacks. Spurred by the OMB, many agency libraries have been reduced in size, both physically and in the number of volumes. And many government libraries also have shorter working hours. At NHTSA, the administrator terminated a contract for outside photocopying services that made it possible for the public, and the automotive industry, to get overnight service on documents in the public file. Now it can take three to four weeks.

On the surface, the suppression of government information may seem to be a policy that is more obnoxious than truly damaging. But in fact it perpetuates the tremendous information imbalance in our society between those who can afford to gather it, study it, and use it, and those who cannot. Government-produced publications, labeling requirements, and other information play a significant role in correcting this imbalance and represent one of the most cost-effective ways to empower citizens.

Beyond the many specific publications and labeling proposals that have been eliminated, the most serious assault on the public's right to know has been the Reagan administration's attack on the Freedom of Information Act (FOIA). This 1966 law, strengthened by amendments in 1974, is one of the most important bulwarks in ensuring that our government is kept accountable to the American people. Just as the Constitution sets up important checks and balances among the three branches of government, the FOIA constitutes an essential citizen "check and balance" on government policies and practices. The Act has proven invaluable to citizen groups in uncovering evidence of unsafe products and law violations, and in petitioning the government. Although the Constitution guarantees the people's right to petition the government for the redress of grievances, without adequate information that right can be meaningless.

But the Reagan administration has launched a lobbying campaign in Congress to make the FOIA more costly, cumbersome, and time-consuming to use. So far, defenders of the FOIA have been able to fend off major revisions in the law, but the pressure for weakening it remains strong.

Meanwhile, Attorney General William French Smith has sent a signal to government agencies implying that delays and resistance in carrying out the spirit of the present law *will* be tolerated. In 1982, he repealed a standard set by the Carter administration that agencies should release information unless it would be "demonstrably harmful." Under Smith's directive, however, the Justice Department stands ready to defend any federal agency against court challenges to their refusal to release information.

In January 1983, Attorney General Smith went even further by issuing new guidelines for waiving fees to obtain documents under the Freedom of Information Act. The most offensive aspect of the guidelines is the instruction to assess whether, in the agency's view, the public has any legitimate interest in the documents. The agency is also instructed to judge whether the requestor is sufficiently "qualified" to understand the information contained in the documents and to convey the "correct" meaning to the public. The FOIA makes no such distinctions. It presumes all Americans should have access to government information.

The Reagan administration's criticism of the Act usually focuses on arguments that it inhibits government performance and costs too much. According to a Justice Department estimate, the Act costs about $45 million a year to administer. That seems a very small price to pay to deter government waste and illegality. The Pentagon spends twice that amount annually on marching bands.

Given the enormous role we have asked the government to play in the relationship between business and consumers, there is a critical need for the citizenry to participate in shaping government decisions as effectively as business does. Beginning in the mid-1970s, funds were allocated by government agencies to assist citizens who otherwise could not afford to be represented in government regulatory decisions. These participation programs were just getting established when Reagan was elected. He eliminated every one. In mid-1982, Michael Horowitz, the general counsel of the Office of Management and Budget, developed legislation to drastically limit the payment of attorney's fees under sixty statutes in cases brought by private citizens and public interest groups against state, local, and federal governments. Often these groups, who do not receive their fees unless they win their case, would not be able to challenge arbitrary government action if fees are not payable. In addition, Horowitz has attempted to issue an OMB regulation (Circular A-122) using the government's leverage over government contractors and grantees to stop their advocacy activities before government agencies and on Capitol Hill. This overreaching caused a firestorm, since it affected defense contractors as well as consumer and poverty groups, and delayed its implementation.

When the curtains of secrecy are thrown over government activities, when the government refuses to reach out and provide citizens with the information they need to exercise their rights, when citizens are de facto excluded from involvement in government decision-making, the control of special interests over our society grows stronger. Only the most powerful gain when government turns off the lights. That is the real waste and fraud in the Reagan administration's war against the production and availability of information.

In 1980, Reagan was elected on a platform of "getting the government off our backs" and "regulatory relief." But what is relief and freedom from government regulations for industry, is hazardous to the health of the public at large. The most controversial regulations, those most opposed by business organizations, are designed to enhance the freedom of the citizenry by protecting them from disease, from death, from injury, from polluted air and water, and from the destruction of the land to maintain our heritage. Do we have more freedom if we can turn on the tap water and drink it without fear or if we have to boil it to assure we don't catch some dreaded disease? Do we have more freedom if we bump into a nylon bag of air in a 35-mile-an-hour crash or if we crush our head without one? Do we have more freedom if our child is injured by a dangerous toy or if she never had it to play with? Ronald Reagan has neither addressed nor answered these questions.

While this administration faithfully represents its narrow ideological concerns of the moment, it is unconcerned about the government's broader mission. As columnist George Will said several years ago, "Government exists not merely to serve individuals' immediate preferences, but to achieve collective purposes for an ongoing nation. Government, unlike the free market, has a duty to look far down the road and consider the interests of citizens yet unborn. The market has a remarkable ability to satisfy the desires of the day."

Indeed, his policies are like Alice in Wonderland. For example, the interest payments on Reagan's budget deficits exceed all the savings from his heavy cuts in social welfare budgets for the years 1982 through 1985. In 1981, Reagan argued that his economic programs would spur the economy and balance the budget by 1985. To accomplish this, social welfare program budgets were cut by $110 billion for the next four years, while military expenditures were increased and taxes were cut. The result has been huge deficits. For 1984 and 1985, they exceed $180 billion. The Congressional Budget Office estimates that the increased spending on interest payments for Reagan's deficits will cost taxpayers $124 billion for 1982 through 1985, thus swallowing up the funds Reagan saved by drastically cutting the social welfare programs.

By 1984, the deficits were a political issue in the election, and an embarrassment. To promote a frugal image, Reagan premiered a report prepared by business executive Peter Grace and a select group of white, male business executives on reducing government costs and improving government management. The Grace Commission identified over $400 billion in "waste" it recommended be cut from federal budgets over three years. Consumer groups complained, however, that the numbers were grossly exaggerated, that programs providing nutrition and health care for the poor (and other social programs) are targeted, and regulatory changes with little budgetary impact are recommended. In addition, many of the commission members are compromised by conflicts of interest, as their companies would benefit from the commission recommendations.

JOAN CLAYBROOK

Retreat
FROM
safety

INFANT FORMULA

INFANT FORMULA ACT OF 1980: ". . . To establish nutritional quality-control record-keeping, notification, and recall requirements necessary to ensure that infant formula is safe and will promote healthy growth."

D r. Shane Roy, a pediatrician in Memphis, Tennessee, was the first to put the pieces of the puzzle together. On June 20, 1979, a baby girl, only six months old, was admitted to his care at the local hospital for "failure to grow." Her condition was diagnosed as metabolic alkalosis, a chemical imbalance in the blood. Later that week another little girl, five months old, was admitted to the same hospital for "failure to thrive." She had the same metabolic condition. Having seen only seven cases of this condition in fourteen years of practice as a pediatrician, Dr. Roy thought it remarkable that he had seen two cases in only one week. He made a mental note that both infants had been fed the formula Neo-Mull-Soy, a product manufactured by Syntex Laboratories in California. About a month later a third infant, a baby boy, was hospitalized in Memphis with the same condition, metabolic alkalosis. When Dr. Roy got the call from the resident on duty, his first question was, "What formula is he receiving?" The answer started a nightmare for thousands of parents, catapulted Congress into action, and shook the public's confidence in the ability of our government to protect the health of our nation's children. That answer was Neo-Mull-Soy.[1]

Commercially prepared infant formulas provide a feeding

alternative or supplement for tens of thousands of infants. For many of these babies, formula is often their sole source of nourishment for the first few months of their lives. Their proper mental and physical development depends on the quality of nutrition they get during this critical period. Children who are fed nutritionally deficient formula can suffer severe mental or physical retardation, illness, or even death.

Babies were "failing to thrive," it was discovered, because the Neo-Mull-Soy formula was drastically deficient in chloride, a nutrient crucial to proper mental and physical growth. In fact, the chloride content was only one-fifth of what the American Academy of Pediatrics' Committee on Nutrition had stated was the minimum required for safe and healthy development.[2] Although much is unknown about the long-term effects of the deficiency, carefully monitored studies comparing children who have metabolic alkalosis with children who have not suffered the disease reveal that infants with the disease demonstrate a greater incidence of memory deficiencies, shortened attention span, and significant learning disabilities.[3] Letters from mothers who fed their children the deficient formula dramatically illustrate the seriousness of the problem:

> My son who was pronounced perfect and healthy at birth and who seemed to be thriving on the formula has been in special education for two and one half years now due to a major speech delay, learning disabilities, and related behavioral, emotional, and socialization problems. . . . This trauma has been a nightmare. . . . the fact that it was completely avoidable makes me sick with anger.

> My son was on Neo-Mull-Soy for the first fifteen months of his life. In the spring of 1979 he started having difficulty in running. Within six months . . . he was close to being completely paralyzed. . . . He is functioning but still cannot run.[4]

Tens of thousands of infants were exposed to the deficient formula before Dr. Roy's discovery led to the nationwide recall in 1979 of two brands of infant formula manufactured by Syntex—Neo-Mull-Soy and Cho-Free.

The Centers for Disease Control documented more than 140 cases of metabolic alkalosis resulting from exposure to these products. An organization of parents named FORMULA was established as the Syntex disaster gained publicity. More than five thousand parents have notified FORMULA after realizing that their children who were fed the deficient formula may suffer various physical and mental disabilities because of it.

But the 1979 Syntex recalls were not isolated cases of a manufacturer's failure to ensure that its infant formula contained all of the nutrients at the proper levels required for safe and healthy growth. In 1951–52, an infant formula called SMA was manufactured by Wyeth Laboratories, a subsidiary of American Home Products and one of the largest infant formula manufacturers in the country. It was deficient in vitamin B_6. The first danger signs in infants were colic or abdominal distress, spitting up, and hyper-irritability. These symptoms were followed by alarming crying, stiffening of the body, and upward rolling of the eyes, all of which became progressively more severe until convulsions seized the baby as often as six or eight times a day. Many of the babies were left brain damaged, with cerebral palsy, and with other disabilities.[5]

In the wake of the Syntex disaster in 1979, Congress and the public were shocked to learn that the content and nutritional quality of this vital food product were unregulated. Led by Representatives Albert Gore, Jr. (Democrat-Tennessee) and Ronald M. Mottl (Democrat-Ohio), the House Subcommittee on Oversight and Investigations of the Committee on Energy and Commerce conducted a thorough investigation of the scope of the Food and Drug Administration's (FDA) authority to protect the public from the marketing of nutritionally deficient infant formula, and of the FDA's and manufacturer's efforts to recall the defective products once the problem was identified.

The subcommittee found that the manufacturer's failure to test the products before putting them on the market allowed the chloride deficiency to go undetected, and that the FDA lacked the specific authority to require manufacturers to test infant formula prior to marketing in order to ensure that each batch contain the proper amount of all essential nutrients.[6] Finally, the subcommittee found that the FDA's efforts to get the two deficient Syntex formulas off the market approached a "total disregard for the health and safety of the affected infants," and that the manufacturer failed to cooperate with the FDA's slow-paced recall of the formula. The products had remained on the market three months after they were determined to be life-threatening.[7]

Congressional reaction was swift. Congress passed the Infant Formula Act of 1980 within months, giving the FDA clear authority to regulate the content and quality of these products, declaring:

> for parents to continue to have confidence in the quality of formula upon which their children depend, they must be assured that formula contains all essential nutrients and has been adequately tested prior to marketing.[8]

Signed into law by President Jimmy Carter on September 26, 1980, the act requires that all infant formulas contain twenty-nine specified "essential" nutrients at designated levels. It directs the FDA to establish quality control procedures to be followed by each manufacturer, including periodic testing, to ensure that all of the essential nutrients are present. The act also governs recall procedures and authorizes the FDA to inspect the factories and records of the manufacturers for compliance with the new law.[9]

Recognizing the urgency of the congressional directive, on December 30, 1980, just three months after the law was enacted, the Carter administration's FDA proposed regulations that were faithful to the new act. The proposal specified detailed quality control procedures consisting of sampling, testing, and analysis of the product during several stages of the manufacturing process to guarantee that it contained all essential nutrients at the appropriate levels, and strict record-keeping requirements.[10]

Enter the Reagan administration. Fifteen months went by and still the final regulations were not issued—this despite the fact that Richard S. Schweiker, Reagan's secretary of Health and Human Services (HHS) and the FDA's boss, had not only sponsored passage of the act in the Senate while he served as senator from Pennsylvania, but had also severely chastised the FDA at Senate hearings in June 1980 for its delay in acting to prevent similar disasters from happening again.

> Senator Schweiker [speaking to the FDA's commissioner, Jere Goyan]: You are telling us this morning that it's going to be another year from now before we get final

regulations. I am really disturbed about that time lag.
. . . I have got to believe there has to be some shortcut
procedure when children's lives are at stake. Surely, we
can come up with something within the bureaucracy to
solve a problem like this.[11]

What Richard Schweiker the senator thought was simply a
matter of bureaucratic inefficiency, Richard Schweiker the secretary of the Department of Health and Human Services quickly
learned was much more formidable—intense industry pressure to
scotch the Carter administration's proposal on the ground that it
would cost too much. The $700-million-a-year infant formula in-
dustry marshaled its forces to oppose the Carter proposal at the
FDA, calling it too burdensome and costly. But the industry had
discovered an even better channel to delay and dilute the regulations—private conversations with the top officials of President
Reagan's Office of Management and Budget (OMB). Under an
executive order issued shortly after he took office, President Reagan directed his regulatory agency heads to send all proposed
regulations through OMB for a "cost/benefit analysis." Under the
order, regulations were not to be issued in final form unless their
benefits to the public clearly outweighed their costs to industry.

While the infant formula industry and OMB were holding
up the issuance of final regulations, another disaster occurred. In
March 1982, two infant formulas manufactured by Wyeth
Laboratories—Nursoy and SMA—had to be recalled. As was the
case with the deficient Wyeth formula thirty years earlier, the
formulas were deficient in the essential nutrient vitamin B_6. This
time some fifty thousand cases of Nursoy totally lacked any vitamin B_6, and 2.5 million cans and bottles of SMA had levels below
those required by the Infant Formula Act, again posing the risk
of serious health problems including convulsions and brain damage for thousands of infants.

On March 11, 1982, the House Subcommittee on Oversight
and Investigations held hearings to examine the circumstances
surrounding the marketing of the deficient formula, the adequacy
of the recall efforts, and the reasons for the FDA's delay in issuing
the proposed quality control regulations in final form. At the
hearing a representative from Wyeth explained that the problem
was caused when an employee mistakenly withdrew the wrong

ingredient from the drums of raw materials, and vitamin B_1 was added to the production of the two formulas instead of vitamin B_6.

Under questioning by Congressman Mottl, a representative of Wyeth admitted that the company does not test its products "for everything" before selling them. It tests, he said, only "for some of the nutrients."[12] Later in the hearings Congressman Gore asked the Wyeth representative:

> On the actual recall, do you think a company with a two-hundred-million-dollar annual advertising budget has any obligation to try to get the message directly to American consumers when an incident like this occurs?

> The reply from the company official: I can't say I thought about it, Mr. Chairman.[13]

After reviewing the circumstances that led to the marketing of the deficient formula, then FDA Commissioner Arthur Hull Hayes admitted that "the proposed regulations would have, if followed by the firm, prevented this problem," since they would have prohibited the shipment of the formula before the manufacturer had laboratory results establishing that the essential nutrients, including vitamin B_6, were present at the required levels.[14]

When asked by Congressman Gore why the FDA had delayed issuing the quality control regulations, Commissioner Hayes testified that the agency had been waiting for the completion of the "independent" cost-benefit analysis required under President Reagan's executive order. He then announced that the economic analysis had since been completed and that, coincidentally, that very day he had transmitted the FDA's recommendations for a final rule to Secretary Schweiker for approval.[15]

On April 20, 1982, almost sixteen months after publication of the proposed regulations, the FDA published a final rule that dropped most of the requirements of the Carter proposal. Instead of establishing detailed quality control procedures, each company is permitted to use whatever system "is best suited to its needs." Moreover, the rule does not require the manufacturer to test the final product for all essential nutrients at designated levels prior to public distribution. Nor does the final ruling even specify any record-keeping requirements to document compliance with the quality control procedures that the manufacturer chooses to employ.[16]

Not surprisingly, the FDA's sole justification for abandoning the proposed quality control and testing procedures was that the new regulations were "more cost effective and more flexible."[17] An internal memorandum from an attorney in the FDA's Office of General Counsel candidly conceded that the final rule "basically reflects the modifications proposed by the industry."[18] Another internal memorandum from Commissioner Hayes to Secretary Schweiker explained that the option of issuing the proposed regulations was rejected because it was "too expensive," and that the FDA had instead incorporated "most" of the proposals put forward by the industry's trade association.[19]

Most incredibly, it turned out that the FDA's "independent" economic analysis was prepared by a consultant, Dr. Dennis L. Heuring, who for the previous eight years had worked for Mead Johnson Co., one of the two largest manufacturers of infant formula, as laboratory manager and then director of Nutritional Quality Control. In fact, Dr. Heuring was also the principal author of Mead Johnson's comments objecting to the Carter proposal on the grounds that it was too specific and too costly. Despite this clear conflict of interest, the FDA paid Dr. Heuring to prepare the economic analysis that became the primary basis for rejecting the Carter proposal in favor of what are essentially no more than voluntary regulations.[20]

On December 1, 1982, Public Citizen, on behalf of three consumer organizations and several parents and their children, filed a lawsuit alleging that the FDA's regulations violated the clear congressional directive of the Infant Formula Act to establish specific quality control, testing, and record-keeping requirements to prevent our nation's children from being exposed any more to unsafe infant formula.[21] Unfortunately, while that lawsuit is still pending, two more defective infant formulas have been sold to the public.

In August 1983, Soyalac, manufactured by Loma Linda Foods of Riverside, California, had to be recalled. It failed to contain the necessary amount of vitamin A, a nutrient designated as "essential" under the Infant Formula Act for normal vision, skin, and tooth formation. Although the deficiency was discovered sometime in May 1983, the company waited until well into July before taking steps to recall the approximately seventy-two hundred cans of the defective product.[22]

Then in September 1983, yet another infant formula had to be recalled when it was discovered to be deficient in the essential nutrients copper, vitamin B_6, and thiamine. The formula, Naturlac, manufactured by a company called Sunrise & Rainbow, contained only 50 percent of the copper required under the Infant Formula Act, and was also 50 percent below the levels of vitamin B_6 and thiamine declared on the product's label. Infants with insufficient amounts of copper can suffer anemia and other blood deficiencies.[23] Thiamine deficiency can result in neurological and intestinal disorders.

With defective infant formula making its way into the market with alarming regularity under the Reagan administration's minimal quality-control regulations, it is obvious to the congressional sponsors that their special legislation to prevent these kinds of tragedies has been rendered ineffectual. As a letter dated July 20, 1983, from seven members of the Senate Committee on Labor and Human Resources to the committee's chairman stated:

> A law is only as effective as the regulations which implement it. Without credible quality control standards, the Infant Formula Act of 1980 will fail to provide America's infants with the minimum protection they deserve. So long as serious doubts remain concerning the efficacy of the FDA quality-control regulations, we place these infants at risk unnecessarily.[24]

Apparently, when Congress thought it could rely on the FDA to protect our nation's most valuable resource—children—from the devastating effects of nutritionally deficient infant formula, it forgot that as administrations change, so do the priorities of the men and women in power. As this book will show, the infant formula debacle is by no means an isolated incident. In no uncertain terms, the Reagan administration's priorities are clear—profits for industry first, protection of the public's health and safety last.

FOOD AND NUTRITION

FOOD STAMP ACT OF 1964: "It is hereby declared to be the policy of Congress, in order to promote the general welfare, that the nation's abundance of food should be utilized cooperatively by the states, the federal government, local governmental units, and other agencies to safeguard the health and well-being of the nation's population and raise levels of nutrition among low-income households."

The American diet is among the best in the world. The selection of foods available to the American public is one of the most varied, and possibly the cleanest. Yet because of limited financial resources among the poor and bad eating habits among many segments of the population, many Americans do not or cannot eat well. The result is that our nation pays a high price for its hungry and its malnourished. In 1977, the General Accounting Office estimated that roughly one-third of our nation's annual health bills ($247 billion in 1980) could be eliminated if Americans ate properly.[1] Beyond the economic costs, poor eating habits and limited diets also exert a toll in human suffering. A Senate Select Committee Report estimates that poor nutrition is significantly related to six of the ten leading causes of death in the United States —heart disease, cancer, cerebrovascular disease, diabetes, arteriosclerosis, and cirrhosis.[2]

The recent recession has had a noticeable impact on the diet of the average American. Record levels of unemployment, the highest since the depression, together with rising food prices boosted by ten years of inflation have limited the public's food-purchasing ability, contributing to a general deterioration in eating habits. Hunger has also increased, once again becoming one of the most widespread problems facing our nation. While many churches and charities have doubled their efforts to feed the poor and needy, the continued presence of long lines at soup kitchens indicates that concerted government action is needed to alleviate the problem.

The federal government continues to be faced with the same issues in formulating its food and nutrition policies. But with a growing number of poor and unemployed, and a stagnating economy, there is a greater sense of urgency that the federal government forge ahead with its appointed tasks: to feed the poor, to supplement the diets of the needy, to protect the food the public eats, and to provide the public with information on diets and food content. But under the Reagan administration, these programs have not been a priority. In fact, they have been cut back.

NUTRITION

For the first one hundred fifty years of our Republic, neither the provision of food nor its quality and cleanliness ranked as a prime responsibility of the federal government. The first government-feeding programs started during the depression, in part to help farmers and the unemployed. But it was during World War II, when hundreds of young men were found to be so malnourished that they were turned down for the draft (their teeth rotting and their muscles poorly developed: a legacy from the depression years) that the federal government addressed the issue of providing young children with adequate nutrition. There is a certain irony in the fact that public attention was focused initially not out of altruistic regard for humanity but to find young men fit for war. In 1946 the government's concern and the enormous postwar agricultural surpluses led to the creation of the federal school-lunch program, which made free meals available to children of poor families, and reduced-price meals available to the needy.

The safety and cleanliness of food and the promotion of decent dietary habits had become part of the responsibility of both the Food and Drug Administration (FDA) and the US Department of Agriculture (USDA) at the turn of the century. The USDA Agricultural Extension Service had developed a tradition of providing information on nutrition to the public, as well as information on how to process, store, and preserve agricultural products and fruits. As far back as the 1890s the USDA researched the relationship between diet and disease.

During the 1960s the USDA expanded the distribution of surplus commodities to help ensure adequate food for the poor, and Congress enacted the food-stamp program. In the late 1960s strong-minded members of Congress—Senators George McGovern, Robert Kennedy, Ernest Hollings, and Hubert Humphrey, and Congressman Thomas Foley—started making a fuss about hunger and malnutrition in America. After the strong case made by the McGovern hearings and reports on the need to correct nutritional deficiencies, the federal government became involved in a number of programs designed to improve the diet of the American people. Senator Robert Dole continued to exert congressional pressure during the following decade. Specially targeted programs, such as nutrition supplements for Women, Infants, and Children (WIC), started in 1972, and funding programs for the elderly were then established; for children there were the school breakfast and lunch programs, the summer lunch program and the child-care food program for private nonprofit or public day-care facilities.

Reagan's Nutrition Budget Cuts

In 1981, Reagan took office riding on his campaign promise to reduce government deficits, to cut the budget, and to "get government off our backs." Reagan had promised cuts in social programs and he got Congress to approve them in his 1981 budget. Nutrition and other low-income supplement programs took a disproportionate share of cuts:

- The budget for child-nutrition programs was cut by 29 percent.[3]
- The budget for the school-breakfast program was cut by 20 percent.[4]
- The budget for summer feeding programs was cut by 25 percent.[5]

Overall domestic food assistance programs at USDA for fiscal year (FY) 1982 through FY 1984 were cut a whopping $8 billion.[6]

In 1982, federal cuts in Aid to Families with Dependent Children (AFDC) totaled more than $1 billion a year, along with cuts of nearly $1 billion in state matching funds.[7] The cuts left 365,000 families with no benefits and another 260,000 with reduced benefits. In nearly half the states those without benefits also lost medical coverage.[8] Reagan's response to those who criticized these cuts was that the states or charitable organizations would pick up the slack. But states themselves faced dwindling resources because of property tax cuts and reduced revenues from the recession. The wide range of federal cuts (Medicaid, unemployment benefits, low-income housing, public service employment, energy assistance, legal services) could not be made up by the states.

In June 1982, President Reagan, referring to social-welfare spending, said, "There have been no budget cuts."[9] A 1983 report by the Congressional Budget Office (CBO) shows that this is flatly incorrect. It analyzed a variety of retirement, health, welfare, nutrition, education, and job-training programs that together account for 96 percent of the government's social spending. It concluded that from FY 1981 to FY 1982:

- The food-stamp program's budget was cut by $1.53 billion.[10]
- Child nutrition programs were cut by $1.02 billion.[11]
- Women, Infants, and Children (WIC) lost $48 million from its budget.[12]

The slashing of the social-welfare programs has had a cumulative and devastating impact on the same group of poor people, and in particular upon the women, children, and elderly of our country. Taking into account the Reagan cuts, consider the following: women are considered to be the fastest-growing poverty group in the nation. Thirty percent of the households headed by women live in poverty.[13] Twenty percent of children under the age of six are living in poverty. At the 1981 poverty rate, the percentage for children under the age of six would grow from 20 to 25 percent by 1990.[14] For the elderly, the poverty rate is approximately 21 percent. If minority status for the elderly is taken into account, the figure jumps dramatically to 36.5 percent.[15]

According to a CBO report issued in August 1983, the social-welfare budgets cuts for FY 1982 through FY 1985 are projected to be about $110 billion.[16] The brunt of these budget cuts, the CBO report states, will be borne by families earning less than $20,000 a year. "Overall, about 40 percent of the federal savings from changes in benefit programs are projected to result from reductions affecting households with 1982 incomes of less than $10,000 —who make up about 23 percent of the population; and another 30 percent will come from reductions affecting households with incomes between $10,000 and $20,000—about 25 percent of the population."[17]

If the combined effect of Reagan's budget and tax cuts in 1981 and 1982 are taken into account, families with annual incomes below $10,000 will lose $20 billion in benefits over the four-year period 1982–1986, while the 1 percent of the population with income over $80,000 per annum will gain $64 billion in after-tax income during the same period.[18]

The CBO report indicates that the average annual reductions in benefits per household are also projected to be greater for households below $10,000 than for any other group, about $430; for those with incomes between $10,000 and $20,000, it is estimated to be $300; for those in higher income categories, it is estimated to be about $140 to $170 per household.[19]

The Reagan administration's budget and tax cuts disregard the worsening reality of poverty in the United States. The Census Bureau reports that between 1981 and 1982, the number of poor people rose from 31.8 million to 34.4 million—the third consecutive annual increase. (A family of four earning an income of less than $9,862 in 1982 is considered to be living below the poverty threshold.) In the face of these statistics, the administration's actions seem rash and will most certainly jeopardize what progress has been made in providing food and income assistance to the poor.[20]

The president, struggling to reverse his image in time for the 1984 election, started openly affirming his commitment to education, civil rights, women, the unemployed, and the hungry. To defuse the issue, in August 1983 he created a Task Force on Food Assistance. The task force was charged with investigating the incidence of hunger in the United States. The deadline for the group's report to the President was January 1984.

Congress, public interest groups, worker organizations, and numerous community groups reacted with anger. They responded:

- that it was Reagan's budget-cutting policies that had exacerbated hunger and caused unemployment;
- that hunger would have been worse had Congress approved all of his proposals and attempted cuts;
- that now was a time for action, not further studies.

Critics were quick to point out that the composition of the task force was not fairly balanced. Bob Greenstein, of the Center on Budget and Policy Priorities, emphasized that the task force "is heavily biased to the right and packed with strong opponents of food programs."[21] Members of the task force included academicians who had previously argued that the food programs were failures and should be cut back significantly, a former Democratic elected official who had a record of advocating cuts in food stamp and welfare programs, and a black former civil rights activist who had criticized public assistance programs.[22]

The Reagan administration's ignorance of the prevalence of hunger in the United States was brought to light in December 1983, when White House counselor, Edwin Meese III, was quoted as saying that he had never seen "any authoritative figures that there are hungry children" in the United States and that he believed that some people visit soup kitchens "because the food is free and . . . that's easier than paying for it."[23] Meese's statements drew an immediate uproar from Congress, anti-hunger activists, and even members of the president's task force on hunger. Former governor Edward J. King, a task force member, said of Meese: "If he's saying there just isn't any hunger, and I don't think he said exactly that, it just isn't so . . . . There are people out there who cannot take care of themselves. And the unemployment, like in Peoria, sticks you right in the face."[24]

Had Meese bothered to check his facts, he might have come across an October 1983 study by the Department of Health and Human Services, which indicated that as many as 500,000 low-income children under the age of six may be suffering from malnutrition.[25]

Reagan's Task Force on Food Assistance submitted its recommendations in January 1984. It concluded that there were local indications of hunger, but that there was no evidence of widespread hunger in the United States. Among its recommendations, the task force suggested that all federal food programs, including the food stamp program, be merged into a single block grant to the states. This proposed change in the implementation of food programs was not well received by congressional leaders, state governors, and anti-hunger activists. Most agreed that federal oversight is crucial in preventing such programs from falling prey to local political and economic pressures.[26]

One of the few constructive recommendations presented by the task force would allow for an increase in the food stamp allotment—from 99 percent to 100 percent of the USDA's lowest-level ("thrifty") food plan. As the *Washington Post* acknowledged in an editorial: "There is plenty of hard evidence that the current allotment is too low to allow many old people and families to get through the month, especially since [the allotment] assumes that the poor have more cash on hand to supplement grocery bills than is usually the case."[27]

Another advisory panel that became involved with food programs was the president's Private Sector Survey on Cost Control, headed by Peter Grace, a business tycoon and friend of the president. The Grace Commission, as it is commonly called, had been charged with the task of recommending to the White House "managerial savings" in government programs. It wound up recommending a whopping $7 billion cut in food stamps.[28]

The Food Research and Action Center (FRAC) and Public Citizen sued the Grace Commission, arguing that the commission was violating the Federal Advisory Committee Act (FACA), which requires that advisory bodies have "balanced" representation. In a partial victory for FRAC and Public Citizen, a federal court ruled that the commission was not sufficiently balanced in its representation to recommend repealing legislation affecting large segments of the population. Specifically, Judge Gerhard Gesell rejected the commission's recommendation to repeal legislation that determined the beneficiaries of food-stamp and school-lunch programs and the amount of benefits distributed. Such recommendations, Judge Gesell argued, "do not fall within the narrow area of cost and management control but fall directly into areas of general national import."[29]

School-Breakfast, Lunch, and Child-Care Programs

In 1946, the school-lunch program was established to ensure that schoolchildren receive at least one nutritious meal a day. Meal plans are designed to provide one-third of the children's daily vitamins, minerals, and proteins.

Under Reagan, federal support for the school-lunch program was cut $1 billion a year by 1983, or nearly 30 percent.[30] As a result:

- 3 million children, 35 percent from low-income homes, no longer receive school lunches.[31]
- 2,700 schools have dropped the school-lunch program.[32]
- 500,000 children, 68 percent from low-income families, no longer receive school breakfasts.[33]

In the tradition of George Orwell's "double-speak," Reagan and his administration manipulated language in order to disguise nutrition budget cuts. At the same time USDA was pushing to cut the child nutrition budget by one-third, it decided to save money by simply redefining snack foods—cookies, doughnuts, pretzels, and pie crust—as bread. Schools could also serve condiments— ketchup, pickles, and mustard—as a "fruit" or "vegetable." According to nutritionist Lynn Parker, of the Food Research and Action Center, the administration was trying to find a way to placate protesting school officials and food service personnel around the country. These officials feared that the 30 percent budget cut in school lunches would mean that large numbers of schools could no longer afford to offer lunch programs. "The administration's solution was to propose a reduction in the amount and nutritional quality of food children would receive at lunch time," Ms. Parker says. "This was not a sensible, fair, or popular solution."[34]

James Johnson, an aide to the Secretary of Agriculture, was quoted in the *Washington Post:* "I think it would be a mistake to say that ketchup per se was classified as a vegetable. . . . Ketchup in combination with other things was classified as a vegetable."

"What other things?" asked the *Post.*

"French fries or hamburgers," was the reply.[35]

The proposed definition change was later withdrawn by the administration amidst a storm of public protest. Budget director David Stockman called the proposed regulations "a bureaucratic goof," although, as USDA defensively pointed out, the plan had already been reviewed and approved by Stockman and the Office of Management and Budget before its public announcement.[36]

Reagan has also tried to do away with the smaller school-breakfast program. This program had been initiated as a pilot program in 1966 and was permanently authorized in 1975. It was established as an aid not only to nutrition but to education, on the theory that a hungry child cannot learn and that it is the country that benefits from an educated, literate populace. After cutting its budget by 20 percent in 1981, the USDA, in 1983, thoroughly evaluated the school-breakfast program. It found that the program increased the likelihood that children ate a breakfast of some sort and that they received a greater intake of milk products. But participants were found to have a smaller intake of vitamin A, vitamin B_6, and iron than those who ate breakfast elsewhere—not a surprising finding, considering that the participants represent the very poor.[37] The Reagan administration seized upon the findings to describe the school-breakfast program as "troubled." To cure its deficiencies, the administration suggested cutting its budget, instead of improving the content of the breakfasts.

Women, Infants, and Children (WIC)

Another program that the Reagan administration targeted is known as Women, Infants, and Children (WIC). It was begun in 1972 following discoveries about the scope of hunger in the United States. A 1967 Field Foundation report, one of a series of reports that publicized the reality of hunger, described the miseries of the poor in Mississippi:

> Wherever we went . . . we saw children in significant numbers who were hungry and sick, children for whom hunger is a daily fact of life, and sickness in many forms an inevitability. The children that we saw were more than malnourished. They were hungry, weak, apathetic. Their lives were being shortened.[38]

Hunger may not be as uncommon today as we would like to believe. In 1980, the United States was ranked fifteenth among nations with a low infant-mortality rate. Of the newborn babies born in the United States, 6.9 percent have birth weights below the international standard of 2.5 kilograms (5.5 lbs)—a figure ranking lower than many other developed countries.[39]

There is a direct relationship between low birth weight and mental and physical retardation. It was to reduce these problems that WIC was founded. To become eligible the pregnant woman applies for enrollment at a local WIC clinic. If she is found to be at nutritional risk and with a low income, she receives a voucher that entitles her to a package of food. It includes fruit juice, cheese, peanut butter, beans, infant formula, and eggs, and infant cereal once the baby is born. She cannot get the food without being enrolled. The health of both mother and baby are monitored on a regular basis. WIC also provides access for vulnerable low-income persons to the health care system. Indirectly, it helps the agriculture and dairy industries by increasing purchases of certain surplus foods. In 1983, approximately 2.35 million people were estimated to have participated in the program.[40] In April 1982, President Reagan, commenting on the WIC program, said, "It's been merged with another program and is in there at much greater money than it has ever had before." Edwin Dale of the OMB acknowledged that "the President possibly misspoke on that one."[41] Reagan in fact tried to reduce WIC's funding by 30 percent in 1982. Congress, however, intervened and maintained WIC as a separate program, and continued funding it at a level of $1.06 billion for FY 1983.[42]

Food Stamps

The food-stamp program has been mentioned prominently by President Reagan in a number of speeches for its "fraud, waste, and abuse." Yet, it has been found responsible for the marked decrease in hunger in the United States. A follow-up to the Field Foundation report of 1967, done a decade later, reported major improvements in the nutritional status of the poor. This was true, they reported, even though overall economic conditions had not improved. They concluded that the increased availability of nutrients through food stamps was responsible for the change, along with other benefits such as WIC and the school-lunch program.[43]

In August 1983, President Reagan said, "I am fully committed to feeding the poor people of this nation. No child, senior citizen, deserted mother, or invalid should have to go to bed hungry in America. . . . If even one American child is forced to go to bed hungry at night, or if one senior citizen is denied the dignity of proper nutrition, that is a national tragedy. We are too generous a people to allow this to happen."[44]

In 1981, the Reagan administration succeeded in getting Congress to cut the food stamp program by approximately $2 billion a year through 1985.[45] Spurred on by their success, the administration came back in 1982, proposing additional cuts. So drastic were these proposed reductions that (according to the CBO) 85 percent of all food stamp households would have had their food stamps reduced or terminated.[46] Ninety-two percent of the disabled and the elderly on food stamps and 94 percent of the working poor would have been cut, with the average working-poor family losing more than $700 a year in food stamps.[47] Overall, six million households, with seventeen million low-income persons, would have lost benefits.[48]

Congress rejected most of these additional cuts, but in 1983 the administration came back again with a new series of proposals to slash food stamp benefits. The CBO has reported that the administration's budget proposal for FY 1984 would cut food stamp benefits for 4 out of every 5 of the poorest households in the program—those with incomes so low that they fall below 50 percent of the poverty line (or below about $5,000 a year for a family of four).[49] Under Reagan's new proposals, one million elderly and disabled households (nearly half of the elderly and disabled in the program) would lose an average of $250 a year in food stamp benefits.[50]

As the administration came under attack for its "insensitivity" to the poor, the president tried to soften his image, and his cabinet stepped in to help. In August 1983, John R. Block, Reagan's forty-seven-year-old secretary of agriculture, himself a millionaire and owner of 3,000 acres in Illinois, spent a week eating the equivalent of a food stamp allotment. His family of four spent the maximum food stamp allotment of $58 a week because he wanted to see how the poorest people ate. Block admitted, "It's impossible to really appreciate the plight of the poor or to pretend to." What he missed most was an ice cream sundae or a beer or soft drink on a sticky, hot August Washington afternoon. His wife, Sue Block, beside him on the podium, was sobered by the amount of time and restraint needed to prepare the food and adhere to the diet.[51]

Food stamp recipients interviewed by the press were not impressed. "That man can go straight to hell," one woman was quoted as saying in the *Washington Post* as she picked up her $120 worth of food stamps for the month of August. Her boyfriend, a cable TV maintenance worker, echoed the common criticism of Block's experiment: "He can do it for a week, just like I can go on a fast for a week, like it's a diet. But he can't prove anything in a week."[52]

Carlton Chapman, a part-time house painter who receives $236 a month in food stamps to help himself, his wife, and five children, said, "Summer's the worst. School's out and the kids don't get their lunches at school."[53] His wife is continually faced with the choice of breaking her food stamp budget or sticking to it and risking her children's health. Her extravagance is to feed her children two pieces of fruit a day. Like most of those interviewed, she has run out of food stamps by the twentieth of every month.

"Food stamps don't cover a whole month, not if you're feeding your children right," said another recipient, who would not be quoted by name. She said the hardest times are when her three-year-old son finishes a meal still hungry.[54]

Other critics have pointed out that Secretary Block was getting an allotment that only 18 percent of the food stamp case-load gets—the maximum. Most households get *much* less in benefits, even though they have little money to buy food after their food stamps run out.[55]

UNCLEAN FOOD

Our earliest government food regulations date back to 1884. In an effort to counter foreign import restrictions on US beef because of contamination, the Bureau of Animal Industry was established. The Bureau was given jurisdiction only over livestock and salted beef that was to be exported.[56] In 1890, as a result of restrictions on US pork exports being imposed by foreign countries (primarily Germany), the United States passed the First Meat Inspection Act. Once again, the government addressed itself only to meats that were exported.[57]

The problem of diseased and contaminated meat prevailed. During the Spanish-American War of 1898, US soldiers died after eating contaminated meat. The scandal prompted Upton Sinclair to expose the meat-packing industry and slaughterhouses in his book *The Jungle*. Congressional hearings on the quality of meats for domestic consumption followed. In 1907, the Second Meat Inspection Act was passed. The act established the first "wholesomeness" standard and stipulated that meat be "sanitary, unadulterated, and properly labeled."[58]

In 1916, the USDA began to develop grading standards for domestic livestock and meat. After numerous revisions, these standards were promulgated in 1926.[59]

Today everyone in the US takes clean food for granted. We presume, when we walk into the supermarket or restaurant, that we will find food that is untainted by contaminants and free from poisonous additives. But clean food does not arrive naturally in our grocery carts. Most food is clean *because* of government standards and inspection. In the United States we have the toughest food regulations in the world, which is why we are free from so many of the diseases and epidemics caused by unclean food.

Since World War II, the problems of inspecting foods have increased dramatically. Chemicals and pesticides never used before are now routinely sprayed on fields, injected into cattle and chickens, or swallowed by fish swimming in polluted waters. Our food is colored with dyes to make it attractive, and adulterated with additives to give it different tastes. The questions have become which levels of contaminants are dangerous to the public's health, and which can be avoided altogether?

Inspecting food is a complex process involving three different government departments and thousands of scientists, administrators, and support staff. The FDA sets levels of human tolerance for such food additives as coloring agents or artificial sweeteners. It also requires the recall of contaminated processed food. The actual inspection of meat and poultry is the duty of the USDA, while pesticides sprayed on food crops must be approved by the Environmental Protection Agency (EPA) before they are marketed.

Meat Inspection

For seventy-seven years the USDA has maintained a program of meat inspection. Today this department is responsible for inspecting 130 million head of livestock a year, 4.07 billion chickens and turkeys in 7,100 establishments, 80 million swine, and 33 million cattle.[60] It is said that Henry Ford got the idea for assembly-line work on cars by watching the disassembling and inspection of carcasses. Inspectors work at split-second speeds.

Kathy Hughes, in *Return to the Jungle*, published by the Center for Study of Responsive Law, describes the process:

Poultry. "One inspector, with the aid of mirrors, views each side of two adjacent birds. [If necessary] he tells a plant employee where to trim [to let him see the bird]. Another inspector grabs each carcass, slits the abdominal cavity and examines . . . the heart. . . ." Total time elapsed: less than 2 seconds.[61]

Cattle. Wielding sharp knives, a number of inspectors are stationed in three positions to slice the head, body, and carcass. At station 1 they slice eight lymph nodes in the head, making four cuts to each node, slice the cheek muscles, and palpate the tongue; at station 2 they check viscera, incising five lymph nodes on lungs, and checking heart, liver, bile ducts, spleen, and rheumino-reticular junctions (this last for wire that may have been eaten by the steer). At station 3 they inspect the carcass, internally and externally, for abcesses. Time elapsed for one steer: less than 60 seconds.[62]

"Inspectors have been complaining loudly and persistently that present line rates compromise their ability to detect contaminated meat," argues Kathy Hughes.[63] Despite their complaints and a GAO report critical of staffing shortages, the Reagan administration is seeking to implement regulations to speed up inspection lines in meat-processing plants, as well as reduce the number of federal meat inspectors.[64]

The Reagan USDA has also undertaken a serious policy shift in the monitoring and rating of individual meat-processing plants. No longer does USDA publicize chronic violators of the law. This step had been a major deterrent to violations of safety standards. Without the notoriety of being labeled in noncompliance, the violators operate with impunity. For example, a recent investigation of Cattle King, a Denver meat-slaughtering plant, by a public-interest group, the Better Government Association, and NBC News revealed that the company continued to supply a major portion of the ground beef used in the school-lunch program, despite its unsanitary plants and spoiled and diseased meat. In fact, Cattle King increased its share of the school-lunch ground-beef market from 14 to 24 percent in one year, in spite of a Canadian ban on Cattle King imports and previous US government convictions of Cattle King owners for meat inspection violations.[65] The "detective work" in this case was done by forces outside the USDA. But public-interest groups with limited resources can investigate only an occasional egregious case such as Cattle King.

One of USDA's most important responsibilities in inspecting meat is to detect the presence of carcinogens, chemicals, hormones, antibiotics, and pesticides. These residues cannot be seen, smelled, tasted, or felt. Sophisticated and time consuming scientific tests are required to determine their presence in meats, whose contamination is often not discovered until after the product has been consumed.

In 1979, cattle that had eaten feed grains contaminated with the highly toxic industrial chemical polychlorinated biphenyl (PCB) from a Montana plant were slaughtered and shipped to fourteen states and two foreign countries before the USDA learned of it. About $20 million worth of meat was withdrawn from the market in 1979.[66] This is not an isolated incident. As Carol Foreman, former assistant secretary for food and consumer services, acknowledges, "There is a good chance that the American public consumes meat with violation levels of carcinogenic and teratogenic chemical residues with some regularity."[67]

The Residue Control Program is an important part of the USDA monitoring system. It oversees the complex meat and poultry production activities of the giant multibillion-dollar industry and monitors its use of chemicals, drugs, and growth promotants. With the advent of many new chemicals used in the production of meat and poultry products, the USDA's Residue Control Program has suffered from a lack of adequate resources. Testifying before Congress at a 1980 budget hearing, Dr. Donald Houston, the administrator of the USDA's Food Safety and Inspection Service, said that to increase monitoring to twenty times the present rate would cost an estimated $92 million. "This option appears unrealistic when viewed against our present budget," Dr. Houston said, "but may turn out to be cost-effective when viewed from the total government-wide budget for controlling toxic substances and the government and private costs associated with a contamination incident."[68]

Despite a recommendation from the GAO in 1979 for more extensive monitoring and the allocation of additional funds to do so in 1980 by Congress, the Reagan administration has limited the program's ability to monitor residues and enforce sanctions against those companies violating the law.[69]

The program is hampered by a modest budget of $18.5 million for 1983 and a staff equivalent to fifty-eight persons working for one year each.[70] Such resources are inadequate when compared to the size of the industry it oversees. About 4.4 billion animals are slaughtered yearly under federal inspection.[71] The Residue Control Program extracts residue samples to test for only 60 out of 143 chemicals listed by the GAO as likely to leave residues above the tolerance level set by the EPA.[72] The FDA estimates that there may be residues from 500 to 600 chemicals in meat.[73]

While the Reagan administration is testing more chemicals —14 more than previously—only 53,816 residue samples were taken in 1982, 6,073 less than the previous year.[74] One reason for the decrease in residue monitoring is that the USDA is shifting money and emphasis away from sampling and enforcement toward producer education. In the last two years, $2 million was reallocated from inspection and laboratory services to educational programs.[75] Though educational programs may be worthwhile, they should not be realized at the expense of consumer protection programs. The inevitable result will be a substantial decline in detection and enforcement activities, and the decreased likelihood of compliance with the law. Carol Foreman, whose duties included supervising the Residue Control Program, believes that the ability to monitor harmful residues has never been good and is getting worse. "With the exception of some new and quicker tests for checking residues, nothing has happened," Ms. Foreman said. "I have always made the assumption that we were missing a good part of the contamination."[76]

Both Ms. Foreman and Rodney Leonard, who was in charge of the USDA's inspection service from 1967 to 1969, believe that the present situation poses a threat to public health: "They need much more intensive sampling," Mr. Leonard said, "so they know where the most severe problems are."[77] But under the Reagan administration's allocation of resources, increased funding for the program seems unlikely.

With the endorsement of the GAO and the USDA, the Carter administration had decided to step up protection against chemical residues violations. It recommended legislation giving the FDA the authority to levy civil penalties on companies for the misuse of drugs in animals.[78] The Reagan administration has dropped all plans for the passage of these laws. USDA officials under Reagan see no need for stronger enforcement power and have promised the industry's representatives that such measures will not be written into meat production legislation. The officials state that the sanctions that are presently available—such as the inspectors' ability to slow production or to condemn cargo—"are both strong and flexible enough to deal with the spectrum of offenses that may occur."[79]

In 1981, the Reagan administration initiated a series of "cooperative agreements" with meat-processing firms, primarily poultry processors, to reduce government oversight by allowing the plants themselves to have substantial control over residue monitoring and enforcement. The model agreement, which serves as the basis for specific agreements between the USDA and individual plants, was developed by a poultry-industry trade association, the National Broiler Council. According to the agreement: "Participants in the cooperative Residue Avoidance Program will encounter decreased surveillance, have latitude in resolving borderline residue problems, and will experience cooperative participation in determining action sequence and nature of press releases in the case of residue incidents."[80] Both Banquet Foods and Louis Rich Co. have entered into "cooperative agreements" with the USDA, despite having had residue violations during the Carter administration.[81]

By limiting the USDA's presence in monitoring residues, the "cooperative agreements" undermine the department's ability to judge whether plants are complying with the law and to punish those plants in violation of the law. "I question the wisdom of allowing individual meat plants, which have had severe residue problems in the past, to conduct their own monitoring programs. If anything, there should be more enforcement on the part of the federal government," says Tom Smith, an economist with Public Voice on Food and Health Policy. "The public pays for the government to inspect meat products. It should not expect the government to assign such responsibility to the regulated industries."[82]

Consumer advocate Ralph Nader summarizes the Reagan approach to meat and poultry inspection this way: "These policies undermine preventive health practices, generate more sickness costs throughout the country, and are more likely to induce even more unsavory practices in less responsible segments of the industry."[83]

The Delaney Clause

In 1958, a New York congressman, James Delaney, sponsored an amendment that prohibited food companies from using additives that had been proven to cause cancer in laboratory animals. Its provisions were extended to color additives in 1960 and to drugs given to animals, which can leave residues in meat, in 1968.

The Delaney Clause places special emphasis on carcinogens. In conjunction with the general safety clause in the food and drug laws, the Delaney Clause has banned the sale of numerous food and color additives found to be carcinogenic. In the late 1970s two additives were discovered to cause tumors in mice: saccharin, a sweetener used in soft drinks and diet foods; and nitrites, used as a preservative in processed meats. The studies on nitrites were variously interpreted, but those on saccharin were clear: the artificial sweetener caused cancer. The FDA moved to issue the legally required ban. Congress, perceiving an overwhelming public demand for the additive, reversed the FDA ban on saccharin. It was the only time that Congress has concluded that a result dictated by the Delaney Clause was inappropriate.

With that victory in hand, followed by the Reagan election victory, the food industry began to pressure the new administration to repeal or weaken the protective Delaney Clause. For two years running, in 1982 and again in 1983, Senator Orrin Hatch of Utah, the chairman of the Senate Committee on Labor and Human Resources, sought major revisions in the food safety laws; for two years they were fought off by opposition from Senator Ted Kennedy (Democrat-Massachusetts) and a coalition of consumer, labor, and senior citizen groups.

The current proposals under consideration would:

- weaken the Delaney Clause, allowing intentional introduction of food additives known to cause cancer in humans and laboratory animals;
- allow the FDA to phase out additives found to be unsafe over a period of years, rather than stop their sale immediately;
- change the definition of "safe" in the law to allow the use of additives with a "small" health risk.

The real debate about the Delaney Clause focuses on who should bear the risks of new food additives: consumers, who could develop cancer and die from eating unsafe additives; or the food industry, which could be financially harmed if the FDA, in an excess of caution, banned a safe additive.

Industry makes three arguments for repealing the Delaney Clause. The first is that the clause is too rigid and requires the FDA to ban an additive even if only a single animal test has shown the additive to be a carcinogen—even if that test is flawed. In fact, this claim is untrue. The FDA has plenty of discretion in deciding how much and what kind of scientific evidence to consider. In the case of saccharin, for example, it waited five years for additional studies to confirm that saccharin causes bladder tumors in animals. "What the Delaney Clause does is to remove the FDA's political discretion to allow carcinogenic additives to be sold," says Bill Schultz, a Public Citizen attorney with years of expertise in food safety.[84]

The second argument is that modern science has made the clause obsolete. Industry representatives claim that sophisticated analytical techniques can now measure such minute quantities of substances—trace amounts of only a few parts per trillion—that low amounts of carcinogens previously undetectable have now become obvious and subject to the Delaney Clause, even though at these low levels they may present no genuine health threat. This claim, too, is false. In a 1979 ruling in the District of Columbia federal district court, the FDA was given the leeway to decide if trace carcinogens pose a hazard or not.[85]

The third argument for repeal is that the scientific assumption behind the law is no longer valid. The Delaney Clause states that "no additive shall be deemed to be safe if it is found to induce cancer when ingested by man or animal. . . ." Industry claims that what causes cancer in animals does not always cause it in humans. Most independent scientists disagree. The food industry has yet to produce an example of such a food additive.[86] In 1960, Dr. Thomas Carney, a vice-president of the Eli Lilly Company, urged Congress not to expand the application of the Delaney Clause to color additives in food. Dr. Carney used this same argument: what causes cancer in animals does not necessarily cause cancer in humans. He cited a drug that doctors were then prescribing to thousands of women to prevent miscarriages—diethylstilbestrol, or DES. While DES had been found to cause cancer in a few species of animals, Dr. Carney argued that a connection to humans' cancers was "most probably mythical."[87] A few years later, DES was shown to cause a rare form of vaginal and cervical cancer in daughters of the pregnant women who had taken the drug. About 80 percent of these daughters are reported to have developed an abnormal vaginal condition known as adenosis as a result of their mothers' use of DES.[88]

The Reagan administration supports industry efforts to repeal the Delaney Clause. It particularly wants to deny a basic scientific assumption of the clause—that animal carcinogens do pose a cancer risk to humans. Bill Schultz, of Public Citizen, advocates a far more prudent approach:

No one has yet identified a single food additive that causes cancer in animals but not in humans. . . . As long as scientists remain uncertain, it is better to heed the warnings of animal test data and not recklessly assume that they do not apply to humans. While the uncertainty persists, industry should bear the risks that it creates. Consumers should not be forced to be guinea pigs for new food additives.[89]

DIETARY GOALS AND CANCER

In 1976, a Senate Select Committee on Nutrition, whose members included Senators George McGovern (Democrat-South Dakota), Robert Dole (Republican-Kansas), Richard Clark (Democrat-Iowa), and Hubert Humphrey (Democrat-Minnesota) issued a report entitled *Dietary Goals for the United States*. The report generated a great deal of controversy by calling for less meat, less salt, less sugar, fewer fats, and more whole grains in the average diet. With this report serving as a political prod, the USDA during the Carter years treated nutrition as a major public health issue. US food companies attempted to blunt the committee's report by spending over $2.3 billion in 1979 enticing the public to buy salt-and sugar-laden junk food.[90]

In 1978, the USDA and the Department of Health, Education, and Welfare (now Health and Human Services) joined together to develop dietary guidelines for the public. A task force of scientists from two departments was appointed to review current data on nutrition and recommend guidelines based on such data. The suggestions that resulted, it was hoped, would be a summary of fundamental scientific knowledge that would be largely undisputed and accepted as fact.[91]

The task force issued seven guidelines. Briefly stated, they were: eat a variety of foods; maintain ideal weight; avoid too much fat (saturated fat and cholesterol); eat foods with adequate fiber; avoid sugar; avoid sodium; and if you drink alcohol, do it in moderation. The producers of processed food products, which are higher in sugar, fat, and sodium, in the words of Carol Foreman, "hemorrhaged."[92] They went to Congress and tried to get the guidelines changed. They went to the USDA. They went to President Carter. No one budged. But the guidelines were popular with the public, if not with the industry. In two years, over seven million copies of *Dietary Guidelines* were distributed.

The Department of Agriculture then issued *Food*, a booklet that sought to help the public follow the guidelines through recipes and dietary recommendations. Over 1.1 million copies of this first *Food* booklet were distributed to the public.[93]

Shortly after Reagan took office, distribution of these materials stopped. In 1980, the USDA planned to put out a second edition, *Food II*, which would include chapters on weight control, and fats and cholesterol. Its printing was delayed. When the Reagan administration assumed office, it blocked the publication even though the booklet assisted the public with information needed to make choices in the marketplace.[94] Instead it gave the rights to *Food II* to the American Dietetic Association, a private organization. The layout, galleys, color plates, and text were given free, too. The book, slick and handsome with color photos of foods, recipes, and suggestions for purchasing wholesome food, was prepared at the taxpayers' expense, yet the American Dietetic Association was given the exclusive right to sell it for $7.50 a copy ($5.00 plus $2.50 handling charges). As of October 1983, only 17,247 copies of *Food II* have been sold.[95]

But limiting the distribution of the guidelines did not satisfy the Reagan administration in tipping its hat to industry. A review board, set up by the USDA, with three members appointed by the FDA, is now rewriting *Dietary Guidelines*. Despite public protest, the board's membership consists of people who have represented the meat, dairy, and egg industries, the primary opponents of the guidelines in the first place. Michael Jacobson, director of the Center for Science in the Public Interest, summed up the problem:

> The *Dietary Guidelines* brochure is the embodiment of our national nutrition policy and the most important nutrition document ever published by the government. USDA under Reagan is being managed by former meat industry executives who have done everything possible to scuttle the nutrition policies and education programs which encourage the reduced consumption of fatty foods, including meat.[96]

Two of the more outspoken critics of the department's *Dietary Guidelines* have been USDA's deputy secretary, Richard Lyng, past president of the American Meat Institute, and its assistant secretary, C.W. McMillan, former lobbyist for the National Cattlemen's Association.

Another book, *Diet, Nutrition, and Cancer,* met a similar fate. In the summer of 1982, a committee of the National Academy of Sciences (NAS) released the report exploring the links between cancer and diet. It advocated that Americans eat less fat, less salt, fewer salt-cured, pickled, and smoked meats, and conversely more fresh fruits and vegetables. Predictably the food producers attacked the report.[97]

The USDA's own nutritionist, Dr. Walter Mertz, one of the NAS panel members, spoke up for the Academy's recommendations at a press conference and offered free of charge various menus and recipes produced by the USDA, which followed the Academy's guidelines to reduce the chance of cancer. Ten thousand requests for menu plans poured in. When the Center for Science in the Public Interest asked for a menu, it took ten months and constant phone calls to get the packet. When the material arrived, it consisted of a complimentary brochure on the Basic Four food groups and a letter stating that government advice now costs from $2 to $5.[98]

The information promised was not supplied because the Reagan administration has made a policy decision not to promote *Dietary Guidelines.* The delay in responding resulted from severe budget cutbacks in the nutrition information programs. By law the USDA is mandated to disseminate information linking dietary choices with disease. Its responsibility was delineated by sections 1403 and 1427 of the Food and Agriculture Act of 1977, which designates the USDA as the chief agency concerned with human nutrition research and information. In the first three years that he was in office, Secretary of Agriculture John Block instituted a number of actions that eroded the USDA's ability to provide nutrition education. By a reorganization order, he eliminated a special Human Nutrition Center. He slated the Nutrition Education and Training Program for extinction by 1984, but Congress insisted that it continue. In 1982, he cut five out of seven employees from the Food and Nutrition Information Center, which serves as a clearinghouse on child nutrition and food service management, and merged the Center into the Human Nutrition Information Service. As a result the Center was forced to stop serving the Head Start program, hospitals, school food workers, and other groups. Responses to requests for information fell from twelve thousand a year to seven thousand.[99]

"I don't think that just because we cut back in staffing," said Mary C. Jarrett, assistant secretary for Food and Consumer Services at USDA, "we are destroying the total function of that agency. . . . We are exploring private sector initiatives that we think are a responsible way of disseminating nutrition information."[100] "These people are not bumblers," one high-level nutrition scientist at USDA said. "They are trashing nutrition administratively, with the intent of doing the whole program in."[101]

FOOD LABELING

"If you want less government regulation," says Carol Foreman, "then the one regulation you want the government involved in is labeling. 'Fellas, do almost anything you want,' you say, 'but tell us on the label what you're doing.' "[102]

In June 1978, the USDA, FDA, and the Federal Trade Commission (FTC) announced hearings on ways to improve the labeling of products. In 1979 they proposed regulations that would provide consumers with substantially more complete and specific information on the labels of processed foods, and that would give the FDA and the USDA wider labeling authority. Among other actions, both agencies proposed to improve the labeling of the sugar, fat, sodium, and potassium content; to study information on improved nutrition; and to increase the "open dating" on foods to tell consumers if the food is fresh.[103]

The Reagan administration dropped all mandatory labeling proposals and instead has asked industry to label its foods voluntarily. Neither industry nor consumers favor the voluntary approach. Although industry prefers it to mandatory standards, it has generally resisted voluntarily putting labels on products, citing among numerous complaints the costs and the confusion to the consumer overloaded by a glut of content labeling. For the consumer, voluntary labeling is of little value, because some products (primarily those with small amounts of sugar, salt, or fat) are labeled and others aren't. It's hard for consumers to make a choice if only some of the products are labeled.

Sodium

In 1970 the FDA undertook a review of all additives on the market that were on the list of substances generally recognized as safe to see if any were unsafe on the basis of new information. They reviewed 460 additives in ten years. One of the more important reversals occurred in 1979 when the Select Committee on Generally Recognized as Safe (GRAS) Substances stated that there was insufficient evidence on sodium chloride to determine that it was not deleterious to the public health. As a result of their finding, the Select Committee favored the "development of guidelines for restricting the amount of salt in processed foods. . . . Adequate labeling of sodium content of foods would help meet these objectives."[104] Thirty senators signed a statement supporting that position. They included Richard Schweiker, who later became secretary of Health and Human Services under Reagan. Representative Margaret Heckler, who later succeeded him at HHS, took a similar position in the House of Representatives.[105]

About fifty million Americans—at least 20 percent of the population—suffer from hypertension, a condition aggravated by a diet high in sodium or salt.[106] Hypertension is the most common cause of serious stroke. It is also associated with heart attacks and kidney failure. The hazards of sodium in connection with hypertension have been known for nearly fifty years, but only in the last twenty has the medical profession recognized that hypertension can be a major killer.[107]

Sodium is found in table salt, in processed, canned, and frozen foods, and in baking soda and sodium ascorbate (added to foods as ascorbic acid, or vitamin C). It is found in all processed meats—smoked, corned, salted, dried, or others prepared with sodium nitrite. It saturates ketchup, soy sauce, frozen dinners, sauerkraut, dill pickles, salted nuts, potato chips, popcorn, cheeses, soups, and hot dogs. Its use is so widespread that Americans are estimated to consume 2,000 to 10,000 mg per day. That is the equivalent of swallowing one to five teaspoons of salt.[108] Most experts agree that the average adult can get along on 1,000 mg or less, and the American Medical Association (AMA) advises 400 mg for those who must limit their intake because of hypertension.[109] The FDA, the National Academy of Sciences, the National Heart, Lung, and Blood Institute, and a variety of other health agencies agree that eating less sodium is beneficial.

For the individual the problem is to tell how much sodium is being consumed, because while labels sometimes show that the food contains sodium, they rarely tell how much. For most Americans, well over 50 percent of all sodium intake comes from processed foods. A serving of fresh peas, for example, contains 3 mg of sodium, but a serving of canned peas can contain 300 to 400 mg because of the salt added in processing.[110]

FDA regulations call for action if an advisory committee questions the safety of an additive. This did not happen with the GRAS recommendation on sodium. Pressured by the food industry, the FDA stalled any follow-up action. In 1981 and again in 1982, the House Subcommittee on Health and the Environment held hearings on labeling the sodium content in certain processed foods. In 1981 the question before the subcommittee was whether to mandate sodium labeling. The subcommittee had considered several options including mandating reductions of sodium in foods or requiring labeling of sodium. The subcommittee eventually favored the labeling alternative. A study by Arthur D. Little Company for the FDA estimated that the total cost of implementation would be less than $50 million, and the possible benefits in excess of $1 billion a year.[111]

In the hearing of September 1982, Dr. Arthur Hayes, then commissioner of the FDA under Reagan, argued the administration's point of view: "We must not mandate unnecessary regulatory requirements that only serve as roadblocks to a good faith effort on the part of industry to deal with this problem. Whatever requirements we feel we must impose have to be clear, consistent, and enforceable."[112]

Congressman Henry Waxman (Democrat-California), the subcommittee chairman, replied, "No one is suggesting we mandate the industry to only put in a certain amount of sodium; we are only suggesting what we ought to have is the ability of the consumer to make a choice based on accurate information."[113] Hayes pleaded for voluntary sodium labeling. Given six months to a year at most, he would know if voluntary labeling worked; he expected 50 percent of the products to have voluntary sodium labeling by the end of 1982. Such labeling still would not be very useful to consumers, since low-sodium products would more likely be labeled and high-sodium products would not. Hayes was not dissuaded from his position by Congressman Scheuer (Democrat-New York), who reminded him that Congress and the FDA had been waiting for voluntary industry action for four or five years already without seeing one speck of progress.[114]

Other witnesses testified against the legislation. The representative of the industry's Salt Institute was upset at singling out sodium and potassium for labeling. He thought it discriminatory. "Providing content information in such a manner can only confuse consumers," he said.[115]

The labeling bill never got out of committee, and another bill the following year also did not pass. In 1982 Commissioner Hayes finally issued a report that the FDA intended to rely on a voluntary labeling effort. He would first ask industry to label the amount of sodium in foods as part of its nutrition labeling; second, he would ask industry to reduce the salt in food. The FDA also finally denied the 1978 petition for sodium reduction from the Center for Science in the Public Interest on the grounds that voluntary control would take care of the problem. As its only recourse, the center sued, arguing that the FDA's action was "arbitrary and capricious."[116] A 1982 FDA review of sodium labeling revealed that only 19 percent of food products checked had been labeled for sodium content.[117]

Mechanically Separated Species (MS[s])

Another labeling dispute involves what is euphemistically called mechanically deboned meat. The USDA calls it mechanically separated species (e.g., mechanically separated beef). It is actually a meat product containing ground-up bone, and it is added to processed meat products, like hot dogs and chili. Unlike sodium, where the issue is whether to tell consumers how much of a known substance they are getting in the products they buy, the issue with MS(s) is whether the label should disclose that the product is different from regular processed meat products and, in particular, that it contains crushed bone. The food watchdog group Community Nutrition Institute charges that the sale of MS(s) constitutes a dishonest business practice unless the product is clearly labeled so that consumers can recognize what is essentially an inferior product, which the meat industry used to discard as garbage. There are also health concerns associated with the substance, since it increases the amount of fat, cholesterol, calcium, fluoride, and lead in the finished product.[118]

MS(s) is made by mechanically separating the muscle tissue of meat from livestock carcasses. After the butcher has removed the large steaks, roasts, and joints by hand, the remaining carcass is put through a machine that crushes the bones, meat, tendons, and gristle and forces the resulting mash through a sieve. The resulting product is a pink, pastelike substance that is added to various meat products.

In 1976 Secretary of Agriculture Earl Butz gave industry the go-ahead, with no limitations, to use MS(s) as a cheap substitute for red meat in products such as hot dogs and chili. The USDA did not require any special labeling for products containing this substance.[119] Several consumer organizations successfully challenged the USDA's decision in federal court. The court struck down the regulations permitting the use of MS(s), on the grounds that they had been issued without affording the public an opportunity to comment on whether crushed bone should be allowed in the food supply. The court also found that the USDA had failed to assess adequately the health and safety consequences of MS(s). Finally, the court held that the USDA could not allow the use of MS(s) without requiring special labeling, since MS(s) is not considered meat under traditional standards accepted by consumers.[120]

In 1977, in keeping with the court's order, the USDA under President Carter conducted safety studies on MS(s). On the basis of those studies, it decided to allow the substance on the market but limited its use to 20 percent of the meat portion of certain processed meat products. In addition, the USDA insisted that if manufacturers use MS(s), they must abide by strict labeling requirements.[121] The label had to read, for instance, "Frankfurters, with mechanically processed beef product" and "Contains up to .51 percent powdered bone." The purpose of the labeling was to enable consumers to make cost comparisons between regular meat products and products containing MS(s).

In April 1979, the meat industry's trade association petitioned the USDA to eliminate the labeling requirements, claiming that the "negative" labeling made it impossible to sell products with MS(s), because consumers would not purchase products that contain bone. The USDA denied the petition and stated that the substantial majority of consumers who commented on the requirements "were against even allowing the product in commerce." The USDA explained that the labeling requirements, therefore, were "an attempt to accommodate this widespread desire to avoid the product, while still permitting it on the market."[122] A month later the meat industry submitted its petition for reconsideration, but again it was denied.

Then President Reagan took office in January 1981. In February the meat industry resubmitted its petition to eliminate the labeling restrictions. This time the USDA agreed with the industry and promptly amended the labeling regulations, so that references to MS(s) and bone in the product name could be deleted. In fact, under the Reagan regulations, there is absolutely no mention of the fact that the product contains bone. Instead the manufacturers can declare that the product contains added "calcium."[123]

In July 1982, Public Citizen, on behalf of other consumer organizations, filed a lawsuit claiming that the regulations not only allow manufacturers to conceal the true nature of products containing MS(s), but also make products containing MS(s) seem nutritionally superior to regular meat products, because they have more calcium. In December 1982, the federal district court upheld the regulations, stating that since the product was not unsafe the USDA could determine the appropriate labeling. The case is now on appeal in the US Court of Appeals.[124]

Meanwhile the USDA also allows the use of MS(s) in processed poultry products, like chicken franks, with no limitation on the amount that can be used and virtually no labeling disclosures. A report issued on May 4, 1983, by the GAO concluded that poultry products containing this substance may be "adulterated and their labels misleading," in violation of the Federal Meat Inspection Act.[125] In response, the USDA has stated that it will do nothing to stop the sale of these products until the legal battle over MS(s) in red-meat products is resolved. In the meantime, the USDA has approved new labels for several red-meat products containing MS(s) that do not tell consumers that such products as hot dogs are any different from regular hot dogs.

The meat industry can now take what used to be discarded as garbage, or at best used in pet foods, and foist it on unsuspecting consumers, with the helping hand of the federal government, which stamps these products "US Inspected and Approved." Since consumers cannot tell the difference, there is no reason for the industry even to make the MS(s) products available at cheaper prices.

A year ago, in proclaiming National Consumers' Week, President Reagan said:

> Honest transactions in a free market between buyers and sellers are at the core of individual, community, and national economic growth. In the final analysis, an effective and efficient system of commerce depends on an informed and educated public.[126]

However, as the MS(s) case shows, President Reagan does not practice what he preaches.

THE COST OF FOOD

Upon entering the White House, the Reagan administration did take on the large and powerful dairy industry. The administration tried repeatedly in its 1981 farm legislation to cut back on the costly dairy-support program. The Carter administration had supported a farm bill with a semiannual adjustment in the price support levels and other changes, which made it lucrative for dairy farmers to produce milk and sell it to the government, regardless of the surplus that built up.

"The [Reagan] administration took on this issue with a concern for the taxpayer and the consumer," says Ellen Haas, director of Public Voice for Food and Health Policy, an organization in the forefront of consumer efforts to cut the levels of farm price supports. "They took a constructive approach, but somehow wound up accommodating the dairy industry. Unfortunately, there has been a minimum of meaningful changes to lower the cost of milk or cut back on dairy price supports."[127] The result is that dairy farmers are still producing too much milk, cheese, and butter, and the poor are standing in line to get free cheese.

Agricultural price supports, which include paying farmers not to grow grain and financing large sugar-growing corporations, are expected to cost taxpayers $21 billion in FY 1983.[128] Compare that expenditure, which flows to 3 percent of the American population, the farm sector, with the cost of the food stamp program of $12 billion, which reaches 22 million people, or 10 percent of the population.[129]

The rate of increase in food prices slowed during 1982 and 1983 because of the deep economic recession. Inflation, however, had taken its toll: higher unemployment, especially among those who had never been unemployed before; and tougher economic conditions for those closest to the bottom of the economic scale. Severe drought and adverse weather conditions have damaged the 1983 crops, and food prices are expected to climb sharply in 1984. Especially hard hit is the corn crop, which provides food for people *and* animals. Cattle are being sold prematurely because of the scarcity of feed grain, which will sharply increase meat costs this spring.

The Reagan administration's Payment-in-Kind (PIK) program for grain is extremely costly to the taxpayer and ill timed. Its estimated cost in 1983 is $12 billion.[130] Under PIK farmers are given grain that is currently being held in reserve as "payment" for not growing grain crops. The program has resulted in a severe shortage of grain, because the grain reserve is being depleted. Less wheat and corn is being grown. Bad weather is expected to further reduce the normal crop size.

The USDA is presently being sued by a coalition of rural public-interest groups on the grounds that the PIK program violates the legal limit of $50,000 in cash subsidies per farmer. The USDA argues that, since it is giving grain grants, the subsidy cap does not apply.

The PIK program is an admission that previous Reagan policies were not working in the agricultural sector. The Reagan plan to let "free market" forces set farm policy has not been realized, and there is probably less price competition in the food industry than in 1980.

Are consumers better off in 1984 because of President Reagan's food and nutrition policies? The evidence shows that they are not. It also suggests that they will not be in a better position for some years in the future, because of the drastic deprivation and health risks to which they are being needlessly subjected.

Administration officials see things differently: they argue that they are merely turning the responsibilities of government back to the private sector, where they belong. This includes letting the food industry supply or withhold information on diet and cancer and continue with the voluntary labeling of products. It is Reagan's proposition that a marketplace left to itself will work, even though an effective marketplace, not to mention public health, depends on informed consumers.

Sadly, it is the poor and needy who will suffer the most from the Reagan administration's food and nutrition policies. With the likelihood of a new round of budget cuts, those who are most in need of the government's help will receive less from food and nutrition programs. Once again they will be the victims of an administration insensitive to the consequences of poverty.

DRUGS

Legislative History of the FEDERAL FOOD, DRUG, AND COS-
METIC ACT OF 1938: [A bill enacted] " . . . to safeguard the
public health against the distribution of drugs which have
not become generally recognized as safe for use . . . among
experts qualified by scientific training and experience to
evaluate the safety of drugs. . . ."

Prescription and over-the-counter (OTC) drugs are
regulated by the Food and Drug Administration (FDA), a division
of the Department of Health and Human Services (HHS). The
origins of the FDA go back to the beginning of the twentieth
century.

Because of its age and prestige, the FDA has never been in
danger of abolition, even under the anti-regulation programs of
the Reagan administration. But for the first time ever, Reagan has
required that all important FDA regulatory decisions be approved
by the secretary of HHS and by the Office of Management and
Budget (OMB). As a result, programs of great benefit to consumers, such as those promoting generic drugs and requiring labeling
or information such as patient package inserts (PPIs), have been
withdrawn, while programs to remove ineffective and unsafe
drugs from the market have been indefinitely delayed. The FDA,
however, has not suffered severe budget and personnel cutbacks
comparable to other health and safety regulatory agencies.

ASPIRIN AND REYE'S SYNDROME

In February 1971, Lois Lafrenière of East Barre, Vermont, gave her
nine-year-old daughter, Leanne, children's aspirin to treat a stom-

ach virus. Although Leanne's condition seemed to improve, a few days later she began vomiting heavily, running a high temperature, and appearing listless. The family doctor prescribed a rectal suppository to relieve the vomiting, but within an hour Leanne became delirious. She was taken to the hospital, and a day later, after falling into a coma, died. An autopsy revealed that Leanne had died of Reye's syndrome, a rare but often fatal disease of unknown origin.[1]

Reye's syndrome has for many years mystified the medical profession. It strikes between six hundred and twelve hundred children a year, 20 to 30 percent of whom die. Permanent brain damage occurs in many of the children who live. The disease usually occurs in children recovering from flu or chicken pox.[2]

In the fall of 1981, the Centers for Disease Control (CDC), a division of HHS, concluded that four independent studies demonstrated that there is a strong link between the use of aspirin and Reye's syndrome. It recommended, therefore, that parents be advised to exercise caution in administering aspirin to treat children with viral illnesses, such as chicken pox and flu.[3]

Public Citizen's Health Research Group immediately urged the FDA to require manufacturers to place a warning label, following the CDC's recommendations, on products containing aspirin, cautioning parents against the use of the product during the flu season and by children with chicken pox. HRG subsequently filed a formal petition with FDA.

Unlike prescription-drug products, over-the-counter products, such as those containing aspirin, can be purchased without a doctor's approval, and it was critical that the warning be placed on the label of the product. On May 17, 1982, after six months had elapsed and the FDA had taken no action, Public Citizen and the American Public Health Association sued the agency to require warning labels on aspirin products.[4]

The FDA, meanwhile, convened its own working group, which also concluded that there is an association between aspirin and Reye's syndrome. On June 4, 1982, Secretary Schweiker announced that the FDA was undertaking an extensive educational campaign to warn parents about the link between aspirin and Reye's syndrome, and would also "require that the label on aspirin products be changed to advise against their use in 'children with flu and chicken pox.' "[5] At this point, it looked as though the Reagan administration would take the action recommended by its own scientists and warn parents about the unsafe use of this product.

But, as has happened repeatedly since 1981, the administration was far more sensitive to pressures from the aspirin industry than to scientific evidence or the needs of consumers. To assure effective responses to complaints from the regulated industry, shortly after he took office President Reagan had ordered that important regulatory decisions by agencies such as the FDA be reviewed by the White House's OMB. After Secretary Schweiker made his announcement in June 1982, his agency transmitted the proposed rule concerning the labeling of aspirin to OMB for final review.

According to an article published in the *Wall Street Journal*,[6] Dr. Joseph M. White, chairman of the Aspirin Foundation of America, reacted by asking the foundation's lawyer if something more could be done to stop the labeling regulation. The aspirin industry claimed that the medical studies supporting the regulation were faulty, that children get Reye's syndrome even without aspirin, and that people would misunderstand the label and possibly stop using aspirin. These arguments had already been made repeatedly by industry, and every government panel that had looked at the issue had rejected the claim that there is no link between aspirin and Reye's syndrome. Disgruntled over losing on the scientific front, but not defeated, the industry turned to the political side of the administration.

Dr. White's lawyer led him to James J. Tozzi, then OMB's deputy administrator for Information and Regulatory Affairs, who, with a staff of eighty (the largest in OMB), was responsible for carrying out EO 12291. Tozzi is described by the *Journal* as a "slim, intense-looking man, who sits behind an almost antiseptically clean desk and tries not to let a listener know whether he agrees with him." A career bureaucrat and OMB hand since the Nixon years, Tozzi had the task of stopping regulations that "don't make sense."

A meeting was arranged between representatives of the Aspirin Foundation and Mr. Tozzi. After some further checking, Tozzi claimed he detected a statistical error in one study. This "error," however, had already been rejected as a basis for discounting the link between aspirin and Reye's syndrome by the pertinent government officials and the two scientific advisory committees. He nevertheless called one doctor, an expert on Reye's syndrome, who confirmed his suspicion that some people in the medical community believed that the link had not been proven *conclusively*. Tozzi apparently never considered whether parents should have been informed about the studies on Reye's syndrome—regardless of whether those studies were absolutely conclusive—while the FDA gathered more definitive information. Tozzi also never explained on what basis it would be appropriate for him to overrule the scientists and outside scientific advisors at the FDA, the HHS, and the Centers for Disease Control.

Instead he sent the rule back "for further study." "It is a wonderful thing," Dr. White told the *Wall Street Journal*, "that the government finally has a system to review these regulations, because it takes a lot of guts to stand up and say 'no' to a proposed rule." Tozzi was also pleased, and has declared, "It's one of the finer things I've ever done."

The proponents of the warning label were outraged. Dr. Sidney M. Wolfe, director of Public Citizen's Health Research Group, claimed that the delay will cause one hundred needless deaths of children every year and many more injuries.

A week after the *Wall Street Journal* story appeared, in June 1983, former secretary of HHS Richard S. Schweiker and Christopher DeMuth, administrator for Information and Regulatory Affairs at OMB, together with George Keyworth, science advisor to the president, wrote a letter to the *Wall Street Journal* stating that the story "is false." The decision to rescind the labeling regulation on aspirin was made, they claimed, by Mr. Schweiker, based on the recommendation of the American Academy of Pediatrics. The financial interests of aspirin manufacturers were never mentioned "and had nothing to do with the decision." Underneath the letter, however, the conservative *Wall Street Journal* declared that it stood by its story.

The aspirin labeling controversy is not over. The administration claims to be still studying the issue, but under the most recent plan, it will be five to seven years before a final decision is reached. Meanwhile, Public Citizen and the American Public Health Association's lawsuit is pending in the US Court of Appeals for the District of Columbia circuit. In the year following the Reagan administration's decision not to require a warning label, there have been 143 more reported cases of children with Reye's syndrome, including 42 deaths. As Dr. Sidney M. Wolfe has observed, "The main prevention program of the Reagan administration is one designed to prevent industry from paying the cost of doing business." [7]

While HHS said it was conducting an educational campaign to warn parents about the link between aspirin and Reye's syndrome, Public Citizen's Health Research Group discovered that, in October 1983, the Reagan administration ordered the FDA to halt the distribution of a half million copies of a consumer pamphlet warning parents about this link. These pamphlets were ready for distribution to 4,200 supermarkets throughout the United States. In addition, HHS also canceled a thirty-second radio spot warning against aspirin use for treating chicken pox and flu, which was scheduled for distribution to 5,000 radio stations. Under pressure from Public Citizen, it then issued a watered-down spot advising against the use of any medication without consulting a physician.

Those parents who are lucky enough to hear about the problem, or who are warned by their physician, can avoid giving their children aspirin during the flu season or when they have chicken pox. Unfortunately, however, those parents who are not so lucky will increase the risks of death and injury to their children by giving them aspirin, as the result of a political decision by the Reagan administration.

REGULATION
OF OVER-THE-COUNTER DRUGS

It is interesting to contrast the aspirin story with the FDA's regulation of Tylenol, a product containing acetaminophen, which is a common substitute for aspirin. In the fall of 1982, seven people died from Tylenol that had been contaminated with cyanide, apparently while on the shelves of drugstores. The tremendous publicity generated from these events understandably upset the over-the-counter (OTC) drug industry. As a result, in an unusual switch by an industry that generally fights every government regulation, the industry's representatives asked the federal government to issue regulations requiring that OTC drugs be packaged to prevent tampering.[8] In this way the industry gained the FDA's seal of approval and assistance in its campaign to assure the public that over-the-counter drugs are safe.

When an industry's interests are at stake, the FDA can act very quickly to issue regulations. The FDA took only one month to issue its tamper-resistant regulations.[9] This example, perhaps more than any other, shows what the Reagan administration's priorities really are. It is not that these particular regulations are unnecessary or even inappropriate. Yet, in case after case, this administration reacts very quickly to protect the interests of industry but resists forcing companies to spend resources to take safety precautions, even when the lives and health of consumers or their children are at risk.

Aspirin and Tylenol are two OTC drug products that work, but many others do not. In a recent book, *Over-the-Counter Pills That Don't Work,* Public Citizen's Health Research Group concluded that two-thirds of the best-selling brands of OTC drugs contain ingredients that lack evidence of safety and effectiveness; even the FDA's own scientific panels agree that about one-third of the best-selling drugs contain ingredients that do not meet the standards of the Federal Food, Drug, and Cosmetic Act.

Many of these products contain a combination of effective and ineffective ingredients. For example, the only safe and effective pain-killing ingredient in Anacin, Bayer Aspirin, Bufferin, and Cope is aspirin. All the other ingredients make no provable difference in the usefulness of the products. They are included to support exaggerated and unproven advertising claims by the $10 billion OTC drug industry.[10]

Since there is nothing unique about OTC pain relievers (or many other OTC products), the industry spends enormous sums of money advertising its particular products. The manufacturers of Anacin tablets and capsules, for example, spent $27.5 million in advertising in 1981. In that same year the five leading headache-remedy product lines spent approximately $150 million.[11]

Under a federal law enacted in 1962, all drugs on the market today, with very limited exceptions, must be proven safe and effective prior to being sold to the public.[12] Because many OTC drugs did not meet this standard, in 1972 the FDA instituted the Over-the-Counter Drug Review to assess the ingredients and claims made for OTC drugs.[13]

The OTC drug industry has resisted meaningful review of its products at every stage. If the review were ever completed, the prices of the brand-name products would fall, since the ineffective ingredients that differentiate those products would have to be eliminated. On the other hand, Public Citizen has pressured the FDA to speed up the review since the mid-1970s to protect consumers against wasting money on high-priced ineffective and possibly unsafe ingredients in OTC products. In 1979, the consumer group won a case eliminating a regulation that had caused some of the delay,[14] and in 1981 it initiated a second lawsuit to challenge that delay.[15] That lawsuit is currently pending before the US Court of Appeals for the District of Columbia circuit. In a report to Congress in April 1982, the GAO concluded that at its current pace the OTC review could not be completed until 1990.[16]

Meanwhile, the FDA under the Reagan administration has brought the OTC review to a virtual standstill. In fact, in a confidential interview with the government's Office of the Comptroller General, the director of the OTC review and his deputy acknowledged, according to the interviewer, that "1990 was not a realistic date for completion of final monographs," and that the review would, in their opinion, be completed "closer to the year 2000."[17] In the meantime, American consumers are being exposed to ineffective and possibly unsafe over-the-counter drugs.

NEW DRUG APPLICATIONS

Unlike OTC drugs, which may be marketed on the basis of their manufacturers' conclusion that they are generally recognized as safe and effective, prescription drugs may not be sold until the FDA has approved a new drug application (NDA) submitted by the company that is seeking permission to sell the drug.[18] The Federal Food, Drug, and Cosmetic Act also requires the drug company to show by means of "substantial evidence" that the drug is safe and effective.[19] The statute defines "substantial evi-

dence" as including "adequate and well-controlled investigations," including "clinical investigations,"[20] which are studies on
human subjects demonstrating that the drug is safe and effective.

In contrast with its snail's pace review of ineffective drugs,
the FDA instituted a program to expedite the approval of new
drug applications shortly after Reagan took office, in spite of the
risks inherent in all new prescription drugs. These risks are
dramatically demonstrated in the case of a drug called Oraflex.

One day in May 1982, while reading scientific journals, Dr.
Sidney M. Wolfe saw an article in a British medical journal reporting several deaths in England from Oraflex. His interest was immediately piqued, since he knew that Oraflex had only recently
been approved by the FDA for use in the US.

The story of Oraflex is a tale of a drug company's overpro-
motion of a drug that has never been proven to be better than
aspirin and of how a consumer watchdog group fought both the
FDA and a major drug company to force the removal of a dangerous drug from the US marketplace.

Benoxaprofen, the chemical name of Oraflex, was first marketed in Great Britain in October 1980 by a subsidiary of Eli
Lilly.[21] Lilly applied for, but was denied, FDA approval to sell
Oraflex in this country in February 1981, but the FDA then approved the drug in May 1982.[22] The purpose of Oraflex is to treat
arthritis, but the studies that Lilly had furnished to the FDA did
not show Oraflex to be any more effective for that purpose than
plain aspirin. Lilly, however, made public claims that its evidence
demonstrated that Oraflex heals the tissues, thus actually curing
arthritis. There is no human evidence to support this claim.

Lilly's campaign worked. Within six weeks five hundred
thousand prescriptions for Oraflex had been filled, probably a
record for sales of a new prescription drug.[23] But at the same time,
Dr. Wolfe was busily checking with the English regulatory authorities to learn more about the foreign experience with this drug,
which had been on the market for two years in England. Lilly had
reported the English deaths to the British authorities, but it did not
similarly inform the FDA officials who were then reviewing the
new drug application. By May 1982, when Oraflex was introduced
into the United States, the number of deaths reported in Britain

had risen to twelve.[24] Public Citizen began warning patients and publicizing the deaths and, in June 1982, formally petitioned Secretary Richard Schweiker to ban the drug immediately as an "imminent hazard" to the public health, "because of a rapidly increasing number of reports of deaths due to liver and kidney damage in people using the drug." The letter also charged there was "no evidence that this drug is any more effective than other drugs in the family of non-steroidal anti-inflammatory drugs . . . a family that includes . . . aspirin." Lilly called the Public Citizen petition "irresponsible" and claimed that it was "without scientific merit."[25]

On June 29, 1982, Lilly cracked for the first time. In a letter addressed to physicians who prescribed the drug, it acknowledged that Oraflex may be dangerous to elderly patients (the primary population for which it was prescribed), and recommended that doctors prescribe for elderly patients only one half the dosage initially recommended.[26] The FDA still did not act.

On July 22, Public Citizen sent another letter to Schweiker, threatening to sue if the drug was not banned. The letter cited new statistics, including a total of forty-five deaths reported in the United Kingdom, one death in the United States suspected of having been caused by Oraflex, and the finding that the four thousand adverse reports filed on benoxaprofen in the United Kingdom represented some 25 percent of *all* adverse reactions for *all* drugs reported since Oraflex had come on the market.[27] The FDA still did not act.

On August 2, 1982, Public Citizen, joined by the American Public Health Association and the National Council of Senior Citizens, sued the FDA to order Lilly to withdraw the drug from the market place. On August 4, England banned the product. By that time, the sales of Oraflex had dropped significantly in the United States, and the pressure on Lilly was mounting. The following day, after a four-hour meeting with the FDA, Eli Lilly "voluntarily" withdrew the drug from the market worldwide.

Then two FDA investigators discovered that Eli Lilly had known all along of the deaths. It had withheld evidence from the FDA of at least eight deaths and ten other cases of nonfatal liver or kidney damage, which had occurred in Great Britain before

April 19, 1982—the official approval date for Oraflex in the United States.[28] By the time Lilly withdrew the drug, Oraflex had caused about fifty deaths in this country, according to Dr. Wolfe.

The Oraflex story continues. The FDA has asked the Justice Department to prosecute Eli Lilly for not reporting the English deaths to the agency. The Justice Department, however, ever sensitive to the interests of the drug industry, has taken the highly unusual course of allowing Lilly to voluntarily submit documents instead of empaneling an investigatory grand jury. It is uncertain whether the prosecution will ever be initiated. A decision not to prosecute Eli Lilly would be consistent with the Reagan administration's general policy of not enforcing federal laws. In fact, studies by Public Citizen demonstrate that enforcement actions brought by the FDA, including criminal prosecutions, regulatory letters, citations, injunctions, and seizures, have decreased about 50 percent during the Reagan administration.[29]

The story of Oraflex also shows the risk of approving prescription drugs too quickly. The United States has the world's most stringent drug laws, and, as a result, American citizens have been spared several drug disasters. The best known is the 1962 thalidomide tragedy, which involved a tranquilizer sold abroad. Thalidomide was used by thousands of pregnant women, who subsequently had babies born with missing limbs and other deformities. The FDA resisted approving thalidomide.

Unlike most of the health and safety regulatory laws, the Federal Food, Drug, and Cosmetic Act requires that drugs be approved by the federal government prior to marketing. There are many drug products approved abroad for which drug manufacturers make claims of effectiveness, but they will never be approved in the United States because there are no acceptable scientific studies demonstrating that they work. In addition, with our more cautious laws, some drugs take a little longer to get approved.

Instead of using its resources to enforce the drug laws or to remove ineffective OTC drugs from the market, the Reagan administration is giving top priority to speeding up the approval of prescription drugs. In some cases, this policy means merely that new drug applications are being processed in a more efficient manner. But the Reagan administration has also proposed weakening the drug approval standards in the United States.

For example, one proposal would place greater reliance on data generated from tests conducted in foreign countries, even though the FDA has very little ability to monitor foreign testing to ensure that it is both accurate and conducted properly. Under a program adopted prior to the Reagan administration, the agency divides applications to market new prescription drugs into two categories. The first is reserved for breakthrough drugs that represent an important medical advance over existing drugs. Of 301 new drugs approved for marketing during the seven-year period January 1, 1974, through December 31, 1980, only 11 percent, according to FDA scientists, offer important therapeutic gains. The FDA currently approves these drugs on an average of ten months after the new drug application is received.[30] No one is suggesting that it can act any more quickly in approving these products.

The second category is reserved for products such as Oraflex, which are not significantly better than products already on the market. Most of the new drug applications submitted to the FDA fall into this category. It currently takes the FDA an average of slightly less than two years to approve these products.[31]

The Reagan administration is proposing to speed up the approval of this second category of new drugs. The main problem with this approach is that it would shift resources from the important task of removing dangerous and ineffective drugs already on the market, and would instead use those resources to speed up the approval of drugs, such as Oraflex, that are not medically important. This emphasis typifies the Reagan administration's priorities, which place the financial interests of industry first, and the health and safety of consumers last.

PATIENT PACKAGE INSERTS

Having decided to shift government resources away from consumer protection laws, it might be presumed that the Reagan regulators are at least interested in helping consumers protect themselves. One program to enhance consumer knowledge adopted at the end of the Carter administration would have required prescription drug manufacturers to include patient package inserts (PPIs) with prescription drugs. PPIs are brochures that give consumers information about the uses for a drug, its possible side effects, and adverse reactions to it, which can be caused by foods and other substances that should not be taken with the drug. Since 1968, the FDA has required PPIs for a handful of drugs: isoproterenol inhalation drug products, oral contraceptives, estrogens, progestins, and a few medical devices, like IUD contraceptives. This type of information is now included with all over-the-counter drugs, but prescription drugs are usually sold with almost no information at all. Instead, the doctor is expected to inform the patient of the proper use of the drug. But it is unrealistic to expect doctors to convey all the information contained in patient package inserts.

In 1974 the FDA began to study the question of extending PPIs to prescription drugs in general. For six years it sponsored meetings, held symposia, and sifted through more than a thousand comments from one hearing alone. In 1980 it issued a final regulation requiring PPIs for ten prescription drugs, covering 300 individual drug products, such as Darvon and Valium, and constituting 16 percent of all new (or nonrefill) prescription drugs in the United States.[32] Seven years of rule-making proceedings backed the decision. The various inserts made statements such as:

- You can become dependent on propoxyphene [Darvon].
- When taking cimetidine [Tagamet], do not use any other drugs, including nonprescription drugs, unless your doctor knows and approves of their use.
- When you take ampicillin, it is important to finish all the prescribed medication even if you begin to feel better. If you do not take all the medication the infection could return.
- Studies show a doubling of the risk of getting gallstones or inflamed gallbladder [in patients taking clofibrate for several years]. One of the studies also suggested that people who take clofibrate have an increased risk of getting cancer.

The regulations were scheduled to take effect in May 1981 for three drugs and in July for two others. The inserts did not seem overly cautious, considering that the Valium family alone, while providing a chemical escape from daily stress, causes more than eight hundred deaths each year,[33] impairs driving, occasionally produces hallucinations or outbursts of rage, and pushes unsuspecting users into drug addiction.

Then Reagan took office. On February 6, 1981, C. Joseph Stetler, representing the American Pharmaceutical Association, met with Richard Schweiker, the new secretary of HHS, to talk about PPIs. On February 18, he wrote to both Secretary Schweiker and Vice-President Bush (at the Vice-President's Task Force on Regulatory Relief), again requesting review of the PPI regulations. Two days later the government began informally notifying industry that the FDA would not require compliance with the regulations. Although it acted without giving the public an opportunity to even comment on its decision, in violation of the Administrative Procedure Act, the administration revoked the program. As a result consumers will not be fully informed about prescription drugs that they use.

Although he defends the decision to halt the PPI program, former Reagan FDA Commissioner Arthur Hayes has acknowledged that almost half of all prescription drugs are taken improperly, and that consumers are "wasting as much as $6 billion each year, causing needless side effects and illness." But he argued that mandatory patient package inserts are merely a "quick fix."[34] Instead, the Reagan administration chose to rely on voluntary efforts by industry to include PPIs with prescription drugs rather than FDA regulation. Not surprisingly, given the opposition of doctors and pharmacists to PPIs, the voluntary program has been a failure.

DRUG SAFETY INFORMATION

Just as the drug companies deny consumers information about prescription drugs, they would also like to withhold from the FDA information about the safety of new drugs. This controversy has centered around the issue of who should control "raw data." Raw data are the medical charts and other information collected as part of a testing program on new drugs, which are submitted to the FDA in support of an application to market a drug. The companies would like to submit summaries of the studies, but not the data supporting them.

Raw data are critical to determining the accuracy of studies on safety and effectiveness. Organizations such as Public Citizen's Health Research Group often review this data when they have questions about the accuracy of a study. The medical officers of the FDA have an important need for access to the data when reviewing new drug applications and believe that it should be sent to the FDA.

Reagan's FDA appointees have proposed eliminating the requirement that drug companies submit raw data in connection with new drug applications.[35] Instead, the data would remain at the company and be available only at the request of FDA medical officers. This approach in no way improves the quality or the speed of new drug approvals. It also will not make drug testing any less expensive, since the raw data will have to be generated either way. The Reagan proposal, if adopted, simply would prevent citizen groups and academic researchers from ever obtaining access to raw data and would make it more difficult and more cumbersome for the FDA medical officers to review such data in connection with their review of new drug applications.[36]

A Public Citizen Health Research Group survey of FDA medical officers on this and other proposed changes to the drug approval process demonstrates that the changes will impair the agency's ability to protect the public from unsafe drugs. Seventy-eight percent said they frequently refer to raw data when reviewing a new drug application; 94 percent were concerned that having to obtain case reports from the drug companies would take significantly more time; 64 percent predicted that not having raw data would worsen the quality of new drug application review; and not a single medical officer thought the proposal would enhance his or her ability to review new drug applications.[37]

GENERIC DRUGS

While consumers are interested in safety first, they are also interested in the price of prescription drugs. For many years the prescription drug industry had excluded competition by convincing state legislatures to adopt very restrictive laws prohibiting prescription drug advertising. Many states also required pharmacists to prescribe the brand-name drug if the brand name appeared on the prescription. The large drug companies then spent huge sums of money familiarizing doctors with the brand names of prescriptions (such as Valium). Not surprisingly, doctors typically put the brand name rather than the longer, chemical name on prescriptions.

All this has changed in recent years. In 1976 the Supreme Court held, in a case brought by attorneys for Public Citizen (*Virginia State Board of Pharmacy* v. *Virginia Citizen Consumers Council*),[38] that the advertising prohibition is unconstitutional; and forty-nine states (every one except Lilly's home state, Indiana) have adopted substitution laws.[39] Those laws generally allow the consumer to purchase the less expensive generic drug, unless the doctor has specifically prohibited substitution in the prescription.

In its approval procedures, the FDA maintains an artificial distinction between brand-name and generic drugs. Generic copies of drugs first marketed after 1962 must be proven to be safe and effective, even if they contain ingredients identical to already approved brand-name drugs. This division has never made any sense, since the agency does not require the same standards for generic copies of drugs first marketed before 1962. For these earlier drugs, the FDA relies on its determination that the brand-name product meets its standards. Companies selling generic drugs may obtain approval of a pre-1962 drug by submitting an abbreviated new drug application, or an ANDA.[40] For several years the FDA has been considering a proposal to extend the ANDA procedures to post-1962 drugs. The FDA under Ronald Reagan, however, has changed this proposal to prohibit the use of ANDAs for the first fifteen years after a post-1962 drug has been approved.[41] The OMB has delayed issuance of the proposed rule. Since the ANDA procedures are not available for post-1962 drugs, there traditionally have been two ways for a generic-drug manufacturer to obtain approval. The first is by submitting published scientific articles and research to the FDA. The second, far more costly avenue is through new studies showing safety and effectiveness.

Shortly after Reagan took office, Secretary Schweiker of HHS required the FDA not to approve post-1962 generic drugs unless the company had submitted these new studies. Public Citizen and several manufacturers of generic drugs sued in federal courts all over the country, and Schweiker subsequently backed down. Currently, the FDA allows drug companies to rely on scientific papers, but if there are no such articles, the generic companies must undertake expensive and duplicative testing to prove that the drugs are safe and effective. This policy has created a high barrier to the approval and marketing of generic drug products.

EXTENSION OF PATENT MONOPOLIES

When Secretary Schweiker failed to undercut generic drugs administratively, he tried the legislative approach. Even though the prescription drug industry is the third most profitable industry in the United States, it has been lobbying vigorously, with the support of the Reagan administration, for a law that would make its profits even greater. That law, the Patent Term Restoration Act, would extend the monopoly patents on prescription drugs by as much as seven additional years.

The large drug companies claim that government regulation delays the marketing of drugs, and as a result, they lose seven or more years of patent life. The proposed patent extension legislation, they argue, would merely "restore" their right to a full seventeen-year monopoly. This, they say, is only fair, since other businesses can take advantage of the full seventeen years of monopoly protection.

These arguments conveniently omit several critical facts. First, for liability reasons, the drug companies would have to conduct time-consuming safety tests even without FDA requirements. Second, the patent laws do not guarantee a seventeen-year marketing monopoly. Instead, they provide seventeen years of protection for development of the product and its sale at monopoly prices. Historically, inventors have far less than seventeen years to market their inventions, because of the normal lag between invention, development, manufacturing, and marketing. Third, the drug companies have often been quite successful at obtaining almost the full seventeen years of protection. In 1980, the eight best-selling drugs enjoyed an average of more than fifteen years of monopoly protection, according to the Office of Technology Assessment.[42]

Moreover, the drug companies engage in the common practice of "evergreening," filing a patent application early to beat out rivals, but then filing new applications that modify or extend the original to postpone the starting date for the seventeen-year patent. Hoffman-LaRoche, for example, used this device to gain twenty-two years of patent protection for Valium.[43]

Not surprisingly, the drug industry's profit picture reflects the benefits of monopoly pricing.[44] At a time when inflation is crippling consumers, particularly the elderly, this industry, with the help of the Reagan administration, is trying to extend its monopoly even further.

Congress created the FDA over seventy-five years ago to protect consumers from dangerous drugs. Yet, under the Reagan administration, the agency has again and again favored the financial interests of the large drug companies over the needs of sick and uninformed consumers. As a result, consumers are being senselessly exposed to drugs with known and unknown health risks, they are being denied important information about the safety of drugs that they use, and they will have to pay exorbitant prices for prescription drug products. The American public deserves more from its government.

PRODUCT SAFETY

CONSUMER PRODUCT SAFETY ACT OF 1972: ". . . A bill to protect consumers against unreasonable risk of injury from hazardous product. . . .

Congress has seldom championed the Consumer Product Safety Commission (CPSC), a small agency regulating a wide variety of consumer products—just about everything except cars, drugs, cigarettes, and firearms. CPSC is popular with a diverse consumer constituency, but consumers rarely have the resources to participate in CPSC battles to make products safer. Often the public is not even aware these battles are waged, but well-stocked industry trade associations, representing almost every product imaginable, have moved to Washington, DC, in droves, primed to fight any CPSC action affecting their clients. With this imbalance of resources among its constituents, CPSC has never risen to the top of the political power curve. In fact, it must spend much of its time fighting OMB and Congress for an annual budget equal to less than the funds spent for two hours of Pentagon operations. In the Reagan administration CPSC has reached its lowest ebb.

The Consumer Product Safety Commission is the smallest and newest of the health and safety regulatory agencies. Most agencies are born in response to sudden death or crisis. Not so the CPSC. It was formed at the recommendation of the National Commission on Product Safety created by President Lyndon Johnson, which issued its final report in 1970: 20 million people a year hurt by household products; 30,000 a year killed; 110,000 disfigured or disabled. The annual economic loss was estimated at $5.5 billion (1970 dollars).[1]

Two years later President Nixon signed into law the Consumer Product Safety Act of 1972, and seven months after that, in May 1973, the independent commission to regulate consumer products came into being. This group became the first, and is still the only independent, health and safety regulatory agency. It has five commissioners, appointed by the president to overlapping seven-year terms. Its task is to ensure the safety of about ten to fifteen thousand products made by about a million companies, and to monitor the recall of tens of millions of products a year. By its own calculations, the commission prevents approximately 215,000 injuries and 300 deaths annually, because of its standards, its recall requirements, and its policing of industrial practices.[2] The Consumer Federation of America (CFA) reports, in a September 1983 study, that in the last five years specific actions of the commission have prevented more than 1.25 million serious injuries and deaths. The CFA calculates this has resulted in economic savings of at least $3.5 billion.[3]

In its ten-year history the agency has recalled more than 300 million dangerously defective products. Its standards for child-resistant medicine bottle tops and package enclosures are estimated to have prevented hundreds of children from dying and thousands of infant poisonings each year. Its standards for cribs save about fifty babies a year and protect hundreds more from injuries that often result in brain damage.[4] It has helped develop voluntary standards to reduce the slipperiness of bathtubs. It has issued mandatory ones to make rotary power mowers safer to operate. It has created standards to insure the safety of architectural glass for storm doors. CPSC protects against flammable children's clothing, sharp edges of children's toys, unvented gas-fired space heaters, and many more possible hazards.

A 1983 poll by Louis Harris showed that most Americans believe that the CPSC is doing a better job protecting consumers than any other federal or state group. They ranked it above Congress in this respect. Almost half of those surveyed wanted to strengthen CPSC, and 88 percent were in favor of CPSC ensuring greater toy safety.[5] An earlier Harris poll, in August 1981, found strong public sentiment against crippling CPSC. By 59 to 32 percent, a majority was opposed to "cutting down the scope and enforcement powers of the CPSC."[6]

In spite of this broad public support for CPSC, since taking office the Reagan administration has tried to stifle the agency. In 1981 David Stockman of OMB slated CPSC for elimination. When that failed, he tried to have the independent agency subsumed under the Department of Commerce,[7] a move that lost by one vote in a subcommittee of the House Energy and Commerce committee. OMB was thus forced to resort to budget cuts to achieve its objectives. Few agencies have experienced the losses of CPSC— its funding was cut by 25 percent in FY 1982, from $42.1 million to $32 million.[8] In FY 1984, Congress finally inched it up to $35 million from the $32 million funding level proposed by Reagan.[9] A massive personnel cut reduced the staff from 889 in FY 1981 to 636 in FY 1983.[10] A GAO report in December 1982 showed that the agency lost 32 percent of its scientific and technical staff in 1981.[11] Moreover, OMB planned to cut the budget further, so that by the end of 1984 its staff would stand at 36 percent below the 1981 level. Eight out of thirteen regional offices were closed by 1982. The impact of the cuts on the ability of the agency to shoulder its health and safety responsibilities has been dramatic. Between 1981 and 1983 inspections dropped 45 percent; recalls dropped 66 percent; investigations of injuries dropped 28 percent; and sample collections for testing dropped 55 percent.[12]

"They're cutting our necks off," said one CPSC staff member, asking that he not be quoted by name. "We've been cut from nine hundred to five hundred. Maybe we were bloated. That happens. . . . Now we've learned to tighten up, but what happens is you lose the best people—young, ambitious."

David Pittle, a former commissioner of CPSC for ten years, disagrees that the agency was ever fat. "For every product not worked on for lack of staff, there will be people killed or injured. It's that simple."[13]

With approximately 28,000 deaths and 130,000 serious injuries each year caused by dangerous products, the CPSC has always had an agenda larger than its capability. Although its budget increased during the Carter years, its list of priorities was drastically cut to focus on the most important projects, such as researching chronic health hazards presented by chemicals in consumer products. Mandatory standards were issued for toy safety, lawnmowers, unstable refuse bins, and citizens' band radio antennas. The commission developed thirty-seven voluntary standards for such products as ladders, playpens, extension cords, and Christmas tree lights, in cooperation with industry groups. It recalled millions of products, including specific models of hair dryers, cribs, snowmobiles, coffee pots, and paint strippers. And it gathered information for warnings to consumers about product hazards.[14]

But under Reagan the CPSC has been so crippled that it has had to postpone research it had under way to update a clothing flammability standard first issued thirty years ago by the Department of Health, Education, and Welfare. The standard has been out of date for years. In Minnesota, a company producing garments complying with this standard has been instructed by a court to pay a $1 million damage award to one of the victims. The court complained that even a garment made out of newspaper could pass the existing standard.[15] The commission has also had to postpone several other significant investigations—into injuries from hot water heaters using corrosive fluids that could pose a fire hazard, and from hot tubs or spas in which sixty-seven people, including twenty-six toddlers, have died in recent years.[16]

The following is a list of some products with their annual injury and death tolls. Research into these products will be curtailed because of the budget cuts:

PROBLEMS NOT TO BE REVIEWED	ANNUAL DEATHS AND INJURIES
Preschool playground equipment	25,000 injuries
Rider lawnmowers	13,800 injuries
Objects thrown from lawnmowers	12,000 injuries
Inflammable wearing apparel	3,000 injuries; 300 deaths
Snow throwers/blowers	2,700 injuries

PROBELMS NOT TO BE REVIEWED	ANNUAL DEATHS AND INJURIES
Kerosene heaters	800 injuries
Bicycle passenger carriers	530 injuries
Carbon monoxide detection systems	350 deaths
Light fixtures	140 injuries; 4,200 fires
Electric clothes dryers	25 injuries[17]

If the 1984 cuts proposed by Reagan (but rejected by Congress) had been instituted, the agency would have been forced to postpone its research on coal- and wood-burning equipment (causing 130,000 injuries and 290 deaths annually) and on fires in upholstered furniture caused by burning cigarettes (resulting in 1,150 deaths and 4,200 injuries annually).[18] CPSC has continued developing voluntary industry standards, which require fewer resources.

Because of its independent status and set terms of office, the CPSC avoided being molded to the Reagan ideology until the end of his third year in office. But now only one Carter appointee (a Republican) still serves on the commission. For the first eight months after Reagan arrived, the commission was without a permanent chairperson, and other members served in an acting capacity. Then Reagan appointed Nancy Steorts, a former Welcome Wagon local club president and public relations consultant, to serve as chairperson. The *Wall Street Journal* commented: "Some critics question the forty-five-year-old chairman's credentials. Her regulatory background is so meager that on her résumé she claimed organizing two inaugural candlelight dinners as 'government experience.' Her four fellow commissioners question her penchant for perquisites and for spending money on promotional activities."[19]

Ms. Steorts stepped on toes without delay. While the agency's budget was being drastically cut, she installed new carpets and curtains in her office, repainted, and constructed a new doorway to avoid sharing a reception area with another commissioner. The redecoration cost $10,000. When complaints surfaced, she responded, "When I came in here, this office was literally filthy."[20]

Steorts then indicated that she would fire the commission's driver because of his informal dress. She insisted he wear a dark suit. When he said he didn't own one, and couldn't afford one on his salary, several top agency officials pitched in and bought him some clothes, to make sure he would not lose his job. "Part of lifting this agency out of its doldrums is maintaining certain standards," Steorts countered.[21]

Citing budget limitations, Steorts reminded agency staff that they must use vacation leave if lunch hours ran more than half an hour. About the same time she hired three consultants in media and business relations, at $84,000 per year.[22]

"The mission of this agency seems almost an annoyance to her," one commissioner commented. "The important thing is to meet the vice-president and go to all the teas. The heart of our work, analyzing what might make a hair dryer electrocute a kid, isn't what occupies her."[23]

In October 1981, the respected executive director of the CPSC, Richard Gross, resigned and wrote a stinging letter to Steorts, accusing her of ignoring the public trust she was charged with protecting. He criticized her unwillingness to trust the agency's staff, her lack of attention to major substantive issues, her failure to follow legal guidelines, and her reluctance to consult her four fellow commissioners. The next day the commission, in a 4 to 1 vote, rejected Steorts' reorganization proposal to meet a $1 million shortfall under the budget cuts. The other commissioners had not received the plan until late the evening before it was to be voted on.[24]

Almost ostracized in the agency during her first months, Steorts had to mend fences. In a surprise move, she decided to vote for a mandatory standard on the most important issue pending in the commission. She voted with the majority, as the commission decided to ban urea formaldehyde foam insulation (UFFI), a product used in many buildings and mobile homes. The decision infuriated the White House. The public pressures on Thorne Auchter at the Occupational Safety and Health Administration (OSHA) and Anne Burford at the Environmental Protection

Agency (EPA) to ban formaldehyde mounted, but both agencies announced that they would not take any action. They said they did not agree with the wisdom of CPSC's decision. Then in April 1983, the Fifth Circuit overruled CPSC. It found that the CPSC's decision was not supported by convincing evidence. The court noted that formaldehyde is ubiquitous, implying that because the substance occurs naturally within living cells, it is not dangerous to humans.[25]

Formaldehyde in its natural state is "bound" within a larger molecule. Cellular processes prevent the formaldehyde from interacting or interfering with other essential molecules. In contrast, formaldehyde released from UFFI is "free"—untied to a larger molecule. When a person inhales air containing free formaldehyde, the formaldehyde readily reacts with molecules within the body, including important proteins and DNA, and can cause cancer and other disabilities.[26] It is because of this potential to interact that free formaldehyde—released from UFFI, particle board, permanent press clothing, and other formaldehyde-containing consumer products—can pose a threat to health.

The decision was a setback for the CPSC, whose morale was already strained. It petitioned the court for a rehearing and was refused. The only option after that was to appeal to the Supreme Court, which three of the five commissioners wanted to do. The Reagan Justice Department refused. They had a credible rationale. The Fifth Circuit decision was very difficult to appeal. "It's been made into a political thing," said one CPSC administrator. "But it's not. Justice got down a bad decision, and it wasn't the kind of case you take to the Supreme Court." The Court takes cases involving constitutional issues, ones that clarify issues of law or resolve disputes between lower courts. This decision on formaldehyde concerns an interpretation of scientific information. The decision took the burden off the White House, as well as EPA and OSHA. Now Reagan had a court of appeals decision as justification for inaction by the other agencies. David Greenberg, legislative director of the Consumer Federation of America, called the Justice Department's action the "dousing of the one bright light for consumers that came out of the Reagan administration."[27]

Chairperson Nancy Steorts said that she still supports the

ban. Foam insulation "presents a risk of injury because of the acute toxicity of the formaldehyde gas it releases. . . . So where does this leave the American consumer?" she asked in a prepared statement. "Back at ground zero."[28]

The CPSC had done everything possible to support its case. Its scientific tests used 960 animals and 240 rats per dose at dose levels ranging from 0 to 15 ppm of formaldehyde. In contrast, the standard program at the National Cancer Institute uses 100 animals per dose. "This was the largest bio-assay of its kind ever done," said one CPSC scientist who worked on the formaldehyde evaluation. The testing was paid for by the Chemical Industry Institute for Toxicology. "If this one was not sufficient for the courts," he continued, "nothing would be."

Based on the finding that 103 of the 240 rats exposed to formaldehyde developed nasal cancers, the CPSC calculated the potential risk of cancer to humans. This assessment, though carried out using accepted scientific and mathematical techniques, simply could not predict precisely the number of cancers that would occur in humans. Yet the court apparently believed that such precision was indispensable for the ban to be upheld. This view not only ignores scientific convention, but it also severely hampers, if not destroys, the ability of a regulatory agency to control human exposure to carcinogens based on animal evidence.

Asked if he was disappointed, the CPSC scientist seemed resigned. "No, we did everything we should. We did the risk assessment. I don't consider lawyers knowledgeable enough to make the decision they did. How can you expect them to know what 'significant risk' is? They're unqualified. People who know agree with our findings. The National Academy of Sciences did a case study on formaldehyde and said we did an excellent job. The *Harvard Environmental Law Review* said we did an excellent job. Why should I be concerned with judges who don't know?"

The Fifth Circuit was not the only court overruling the CPSC. A week later the US Court of Appeals DC circuit ruled that the CPSC lacks the authority to impose civil penalties on its own. According to the appellate court, the CPSC must sue the companies in federal court rather than use its own administrative procedures to impose civil penalties.[29] Many agencies have this power, and it has been conservatively used by the CPSC. Members of the commission believe that the decision will diminish the willingness of companies to negotiate for rapid recalls of unsafe products from the marketplace. "There is a bargaining process in arranging a recall," explains Commissioner Stuart M. Statler. He believes that the court's decision undermines the commission's leverage and could result in delay and less effective recalls.[30] While the White House has not been able to push through legislation to exercise direct control over the CPSC, except through budget cuts, the court decisions have been very effective in curbing the agency.

Although one of the purposes stated in the Consumer Product Safety Act is "to assist consumers in evaluating the comparative safety of consumer products,"[31] the Supreme Court has placed severe restrictions on the agency's authority to disclose information about product performance and causes of injury. The decision grew out of a suit by GTE Sylvania to protect alleged trade secrets and its own reputation, by preventing CPSC from disclosing information about injuries from its products. The case involved fires associated with television sets. The CPSC had sought statistics on injuries in an effort to discern the hazard. GTE Sylvania, as well as other companies, provided the data, but when CPSC wanted to release it in response to a request covered by the Freedom of Information Act (FOIA), the company objected. The Supreme Court held in 1980 that the CPSC could not release information identifying the product of a manufacturer in response to a FOIA request without first letting the manufacturer know and giving it time to respond.[32]

Under the Consumer Product Safety Act, as interpreted by the Court, CPSC cannot even provide information on a product recall or answer a FOIA request without lengthy delays. CPSC must give the manufacturer of any named product a chance to object and to seek a court injunction barring the release. One example of how this restriction confines CPSC is shown by the difficulty Public Citizen's Health Research Group faced when it requested all letters that the CPSC had received between certain dates from consumers complaining about the effects of formaldehyde in mobile homes. By law, a FOIA request must be answered within ten days. It took CPSC thirteen months to respond to the request. When the material arrived, it included a copy of an article from the *Louisville Courier-Journal:* "Man's Death Fuels Concern about Fumes in Mobile Homes." Absurdly, the names of each person in the article had been crossed out, and black boxes covered the eyes of people in the photos. The agency seemed to be unreasonably diligent in interpreting the disclosure limitations.[33]

In 1981 the Congress further tightened the authority of the CPSC to disclose information. It prohibited the agency from releasing any information obtained from a company concerning defects, violations of standards, and fatalities caused by product hazards, unless the company is sued by CPSC, agrees to a settlement, or permits the release. This additional prohibition significantly hinders the Commission's investigative activities because it is not able, as are other agencies, to alert the public during a pending case. This not only prevents the CPSC from warning consumers of a potential danger, but also restricts its ability to gather consumer case histories which illustrate the severity of a product hazard. In addition, even after a recall has been conducted, CPSC is still forbidden to make public accident data in those cases in which an injury cannot be explicitly proven to be caused by the product.[34] "It's a form of censorship," Commissioner Statler told a House subcommittee. "The Consumer Product Safety Commission is the only health or safety federal agency which must undergo these egregious delays before disclosing vital safety information."[35]

To avoid delays in publicizing a recall, the agency must withhold vital information. For example, a press release about the February 1983 recall of 240,000 Rototillers did not mention that thirty-seven accidents and seven limb amputations had been associated with the garden machines.[36] The Roper Corporation of Illinois manufactured the Rototillers, which were distributed through Sears, Roebuck, and Co. The companies maintained that the Rototillers are safe if used properly. They were concerned that publishing the accident reports would increase their product liability suits.

"The section's safeguards," said Statler, "were designed to protect firms from misleading or inaccurate publicity coming out of the agency, not accurate information a firm may be uncomfortable about, such as the numbers of infants killed from an ill-designed crib, or the number of amputations of legs and feet from a defective Rototiller."[37]

But since the CPSC must, in effect, obtain the permission of the company to release any information concerning the details about recalls, the news release could announce only that an investigation was under way. "From the consumer's perspective," said former commissioner David Pittle, "CPSC is the only health and safety agency in Washington that does not routinely give out consumer complaints under the FOIA. FDA does. EPA does. NHTSA [the National Highway Traffic Safety Association] does. OSHA does. CPSC does not—and that makes no sense."[38]

These limitations also waste significant agency resources at a time when the Reagan budget has cut the number of enforcement personnel from 87 to 50 in the Washington office and from 123 to 89 in the field. During the same period, the number of recall campaigns both for enforcement of safety standards and for defects has dropped. Agency staff have determined that about 50 percent of the recall campaigns initiated by companies are less serious than the cases that CPSC discovers. Thus, the cutback in personnel and information is particularly harmful because it stifles CPSC's ability to protect consumers from millions of hazardous products. Each year at least several million products are recalled.[39]

Although the OMB does not have the authority to review the rule making of independent agencies such as CPSC, directions to the staff from Chairperson Steorts and the Reagan budget cuts adversely affected agency research and rule-making activity. In 1982, for example, the Commission focused on eleven product hazard areas. In only three (formaldehyde, omnidirectional CB antennas, and decorative cutout designs on cribs) were standards issued. In another area, the existing standard for poison-prevention packaging to protect children was reviewed with an eye to reducing the requirements. The rest of the projects were merely cooperative ventures with the so-called regulated industries, some of which have been pending for years. Four involved fire problems: house wiring and circuit breakers; plastic flammability in cookware, toys, and furniture; upholstered furniture; and wood- and coal-burning heating equipment. The remaining concerned deadly chain saws, the toxicity of dyes and finishes, and indoor air quality.[40]

In June 1983, the CPSC authorization bill to extend the life of the agency came before the House of Representatives. It included a provision to remove some of the limits on disclosing information. The timing was terrible. The US Supreme Court in the previous week had just declared Congress's legislative veto unconstitutional. Members were fond of putting this device into agency statutes allowing Congress to veto agency decisions. After the court's declaration the members of Congress were frustrated and confused. The court's ruling meant that Congress could no longer reject the regulations promulgated by agencies except by passing a bill through both the House and Senate, and by getting it signed by the president. Congressional response was swift.

"We should be very careful," said James T. Broyhill, a Republican representative from North Carolina, "as we delegate those lawmaking powers to these independent commissions, especially because now the legislative veto . . . has been overturned by the Supreme Court last week."[41]

Throughout the debate on whether the budget should be raised or cut, on whether the CPSC could function with stripped-down numbers of personnel, there were frequent references to the legislative veto. The members of Congress could not get this affront to their own power off their minds.

A drastically weakened CPSC authorization bill passed the House on June 29, 1983, by a vote of 238 to 177. It permits the crippled agency to stagger on, but without increasing its funding ceiling or personnel level. Congressman Elliott Levitas (Democrat-Georgia) successfully tacked on an amendment requiring that both houses of Congress must pass any CPSC standard and the president must sign it into law before it can take effect. Then Congressman Henry Waxman (Democrat-California) proposed a substitute amendment, making CPSC's safety rules concerning products final after ninety days unless Congress has intervened. In that way Congress could overturn any action it disapproved of but would not have to debate every rule. The full House passed that amendment as well, even though it conflicted with the Levitas amendment. The contradictions between the Waxman and Levitas amendments were left for the Senate to resolve.

The bill that the House of Representatives finally passed was opposed by Public Citizen's Congress Watch, the Consumer Federation of America (CFA), the AFL-CIO, the National Council of Senior Citizens, Consumers Union, the American Academy of Pediatrics, the International Association of Machinists, and the International Ladies Garment Workers Union. It was supported by David Stockman and by Vice-President Bush. With this impasse, it is unlikely to be enacted into law.

While the CPSC budget cuts reflected the Reagan philosophy as early as 1981, it was not until late 1983 that Reagan had the opportunity to appoint a majority of the commission members. The agency's independent structure and seven-year terms of office had protected it from the worst ravages of antiregulation fervor that spread throughout the executive agencies in 1981. That is why David Stockman wanted to abolish the Consumer Product Safety Commission and subsume its functions—or at least pretend to do so—under the Department of Commerce. But now that isn't necessary. The agency is wounded from budgetary and staffing cuts, and the majority of commissioners won't press for any consumer initiatives.

THE HEALTH AND SAFETY OF WORKERS

OCCUPATIONAL SAFETY AND HEALTH ACT OF 1970:
". . . To assure so far as possible every working man and woman in the nation safe and healthful working conditions and to preserve our human resources."

"I bet everyone in this room has, at one time or another, climbed a ladder," Ronald Reagan once told a business audience. "How we did it without a hundred forty-four rules and regulations about ladder climbing, I'll never know. The first [rule] is: In order to climb a ladder, you begin by facing it."[1]

Jokes like these about the Occupational Safety and Health Administration (OSHA) had become standard humor among business audiences before 1980—even though few people realized that industry itself had written OSHA's many "nitpicking" standards. Still, OSHA was a ready target for cheap shots and a scapegoat for antiregulatory resentments.

Once Ronald Reagan moved into the White House in January 1981, however, the kidding about OSHA became something of a sick joke for American workers. In fact, that was precisely the terminology that Leon Kruchten used in the aftermath of his near electrocution on New Year's Eve of 1981. While trying to repair a power outage at the Oscar Mayer meat-packing plant in Madison, Wisconsin, Kruchten was severely burned and lost an arm. His supervisor's arm was also amputated as a result of the accident. One month later OSHA investigator Gerald Madjeska concluded that Oscar Mayer had failed to follow OSHA safety procedures on its electrical equipment and proposed that the company be fined $640.

By this time, however, the Reagan administration had assumed control of OSHA and had instituted a new regime of "cooperation." After an "informal conference" between company representatives, agency officials, and a shop steward, the fine was dropped and the citation reduced to "nonserious." Kruchten, who has been through eleven operations since the accident and who is now back at work at Oscar Mayer, terms OSHA's citation "a joke."[2]

In 1981, the workers of the Beloit Corporation, of Beloit, Wisconsin, were the punchlines of a stale joke themselves. They were suffering from exceedingly high levels of silica dust and noise, generated by Beloit's metal-casting foundry, which produces paper-making machinery. In 1974, OSHA presented the company with citations for the health hazards and gave it three years to correct them. The company delayed correcting the major hazards. In 1980, the union filed another complaint with OSHA. In January 1981, OSHA issued thirteen citations against the company and gave it a year to make corrections. But when OSHA's inspectors returned in February 1982, they found the same violations.[3]

When OSHA charged the Beloit Corporation with more infractions (but not for areas previously cited), the company asked for an "informal conference" to resolve the dispute. Once again "cooperation" carried the day, and the Beloit Corporation's fines were reduced more than 80 percent, from $1,620 to $300. Union representatives tried to attend but were excluded and informed of the decision after the fact.[4]

The first sign that OSHA was in for a four-year depression came when President Reagan announced his nominee for its top post, Thorne Auchter. Reagan did not follow the example of Presidents Ford and Carter, who appointed respected scientists, with experience in occupational safety and health matters. Instead, he tapped Auchter, a politically ambitious businessman, whose full-time job since graduating from college in 1968 had been working at his family's construction company in Florida, first as a construction supervisor and then as executive vice-president. Although he had once served on a governor's task force for establishing a state OSHA program, Auchter's company did not have an exemplary record in job safety. During the 1970s, it was cited for forty-eight safety violations; six of them were considered serious and incurred fines totaling $1,200.[5]

As the newly appointed assistant secretary of labor for OSHA, Auchter was candid about this conviction that OSHA should retreat from its role as policeman of the workplace. Under the new Reagan philosophy concerning workplace protection, "consultation and education will be ... improved," he told a union audience in June 1981. "The states will play a larger role. We will begin encouraging employers to do self-inspection of their workplaces. And OSHA will become the catalyst to encourage various employer/employee approaches to workplace safety and health."[6] Although Auchter's vision of improved workplace protection resembles that of the pre-OSHA era—voluntary and largely ineffective—he insists to this day that the "cooperative" approach greatly improves OSHA's impact.

The key, Auchter explained, is to transform OSHA from a strict disciplinarian into a solicitous educator. The confrontations between OSHA and business had to stop, he told the New York Chamber of Commerce and Industry: "OSHA has always been in an adversarial position. This adversarial spirit has hampered the effective functioning of the agency long enough. ... The OSHA of today is a cooperative regulator."[7]

Auchter has not been so cooperative himself with members of Congress inquiring into the agency's performance. Factual inquiries have been dismissed by peremptory, uninformed replies, or, in instances of accusatory challenges, by curt retorts of "that is a bunch of hogwash."[8]

As to OSHA's mission "to assure as far as possible every man and woman in the nation safe and healthful working conditions," Auchter's definition of "cooperative" is a subterfuge for deregulation. During Auchter's term, the agency has not issued a single new health standard. Existing standards have been weakened or revoked entirely. Emergency temporary standards (intended to give quick protection to workers while permanent standards are being developed) have been resisted by Auchter, until the federal courts themselves have directed the agency to take action.

Auchter's alternative to standards requiring improvement in the workplace environment is the use of worker equipment to protect against hazards. This view caused Lane Kirkland, AFL-CIO president, to respond, "This means that, instead of reducing noise through engineering controls, employers force workers to wear earplugs. Instead of removing unsafe concentrations of dust or of chemicals, employers encase the workers in respirators. The worker is engineered, not the workplace."[9]

OSHA inspections and the enforcement of standards have drastically declined. Information and research to help workers and the scientific community have been curtailed. The lasting institutional damage has grown worse, as OSHA's highly skilled, professional staff have been fired, demoted, or reassigned to less appropriate jobs. Other staff, disgusted and demoralized, have quit. "The gradual assembly of scientific and technical talent has been dissipated. . . . The effective deployment of a trained and competent enforcement corps has been relegated to paper inspections and compromised citations," laments Bertram Cottine, a former commissioner of the Occupational Safety and Health Review Commission.[10]

"Every other administrator at least said [that he was] trying to carry out the congressional mandate," charged Tony Mazzocchi, former vice-president of the Oil, Chemical, and Atomic Workers, and a leading expert on occupational health. "There may have been delays, . . . but here is an individual dedicated to dismantling the [regulatory] apparatus."[11] What is most notable about the Reagan administration's handling of OSHA and the Review Commission is its intense politicization. Auchter had been a Reagan Florida fund raiser; the chairman of the OSHA Review Commission had been the vice-chairman of the Texas Reagan-Bush Committee; the executive director of the commission had been the national director of the Young Americans for Freedom; and the commission's general counsel had been the former Republican candidate for mayor of New Orleans. As Bertram Cottine concluded, "Even the selling of OSHA under the Nixon administration [in exchange for campaign contributions] pales by comparison."[12]

A BRIEF HISTORY OF OSHA

"Occupational health and safety always has been the illegitimate child at the family reunion," former AFL-CIO union official George Taylor once told a congressional hearing. "No one gives a damn. If twenty-three people get swine flu, the whole government is turned upside down, but you can have carnage in the workplace and no one cares."[13]

By the late 1960s, the toll taken by unsafe workplaces was finally penetrating the apathy and abstractions that had allowed this national epidemic to go unaddressed. Amputations, cuts and lacerations, respiratory diseases, muscle disorders, and dozens of kinds of cancer were everyday events. This distasteful, unnecessary human wreckage was highlighted by statistics, grisly disasters, and a series of congressional hearings held after President Lyndon Johnson proposed a federal occupational safety and health program in his Manpower Message to Congress in January 1968.

Although the rate of industrial accidents had risen by 29 percent between 1961 and 1970, it was a horrible mining explosion in November 1968 that galvanized Congress to take action against job hazards. The death of seventy-eight miners in Farmington, Virginia, led to passage of the Coal Mine Health and Safety Act of 1969, which in turn fueled the momentum for enactment of the Occupational Safety and Health Act of 1970.[14]

The new law established OSHA as part of the Department of Labor and created a research arm, the National Institute of Occupational Safety and Health (NIOSH), to be administered, along with the other health research institutes, by the Department of Health and Human Services. Finally, the 1970 law created an independent Occupational Safety and Health Review Commission to review any enforcement disputes between OSHA and recalcitrant companies or dissatisfied workers.

By establishing a separate federal agency for occupational dangers, Congress sought to focus more attention on a problem that had been pursued ineffectually (if at all) by most states and virtually ignored by most companies. Because of the new law, research into health hazards, which had hardly been studied at all, would be intensified; professionals would be encouraged to study industrial hygiene, epidemiology, toxicology, and related disciplines; new educational and training programs would be instituted for workers; publications and notices to alert workers to possible hazards would be issued to reduce risks in the workplace.

But the heart of the new Occupational Safety and Health Act was the authority to issue and enforce safety as well as health standards for specific hazards. In addition to an all-purpose "general duty" clause, which applied to all workplaces, OSHA could regulate the hazards of specific substances, machinery, and job conditions. For the first time, millions of workers in the nation's petrochemical plants, auto factories, textile mills, steel mills, construction sites, and shipyards enjoyed formal legal rights and protections against unscrupulous or ignorant employers.[15]

However ambitious the 1970 statute, its execution by the first OSHA administrators was dismal. Rather than aggressively moving against the most serious job dangers, the first Republican-appointed administrators dwelt on the trivial and noncontroversial. In an attempt to avoid significant new standards, the industry pressed OSHA to adopt thousands of workplace guidelines that industry groups had voluntarily developed for themselves years earlier. The standards dealt primarily with minor safety matters, such as the height of fire extinguishers on walls, the distance between rungs of ladders, and the shape and placement of toilets. OSHA complied with industry's requests and adopted its "consensus guidelines" as mandatory federal standards. And so the stage was set for the jokes and ribbing about OSHA.

Recognizing that it was easier and less politically damaging to go after the trivial job hazards, OSHA inspectors spent an inordinate amount of time enforcing those regulations—an ironic retribution to the businesses that had pressed for their adoption. By 1975, the uproar in the business community against OSHA had reached a high pitch, and bills were introduced in Congress to exempt small businesses and provide other relief. Dr. Morton Corn, appointed OSHA administrator by President Gerald Ford in 1975, tried to increase training of staff and upgrade health standards, but his term of office was cut short when Ford did not get re-elected.

The cause of occupational safety and health might well have been permanently discredited if President Carter had not appointed Dr. Eula Bingham as the OSHA administrator in 1977. An eminent toxicologist, Dr. Bingham quickly set about instituting new "common sense priorities," including the repeal of 928 "nit-picking" regulations. Dr. Bingham beefed up the agency's scientific staff and analyses, focused new attention on health hazards (chemicals, gases, dusts), and issued a raft of new standards for cotton dust, arsenic, lead, benzene, the pesticide DBCP, acrylonitrile, and workers' access to medical records.

Enforcement, too, was diligently pursued. More citations were issued, stiffer penalties levied, and many more cases referred to the Justice Department for possible criminal action. Notwithstanding this new get-tough attitude, Dr. Bingham also improved the agency's outreach to businesses, to help them comply with OSHA's standards. Dr. Bingham knew that the changes that OSHA was meant to bring about would require adjustments that might be painful, inconvenient, and costly. But she was adamant that OSHA be the catalyst for change and that costs play a secondary role. "This idea of using workers' bodies to drive the wheel is a philosophy untenable to me. I am in the business of preventing sickness and injury, not using bodies . . . [, which will] drive up the cost so that business will find it more profitable to comply."[16]

The best measure of OSHA's impact under Bingham may be industry's reaction: it fought nearly every standard tooth and nail and bitterly contested OSHA's enforcement actions. From 1973 to 1977, industry challenged some 6 percent of OSHA's enforcement actions. But by the end of 1980, approximately 25 percent of all violations were being contested by industry.

A key measure of OSHA's new resolve was its issuance of new standards. In the agency's first six years, only four major health standards had been developed (for asbestos, vinyl chloride, coke oven emissions, and a group of fourteen carcinogens). During Dr. Bingham's tenure, however, OSHA issued seven additional major health standards—twice as many per year as had been issued previously—and six new safety standards.

Perhaps the most significant legacy of the Bingham years was the wholesale renovation of OSHA's research, analysis, and regulatory apparatus. A new *esprit de corps* invigorated an ener-

getic staff of professionals, who went about their work with a
dedication and rigor that the agency had not seen before. This
transformation, in turn, radiated out to OSHA's many constituen-
cies. Unions began to take a new interest in health and safety
issues; more students entered graduate programs in industrial
safety and hygiene; academic research in these areas was buoyed
by new federal funds; businesses created their own in-house staffs
to deal with occupational health and safety issues; and workers at
the shop floor level began to exercise their new rights, and to take
cognizance of the threats they faced at work each day.

By 1981, when Ronald Reagan took office, OSHA possessed
the legal mandate and the organizational and scientific expertise
to move with dispatch to reduce the risk of being a worker in
America. The challenge to improve the safety and health of 46
million workers in 3 million workplaces was enormous. And the
need was still great: 5½ million on-the-job injuries (hospital treatment required for 3.3 million);[17] at least 100,000 worker deaths each
year from exposure to deadly chemicals and other safety hazards;
and 390,000 new cases of occupational disease.[18] Recent figures
show that of the 38 million workers in manufacturing industries,
1.7 million are exposed to a potential carcinogen each year. Figures
derived from the NIOSH survey of occupational hazards indicate
that about 10.7 million workers are exposed on their jobs to at least
eleven of the hundreds of cancer-causing substances known.[19]
Workplace carcinogens are believed to cause an estimated 23 percent to 38 percent of all deaths resulting from cancer each year.

"Beyond these statistics," Lane Kirkland reminds us, "are
people. Men and women working in small mill towns, in big cities.
. . . They are people like . . . Jimmy Good, whose lungs carry the
terrible burden of asbestos particles; like Leon Kruchten, who lost
an arm from electrocution . . . and uncounted thousands whose
lives and livelihoods have been terminated or damaged as they
sought to earn decent livings."[20]

STANDARD SETTING CHARADE

Thorne Auchter makes no apologies for his lack of training or
interest in the science of occupational health. "I'm not a scientist,"
he told the authors of *Reagan's Ruling Class.* "I'm a manager and
a regulator." As if to advertise this identity to visitors, Auchter's

office is plastered with elaborate flow charts and management graphs[21] plotting decision-making nodes, and a sargasso soup of lines, arrows, and contingencies for setting OSHA's standards.

Few of these formalities seemed to matter in February 1981, when the new Reagan administration summarily stopped the implementation of several standards that OSHA had prepared late in the Carter administration. The "walk-around pay" standard, issued a month earlier, required employers to pay employees for time spent involved with OSHA inspections—a provision that prevented workers from suffering a financial penalty for participation. It also improved the thoroughness of OSHA inspections, since workers were present. Postponed by Labor Secretary Raymond Donovan for further "review," the walk-around pay requirement has been forgotten by OSHA.

Also jettisoned in February 1981 was OSHA's landmark "generic cancer policy," which laid down uniform scientific guidelines for identifying, classifying, and regulating cancer-causing substances. The standard represented a major advance over previous carcinogen regulation, because it established consistent scientific and regulatory principles, thus expediting the regulation of carcinogens. No longer would OSHA have to undergo the time-consuming, costly process of rearguing the same scientific debates (i.e., that animal carcinogens pose a risk to humans) each time it wanted to regulate a dangerous substance.

Once OSHA suspended the generic cancer policy, the issue was largely taken over by a task force, under the supervision of the White House Office of Science and Technology Policy, which planned to issue a government-wide policy for regulating carcinogens. But this review, whose deliberations have been ridiculed by the scientific community, has yet to result in a final, public document.

Another important Carter administration OSHA standard, for hearing-conservation programs for workers exposed to noise, was delayed eight months, until August 1981, before the Reagan administration allowed certain parts to take effect. In August, OSHA also proposed weakening the provisions for monitoring noise exposure levels, hearing tests, and worker training. In March 1983, a scaled-down final revised hearing-conservation standard was issued.

OSHA lost no time in scuttling a comprehensive "right-to-know" labeling standard, which had been proposed by the previous administration in January 1981. The rules would have required more than 300,000 companies that make, import, or process chemicals to tell workers about the chemicals that they are exposed to and what risks the chemicals pose. A much weaker standard was proposed in March 1982 and issued as a final regulation in November 1983.

The delays and gutting of standards were motivated primarily by political considerations. Yet when called to account, Auchter has piously claimed that OSHA's standards-setting is governed by the strict dictates of science and law: "Underlying OSHA's approach to standards-setting is the determination that this agency will undertake regulatory action only when sound, objective data demonstrate a need for regulation. Development of occupational safety and health standards is a lengthy and complex process. Certain long-established procedures and principles must be observed."[22]

Auchter's professed concern for procedures has helped insulate him from his critics both inside and outside the administration. On the one hand, by heaping one procedural review on top of another, followed by more analysis and endless bureaucratic hurdles, Auchter has portrayed himself as the conscientious regulator, whose hands, alas, are tied. But on the other hand, Auchter's preoccupation with procedure has aroused the ire of the Office of Management and Budget—and its deregulation czar Christopher DeMuth—who gripes that Auchter has not deregulated swiftly enough. In August 1982, DeMuth wrote to the Department of Labor, complaining that "all four of OSHA's [regulatory] reviews are behind schedule." DeMuth suggested that rather than work on new health standards, OSHA should spend more of its resources correcting "the slippage on the task force review."[23]

If Auchter's penchant for procedure is expedient, it is certainly not consistent with his promoting "the most ambitious regulatory agenda that OSHA has ever had." Auchter has boasted that he will issue fifteen health and twenty-three safety standards by the end of 1984[24]—a fatuous claim, considering that in the entire ten years before Auchter took over, OSHA had managed to issue only forty standards. His "ambitious" agenda begins to make sense when it is discovered that nearly every proposed standard would actually *weaken* existing regulations, not advance their protection. In fact, the four tougher standards that Auchter has agreed to issue—for ethylene oxide, benzene, ethylene dibromide (EDB), and asbestos—have been forced on him by the courts or by unrelenting pressure from unions and consumer groups. Furthermore, efforts by unions to push through other tough *new* standards have been rejected or postponed indefinitely.

Despite the concerns of many powerful trade unions, Auchter managed to keep his agency's foot-dragging and acts of bureaucratic sabotage out of the headlines for two years. Trade unions were so preoccupied by their members' economic plight that Auchter's policies did not get sufficient attention. Additionally, the press was on the trail of a more sizzling regulatory scandal by December 1982: that of Anne Burford and the Environmental Protection Agency's sweetheart deals, suppression of information, contempt for the law, and neglect for the public's physical safety.

By March 1983, the press, still giddy from its exposés of wrongdoing at EPA, started nosing around at other regulatory agencies, including OSHA. Thorne Auchter quickly saw that his official behavior would come under closer scrutiny, and that his politics of procedural delay were a less than credible excuse for his behavior. By March 21, 1983—only two weeks after Anne Burford's departure—a *Business Week* headline announced a new shift in Auchter's policies: "OSHA's Unexpected Bite Has the OMB Bristling." To industry's great surprise and dismay, Auchter was asserting that OSHA's revised standards protecting workers' hearing, though significantly weakened from the Carter proposal, be enacted over the OMB's objections.

Auchter's uncharacteristic outburst of independence struck many skeptical reporters as a public relations ploy. Auchter's top aides, who in the past had criticized the press's use of unnamed sources, were suddenly whispering to reporters their inside tip that Auchter was fighting OMB. "It's a bit hard to picture him standing up on his own back legs to OMB," one labor official told the *Washington Post*. "He always has been a good lieutenant in the past."[25]

The truth of this suspicion was bolstered six months later

when an internal memo obtained by the *Washington Post* confirmed OSHA's intent to cut back its standard-setting activity on all but six hazardous substances found in the workplace. An internal task force established by Auchter in 1981 to review OSHA's rule-making history recommended that the agency stop any ongoing work on setting standards for 116 potentially hazardous substances, including known carcinogens such as beryllium, cadmium, chromium compounds, and nickel. Also included were industrial solvents such as toluene and trichloroethylene. In one candid passage, the memo pointed out that by deleting these substances from its workload, OSHA "would notify the regulated industries that OSHA has no intention of moving on these chemicals, relieving them of any anxieties about possible impacts on their markets or production." A section entitled "Factual Issues," which would presumably discuss the scientific merit of discontinuing work on the 116 substances, was scratched out and replaced with a handwritten note reading, "There are no factual issues to be considered."

Recognizing the volatility of the message, the memo acknowledged, "If this proposal [to eliminate the consideration of 116 substances from standard-setting] were announced, it would immediately bring attention to the fact that OSHA had not completed work on 116 substances. This cannot be good publicity for the agency." The memo also argued against announcing elimination of the agency's work of setting standards, because "agency critics will imply that the sole motive for this revocation is to impede future rule making for these substances," and "the action will be seen as another attempt by the agency to avoid its statutory duties, or as another indication that the agency is unwilling to improve safety and health for workers."[26]

STANDARD-SETTING UNDER REAGAN'S OSHA

The memo might just as well have been written about OSHA's many other standard-setting projects, for both permanent and emergency temporary standards. Top officials at OSHA have frequently brushed aside scientific evidence when deciding on how to proceed with standards. And when the facts about a health hazard have been inconveniently incriminating, Auchter has wrapped himself in the chains and handcuffs of procedure, only to complain that budget limitations and legal impediments prevent him from acting as fast as he would like. A review of seven specific decisions provides some telling insights into Auchter's *real* concern about developing health standards.

Cotton Dust

Of the nation's 560,000 textile workers exposed to cotton dust, 100,000 suffer from acute byssinosis,[27] a crippling lung disease, marked by chest tightness, wheezing, and shortness of breath. At least 35,000 workers are already permanently disabled by the disease, commonly known as brown lung.[28] There is no established threshold of cotton dust exposure below which no disease will occur.[29] The disease worsens with continued exposure and may progress to a chronic, disabling stage even after a worker is no longer exposed to cotton dust. At its irreversible stage, the worker's lung tissue itself is destroyed, and death may result from infection, or respiratory or heart failure. The physical effects of brown lung are devastating. Listen to Grover Hardin describe his plight: "Since I've had this brown lung, I have come to the point where I can't do much of anything. It cuts my breath down to where I have difficulty even changing clothes, shaving, or taking a bath. Even talking I can't do sometimes—I have to stop to catch my breath; it's that bad. I haven't been able to work a lick at nothing since nineteen sixty-two. I had to leave the mill at the age of fifty-four. I tried to keep working, but I just couldn't."[30] Until the publicity generated by OSHA, most cotton mill workers had never heard of byssinosis, and many who could no longer do their jobs had been forced to retire early, with little or no pension.

Cotton dust was first subject to "consensus guidelines" that were developed by the textile industry in 1969 and adopted by OSHA in 1971. But the level of exposure was set so that one in four workers still contracted byssinosis. After several years of intense research and analysis, Dr. Bingham issued a new, stricter cotton dust standard in 1978. It required companies to install engineering controls to reduce the dust levels (instead of just using respirators), and to provide periodic medical examinations for workers.

The industry challenged the standard in federal court and

eventually won a hearing before the Supreme Court in 1981. The companies argued that OSHA should conduct a cost-benefit analysis before determining whether to regulate cotton dust; and that health criteria alone should not be decisive.

Once the Reagan administration was settled into office, however, textile companies no longer needed a court ruling to overturn the agency's standard—it could be accomplished administratively through Reagan's OSHA. Accordingly, after consultation with the industry, the Reagan administration asked the Supreme Court to suspend its review of the case and return it to OSHA for revision. Wisely, the court denied the request and in June 1981 upheld the cotton dust standard. Based on the Occupational Safety and Health Act, the overriding criteria for determining the agency's standards must be the threat to workers' health, said the court, not cost-benefit analyses.[31]

Despite the clear direction in the Supreme Court's decision, OSHA proposed a revised cotton-dust standard in June 1983 that would exclude at least 340,000 exposed workers in nontextile and knitting industries from the standard's protection.[32] (Textile workers, however, would continue to be protected.) In addition, the proposed revision would allow employers to seek exemptions from current monitoring, training, and medical surveillance requirements, and to delay the installation of engineering controls for some sections of the industry for two years. Also not included under the proposed revision are "medical removal protection" rights, which allow workers to transfer to another job without economic loss if a respirator cannot be worn and dust or other hazardous substances exceed permissible levels. To his credit, Auchter resisted White House pressure to permit use of respirators—which are hot, heavy, and only partly effective—in place of engineering controls with air-filtering equipment.

In his persistence to weaken the cotton dust standard, Auchter ignored the congressional testimony of his own colleague and NIOSH's director, J. Donald Millar. On September 22, 1982, Millar told Congress, "NIOSH is not aware of any new scientific information that warrants a change in the recommendations . . . and we see no justification for re-opening [an] inquiry into the efficacy of the [original cotton dust] standard."[33] While lamenting his agency's limited assets on the one hand, Auchter simultaneously has invested precious OSHA resources in weakening a standard that most of the textile industry was already meeting[34] and that workers desperately needed.

The cotton dust standard has served another purpose. It has helped to increase the textile industry's competitiveness. According to Eric Frumin, director of occupational safety and health for the Amalgamated Clothing and Textile Workers Union, AFL-CIO, "It makes good business sense to install the kind of equipment that is needed to comply with the standard." For years the textile industry had resisted making new investments in automated equipment (which also controls cotton dust), but eventually many companies realized that protecting their workers' health and improving productivity went hand in hand. Now those companies' products are more competitive with imports.[35]

The Lead Standard

In 1978, OSHA issued a landmark standard to protect approximately 835,000 people in 120 occupations, who work with the one million tons of lead mined and processed each year in the United States. The health hazards of lead have been well known for centuries. In its most severe form, lead poisoning can be fatal. It can cause serious harm to the central nervous system, including motor and brain damage, and it can limit kidney function. Lead can cause loss of appetite and nausea, constipation, anemia, colic, tremors, weakness, and numbness. Sterility in men and birth defects among children have also been associated with significant exposures to lead.[36]

Once again, even though the scientific documentation of the hazard was overwhelming, a coalition of lead-related industries challenged OSHA's standard in court. But in August 1980, the US Court of Appeals upheld the standard and instructed the agency to enforce it.[37] Auchter, however, has proposed numerous modifications, postponed the effective date for certain protection clauses, and allowed deadlines to be extended.

He first tried to delay the date that the standard would take effect by insisting that OSHA perform a cost-benefit analysis, but the Supreme Court denied his request for delay. Auchter then granted some of the major lead industries' exemptions, for several years, from the requirements that they submit written plans explaining how they would comply with the standard. In September 1982, the United Steel Workers of America filed suit to set aside the new provisions that would weaken the standard, and to require the original standard to remain in effect.[38]

Auchter also delayed the "medical removal protection" rule, a requirement in the standard that employees be automatically removed from their jobs when the level of lead in their blood reaches a "trigger point" of 50 Mg per 100 g of blood. The worker is shifted to another job, with no loss of pay or seniority. After repeated delays, the lower "trigger level" finally took effect.

Emergency Temporary Standards (ETS)

In writing the statute for the OSHA, Congress recognized that some health hazards may be particularly acute and warrant immediate attention. Because it could take OSHA at least two to three years to promulgate a permanent health standard, Congress empowered the agency to issue interim regulations, or emergency temporary standards (ETS), if workers "are exposed to grave dangers from exposure to substances or agents determined to be toxic or physically harmful, or from new hazards."

Since Auchter took office, labor unions and public interest groups have petitioned OSHA to issue emergency temporary standards for five cancer-causing substances: benzene (a widely used industrial solvent), formaldehyde (a chemical used in dozens of industrial processes), ethylene oxide (a sterilizer used in hospitals), ethylene dibromide (a fumigant used on fruits, grains, and vegetables), and asbestos. The first four petitions were denied by Auchter, a rejection rate that greatly angered Congressman David Obey (Democrat-Wisconsin), one of Auchter's foremost critics in Congress.

Why had OSHA not issued a single emergency standard over the preceding two and a half years, even though no one disputed the deadly effects of the chemicals in question? Congressman Obey put that question to Auchter at hearings before a House labor appropriations subcommittee in March 1983. Auchter blamed procedural shackles for his behavior, saying, "At what point do you violate legal and administrative procedures and go straight to action on the emergency process? Clearly each one of these three instances that you have mentioned [ethylene oxide, ethylene di-bromide, and formaldehyde] do not meet the test based on emergency."

> CONGRESSMAN OBEY: You made that quite clear in the argument that you made before the court, but the fact remains that your own scientists have indicated that [with formaldehyde exposure] you will have six extra deaths per thousand from that. . . .
>
> MR. AUCHTER: Over a working lifetime.
>
> CONGRESSMAN OBEY: Correct, and if you don't get it [cancer], I suppose it is not a grave danger, a serious emergency, but if you do, it could be pretty troublesome.[39]

Auchter's routine excuse has been the likelihood the courts would overrule any emergency standards. He cites four instances in the past in which emergency standards had been struck down by the courts. But Auchter's predictions about federal court reaction to his inaction has not been on target. In fact, the courts recently have chastised his agency for *failing* to issue standards in cases in which it had been so clearly warranted (ethylene oxide), and for insisting on cost-benefit analyses when the law does not permit such a balancing test (cotton dust).

Ethylene Oxide (EtO)

Ethylene oxide (EtO) was first developed as a poison gas in World War I. It is valuable as a sterilizing agent, fumigant, pesticide, and chemical additive, widely used in producing automotive antifreeze, textiles, films, bottles, and detergents. EtO is also a critical component of the sterilization process in hospitals and other health care facilities, which inject the gas into sealed vessels containing objects to be sterilized. After sterilization, the gas is vented —and at this point health care workers are exposed to sudden, high bursts of the dangerous gas.

The existing OSHA standard for exposure to ethylene oxide, on the books since 1971, permits exposure of 50 parts per million (ppm), averaged over an eight-hour period. Yet at levels well below 50 ppm, EtO is now known to cause leukemia and lymphoma, as well as mutagenic and chromosomal damage. At 50 ppm, it is estimated that 40 to 500 people out of every 1,000 exposed will die of cancer. Indeed, studies on humans have found genetic damage at as low as .5 ppm, and many scientists believe that there is no "minimal exposure" threshold that can be considered truly "safe."

One study, in 1981, showed that 3 of 230 persons working near a sterilizer for only four to nine years (only a small fraction of the average worklife) contracted leukemia. This statistic represents a rate fifteen times higher than anticipated. The EtO levels in the area were less than half of OSHA's permissible 50 ppm exposure limit.[40] Another report, also in 1981, by the Mitre Company think-tank found that EtO levels near some health care facilities' sterilization equipment were as high as 500 ppm. A NIOSH survey of four Washington, DC, hospitals found levels of 600 ppm near the sterilizer door, and of 8,000 ppm above an open drain.[41]

Time-weighted average (TWA) is a complicated measure for levels of exposure to gases. TWA measures the amount of exposure over an average period of time, usually over an eight-hour period. Many workers, however, receive higher concentrations—100 ppm to 600 ppm, a huge dose—in one brief period and then nothing for the remainder of the day. No one can predict what damage ensues.

EtO is so dangerous that many companies, such as Rohm and Haas, a plastics and chemical company, have voluntarily reduced exposure to 1 ppm over an eight-hour, time-weighted average, with peak short-term levels no higher than 5 ppm. Ten of twenty-three California hospitals have maintained an estimated average exposure of under 1 ppm. It is neither difficult nor expensive to reduce exposure to 1 ppm or less. One study showed the cost to a hospital would come to about $1,000 or $2,000 per sterilizer. Three California hospitals reduced exposure from 10 ppm to 1 ppm simply by repairing leaks in their equipment. One hospital informed OSHA that "control of worker exposure to ethylene oxide in the hospital environment is possible, practical, and inexpensive."[42]

On September 28, 1981, Thorne Auchter denied a petition from Public Citizen and the American Federation of State, County, and Municipal Employees (AFSCME), a union representing thousands of hospital workers, to issue a temporary emergency standard reducing EtO exposure from 50 to 1 ppm over an eight-hour TWA. Public Citizen had summarized some of the recent evidence of the health risk. One study by the Finnish government, for example, showed that the chemical was associated with a three-fold increase in miscarriages among female workers at levels less than one-hundredth of the legal US limit of 50 ppm. The data suggest that EtO may have been responsible for at least twenty-five hundred miscarriages among US hospital workers. Various other studies have linked EtO to an increased incidence of cancer and genetic damage at legal exposure levels, and experiments with EtO on animals have resulted in a higher incidence of leukemia, and chromosome and sperm damage.[43]

In 1982, when pressed to explain his refusal to issue an emergency temporary standard, Auchter responded, "I only go by what our attorneys tell me."[44] But a year later congressional investigators discovered that Auchter's only written communication with his legal advisors occurred on October 5, 1981, a week after he denied the petition. On that date, Auchter received a memo from his solicitors' office, stating that if OSHA decided to issue an emergency temporary standard on EtO (and also on another chemical, EDB), the lawyers could defend the move in court. A respectable legal argument could be made either way.[45]

Auchter also ignored the advice of his scientists in denying the ethylene oxide petition. Several weeks before the denial letter was issued, OSHA's top scientists had urged Auchter to issue an emergency standard, or at the very least initiate regulation proceedings—and circulate a warning promptly, citing the grave dangers of exposure to EtO. Auchter ignored his advisors and simply denied the petition.

Auchter's denial triggered the first legal challenge to OSHA's inaction. In late 1981, Public Citizen and AFSCME brought suit to compel OSHA to regulate EtO promptly. After a legal battle of a year and a half, the US Court of Appeals in the District of Columbia found that OSHA had acted unreasonably in not promptly promulgating an EtO standard, and ordered the agency to issue a proposed regulation within thirty days and get a final standard on the books within a year. The court ruled that "[b]eyond question the record shows a significant risk that some workers and the children they will hereafter conceive are subject to grave danger from the employees' exposure to EtO."[46]

The court used harsh words condemning OSHA for dragging its feet by failing to "give due regard to the urgency of the need" for a new standard, and commanded OSHA to proceed with expediting a regulation.

At Auchter's appropriations hearing shortly after the court decision, Congressman David Obey was incensed:

> Last year you indicated to us that the major reason you had not proceeded with promulgating an emergency temporary standard is because you did not want to be challenged in court and have the standard go down the tubes. . . . Let me just suggest that . . . given the great reluctance of your agency to approve requests for emergency temporary standards, because of your legal interpretation, perhaps the best thing for you to do would be to routinely turn them all down, so that you could be challenged in a friendly court and thereby be ordered to move faster. . . . That is the logic of the position you take. . . .[47]

Despite the court's command and the anger among members of Congress, OSHA continued to mishandle the EtO standard. In April 1983, OSHA issued a proposed standard without a ceiling on short-term exposure, saying it did not have time to include it. Short-term exposure limits are considered essential to prevent harm to hospital workers, who often receive high exposure levels for short periods of time. But in June 1983, shortly after a secret meeting with Arlin G. Voress, a top official of Union Carbide, Auchter's director of health standards, R. Leonard Vance, blocked agency activities to make it possible to include short-term exposure requirements. Vance canceled a proposed study of short-term exposures, directed an agency employee not to ask questions about short-term exposure at an agency hearing, and tried to prevent a private expert from testifying. Union Carbide is opposed to a short-term exposure limit. Representative George Miller (Democrat-California) held a hearing in October 1983 to put all these facts on the record and discourage future misbehavior.[48]

Benzene

Benzene, a chemical widely used in the petrochemical and rubber industries, causes cancer, leukemia, blood disorders, and other serious illnesses. Despite the fact that it is a well-recognized threat to health, the Reagan administration has not acted to reduce the federal "permissible exposure levels" of 10 ppm, set in 1971.

Dr. Bingham had tried to lower the exposure standard for benzene in 1977 by issuing an emergency temporary standard that lowered the 10 ppm requirement to 1 ppm over an eight-hour time-weighted-average. A permanent standard followed a year later, in 1978. But when the chemical industry challenged the stricter benzene regulation, the US Court of Appeals for the Fifth Circuit concurred and threw out the standard, a judgment that the Supreme Court affirmed in 1980. The crux of its ruling was that OSHA could not require companies to reduce chemical exposure to the "lowest feasible level," even if there was a strong risk of cancer, unless OSHA could show that the new standard would eliminate a "significant risk of material health impairment."[49]

To meet this Court requirement, OSHA had prepared a "risk assessment" (an epidemiological estimate of the number of people at risk and the severity of the health damage) in the late 1970s. But for Auchter to issue a new benzene standard, a contemporary, updated risk assessment was needed—a task that could be completed in six months to a year. Instead of forging ahead to produce a new risk assessment, OSHA let two years pass with no action.

By late 1982, OSHA completed and published its new risk assessment. The results were sobering: according to OSHA's own data, an estimated 800,000 workers are exposed to benzene, of which about 35,000 workers are regularly exposed to more than 1 ppm of benzene. Based on exposure to benzene at the current permissible level of 10 ppm, OSHA's own calculations showed that 1,540 to 7,245 excess cases of leukemia could be expected during the lifetimes of benzene-exposed workers.[50] Each year of delay in tightening the benzene standard has meant that another 34 to 161 workers, exposed to 10 ppm of benzene, get leukemia.[51] These risk estimates do not even include the serious nonmalignant blood diseases and chromosomal damage that are even more common than leukemia.

On April 14, 1983, several labor unions and Public Citizen petitioned OSHA for an emergency temporary standard on benzene.[52] Auchter denied the petition but promised to expedite the proceedings for a ruling on a permanent standard, which would be effective, he said, in 1984: "We share the concern that benzene has the capacity to pose a very serious risk to workers." In turning down the petition, Auchter wrote Dr. Sidney M. Wolfe, director of Public Citizen's Health Research Group: "Courts have vacated three other OSHA emergency temporary standards on their merits, while upholding only one ETS." (Auchter did not mention that four others were never challenged.) "Any decision to issue an ETS," he said, "must be made in the light of this legal background."[53] But the petitioners were more impressed by Auchter's informal comment to Dr. Wolfe at a private meeting, in May 1983. When asked why OSHA had done nothing about benzene for almost two and a half years, he answered, "Because it wasn't a hot press item."[54]

Ethylene Dibromide (EDB)

Most pesticides perpetrate their damage gradually: cancer, birth defects, nerve damage show up years after the first exposure. But not so with EDB. "EDB is different," noted NBC's "First Camera" program in September 1983. "Given to laboratory rats in normal doses, EDB does not cause them to get cancer; it causes them to drop dead instantly."[55] Widely used as a soil, fruit, and grain fumigant, EDB is now considered one of the most dangerous carcinogens known. But the hundred thousand warehouse workers, truckers, and dock handlers who frequently are exposed to EDB are rarely told of its insidious characteristics.

No one told David Smith. While working weekends fumigating grain in a Minneapolis flour mill, he got some of the liquid fumigant on his hands, and within an hour he was dizzy. "It was as if my whole body was starting to go numb." By the time he got to the ground floor, he could not walk: "I crawled into the locker room." Smith was rushed to the hospital and placed in intensive care. His pulse rate dropped to twenty-nine beats per minute (seventy-two is normal). Five days passed before doctors could be sure that Smith would survive.[56]

And no one told two chemical workers in Bakersfield, California, whose story was recently told on NBC. They "died gruesome deaths after they were exposed to a fraction of an ounce of EDB. . . . As Robert Harris was rushed to a hospital, paramedics stripped James Harris to his underwear and hosed him down with water to try to save his life. He died 72 hours later."[57] The company was fined over $50,000 by Cal/OSHA for EDB violations.

A decade ago, in 1974, the National Cancer Institute issued a notice that EDB was a carcinogen.[58] More recent research has shown that it can cause birth defects and male sterility. In 1977, NIOSH recommended that the exposure levels of EDB be significantly reduced below the existing limit of 20 ppm. Still nothing was done.

Then in 1981, the spraying of the Mediterranean fruit fly with EDB revived the concern about the chemical, especially among the Teamsters, the AFL-CIO, and the Longshoremen's union, whose members were exposed to EDB. In September 1981, the labor federation and the two unions petitioned OSHA for an emergency temporary standard to reduce the exposure limit drastically. Predictably, Auchter rejected the petition three months later, claiming that OSHA did not know enough either about the amount of workers' exposure to EDB or the number of workers involved. Furthermore, he claimed that a standard defending a lower level of exposure to EDB would not stand up in court.[59]

In 1982, J. Donald Millar, director of NIOSH, urged Auchter to reconsider this decision in the face of the "mounting evidence" of EDB's toxicity. But Auchter again refused to budge. Meanwhile, the government's own research began to provide more damning evidence against EDB. One study performed by EPA refers to the risk of cancer from EDB as being "among the highest the agency [has] ever confronted." Another EPA study showed that at OSHA's current maximum limit of exposure to EDB (20 ppm), death from cancer could be expected for 999 out of every 1,000 workers.[60] A risk assessment prepared by David Brown from Northeastern University in Boston showed that at 10 ppm (half OSHA's limit), approximately 270 workers out of 1,000 would probably develop cancer. The National Cancer Institute also conducted a study using 10 ppm as the exposure rate and found that 40 percent of the rats developed cancer. This is particularly surprising, because in these types of studies the animals are usually given massive doses to approximate a lifetime of human exposure.[61]

In March 1983, Congressman David Obey asked Auchter about EDB at OSHA's appropriations hearings. He wanted to know why OSHA had not issued the emergency temporary standard for EDB after Department of Labor attorneys in a memo on October 5, 1981, had told Auchter that "a respectable argument could be made . . . [in court] in support of the ETS, and that we would have a reasonably good chance of success."[62]

> CONGRESSMAN OBEY: But didn't they [attorneys from the Labor Department] tell you that 40 percent of the animals developed cancer after being exposed to [only] ten parts per million?
>
> MR. AUCHTER: Yes.
>
> CONGRESSMAN OBEY: That is very high. That is not just the run of the mill report, is it?
>
> MR. AUCHTER: Oh, no, that is extremely high. Ethylene dibromide is a bad actor.
>
> CONGRESSMAN OBEY: Did your lawyers find that EDB met the test of "grave danger"?
>
> MR. AUCHTER: Yes.

Auchter finally responded to Congressman Obey's attack by citing the labor solicitors' memo, which concludes that "arguments could be made on either side. . . ." After more prodding by Obey, Auchter explained further:

> I think you have a fair understanding of what occurs if we issue an emergency temporary standard, not only legal challenges, but we must promulgate a final rule within six months.
>
> That throws our whole standards activity into total disarray. When that occurs, we have to change the make-up of our teams and postpone work on standards which we believe should have priority."[63]

Anger over Auchter's refusal to act exploded in September 1983, and it got the agency moving. Congressman George Miller

(Democrat-California) convened a hearing to find out why EPA and OSHA had not acted to control exposure to EDB. Miller produced recommendations from OSHA's staff, labeling the current standard outdated and inadequate. When Auchter repeated his well-worn excuse about the possibility of losing a court challenge if he issued an emergency standard, Miller bellowed:

> It was a question of whether you wanted to go to court on workers' behalf. Those workers came to you and asked you to take a risk. What would have been the harm if you lost? Your pride? Your agency's batting average? The bottom line is you did nothing and workers are still being covered by a twelve-year-old standard everybody agrees is inadequate.[64]

Auchter tried to take credit for having sent an alert to industries in which workers might be exposed to EDB, warning of the dangers and recommending precautions. But he was asked why he sent out a cursory three-page notice rather than a comprehensive thirty-three-page health hazard alert prepared by his staff, which gave workers specific suggestions to protect them from the chemical. Auchter said he "simplified" the memo so that workers could understand it.[65]

Candy Harris, the widow of Robert Harris, thinks Auchter is wrong. "I don't think they had the right to omit one iota of information. They had a duty to make available all information they had; they are partly responsible for Robert's accident."[66]

Auchter would not concede. He contended that an emergency standard was not necessary because worker exposure is seasonal and intermittent. Finally, in late September 1983, both EPA and OSHA issued proposed standards to limit EDB exposures. OSHA even admitted that "risks from EDB exposure appear to be far greater than for any other hazard that OSHA has regulated in the past."[67] OMB intervened in the process and temporarily held up the OSHA's proposal. It removed the requirement for medical testing for some exposed workers because "it is not clear how these tests will reduce the cancer incidence of EDB exposure."[68] OSHA indicated it would take six months or more before a new standard would be issued to lower the permissible exposure to 0.1 ppm.

With all the attention given to the congressional hearings by the media, the public started paying attention, too, because it became evident that what contaminated workers also affected everyone in the marketplace. As NBC informed the citizenry on September 25, 1983:

> For more than six years, federal officials have known EDB is a potent cause of cancer and one of the most poisonous pesticides in existence, yet they have done little to control its use. More EDB is used now than ever before to kill insects that feed on crops. Because of this, it is now showing up in alarming amounts in oranges, grapefruit, and grain.
>
> But federal officials have kept these findings from the public. Example: School lunches. In 1980, the Environmental Protection Agency—EPA—found the pesticide in every sample of flour that was to be used in the school lunch program. Nationwide, that program feeds 23 million children each year.[69]

Asbestos

It is rumored that Thorne Auchter finally "got religion" on asbestos during a meeting with labor leaders in April 1983. Dr. Irving Selikoff, of the Mount Sinai School of Medicine, the scientific dean of health conditions in the workplace, cornered Auchter and lectured him about one of the largest killers of workers in America. Known for his persuasive presentations, Selikoff got what he was after. Auchter reportedly telephoned his staff and ordered them to get a standard ready.

Auchter's conversion came after several of the most intense weeks of his tenure. Just a few days after Anne Burford left the EPA, in March 1983, Auchter was called to the mat by members of Congress for his abysmal record of setting regulatory standards —"goose eggs," as Congressman Obey put it. Other members of Congress leveled serious criticism of Auchter's first two years. In the highly charged political climate surrounding the EPA scandals, Auchter was undergoing heavy fire and knew his number might be next if he did not take action against *some* health hazard.

It was an unusual series of events that made asbestos the

prime candidate for a new OSHA standard. In trying to justify its inaction against EtO, Auchter's attorneys told the US Court of Appeals in February 1983 that the agency was working instead on a new standard for asbestos—work that would be disrupted if the court suddenly ordered OSHA to issue an emergency standard for EtO. To show that it was serious about asbestos, OSHA attached its asbestos risk assessment study to the court documents. It had been completed eighteen months earlier, in August 1981. The agency apparently thought that the study would not be noticed. It was, after all, an auxiliary document in a case dealing with another chemical altogether, ethylene oxide.

In fact, the existence of a thorough risk assessment of asbestos—a document that would be the centerpiece of any new health standard—was big news, indeed. The inclusion of the study in the court papers was the first indication that OSHA had any interest in an asbestos standard, and it was the first time that it was publicly known that a formal risk assessment had been completed. What is more important, the risk assessment confirmed what most workers knew: that asbestos was indeed a serious hazard in the workplace and deserved a strict OSHA standard.

The confluence of these events—the EPA scandals, Auchter's searing congressional appearance at the appropriations hearing in March 1983, the quiet release of a key scientific study on asbestos, and Dr. Selikoff's skillful use of this information to lobby Auchter—must have triggered a reaction in Auchter. In April 1983, he revealed that OSHA would propose an asbestos standard soon. The initiative, he evidently hoped, would ease the persistent criticism of his bias toward industry.

OSHA had first issued an asbestos standard in 1972, establishing a permissible limit of two million fibers per cubic meter of air. The risk assessment of August 1981 revealed that under the 1972 standard, 18,400 to 598,000 deaths from lung cancer would result in the exposed population of 2.3 million workers. These deaths are in addition to the 200,000 deaths from cancer that Selikoff's associate at Mt. Sinai, Dr. William Nicholson, estimated will occur over the next twenty years, from the legacy of asbestos exposure from World War II to 1972.[70] Asbestos was used extensively during the war by Navy shipbuilders, and thereafter to insulate schools, post offices, houses, office buildings, factories, oil refineries, and chemical plants, as well as pipes and all types of heating equipment. Thirty-five million tons of asbestos are now in place.

The dangers of asbestos have been known for years. Numerous reports appeared in the British medical literature between 1900 and 1920 on asbestosis, and in medical literature in the United States after 1920. Between 1935 and 1938, the first reports appeared in the US medical literature linking asbestos with cancer, and in 1942 linking asbestos with lung cancer. In 1964, Dr. Selikoff published the first epidemiological study linking asbestos with mesothelioma.[71]

OSHA first indicated that it would lower the exposure levels in 1975. By 1980, new studies were completed to justify this action, and the NIOSH and OSHA Asbestos Working Group reported, in April 1980, that "immediate action" was necessary. A schedule released in November 1980 predicted that the standard would be completed by the winter of 1981.

But within days after the November 1980 election, David Stockman announced that the Reagan administration was preparing to rescind the regulations that were being prepared concerning asbestos. And in January 1982, Auchter actually revoked the schedule established by the Carter administration. He did this five months after his agency had completed the devastating risk assessment in August 1981. Auchter's three years of delay in strengthening the asbestos standard will cause between 7,200 and 72,000 excess cancer deaths, according to Dr. Nicholson's calculations.[72]

What ultimately sparked Auchter were not the grim statistics but the steady political pressure facing the administration. By late August 1983, word was coming out of OSHA that the Labor Department was seriously considering issuance of an emergency temporary standard on asbestos, a significant departure from its past opposition to fast-track rulemaking. With the election not far away, OSHA officials "are trying to look like they have a better position on worker protection," and an emergency temporary standard "strategically isn't a bad move," commented one labor official.[73]

Finally, on November 2, 1983, eight years after OSHA first indicated it would lower the exposure levels and eight months after Auchter said he was "speeding" OSHA's work on tightening the existing standard, the Reagan administration issued its first emergency ruling, an emergency temporary standard which lowered the legal asbestos exposure level by 75 percent. Sheldon Samuels, director of health and safety of the Industrial Union Department of the AFL-CIO, said that he was pleased about the move but that "the real test is whether they have put into place the enforcement mechanism. It's the quality, rather than the quantity, of enforcement."[74]

The asbestos story has a final irony. In the early 1970s, a number of diseased workers started suing asbestos manufacturers for their failure to warn employees about the dangers of asbestos. Johns-Manville, one major manufacturer, was faced with so many lawsuits that it decided to file for bankruptcy in 1982, even though it was financially solvent. Its bankruptcy was based on the future liability claims that the courts might award against the company. Johns-Manville's cynical strategy is just another reason why an effective OSHA is needed. After the fact claims not only don't protect workers; they can potentially damage companies who made handsome profits by covering up the hazards for years.

ENFORCEMENT

No one in the Reagan administration has ever proposed a "voluntary" approach when it comes to food stamp fraud or illegal immigration. "Law and order" in these areas is a brisk, menacing enterprise that has thousands of federal enforcers vigilantly patrolling their turf for violations of the law.

Mention safety and health in the workplace, however, and Reagan's enforcers are decidedly more casual. "Our job is health and safety," explained Thorne Auchter. "We're not interested in crime and punishment."[75] His top deputy, Patrick R. Tyson, concurs: "We're not out there pushing for penalties, because we don't think they're that important."[76] Needless to say, American business has been pleased that its transgressions against people's health are treated more sympathetically by the government. Since Auchter took office, enforcement of the occupational safety and health requirements under the law has plunged in every relevant category. This fact is documented in a study by Public Citizen comparing OSHA safety and health enforcement activities during the first eight months of fiscal year 1982 to a similar period in fiscal year 1980:[77]

Number of workers covered	
(1.5 million fewer)	Down 41%
Workplace inspections	Down 17%
accident	Down 10%
response to workers' complaints	Down 54%
general schedule	Up 29%
follow-up after violation	Down 86%
Violations	
serious	Down 50%
willful	Down 86%
repeated	Down 65%
Total penalties imposed	Down 67%
for failure to abate hazards	Down 79%
Average hours per inspection	
safety	Down 18%
health	Down 13%

Although the number of general schedule inspections increased by 29 percent, this makes the overall decrease in violations found all the more striking. To bolster its inspection figures in responding to critiques about reductions in enforcement actions, OSHA often cites inspections where only records are inspected, not the workplace. But OSHA cannot dispute that the number of inspection personnel has dropped from 1,328 to 981 since Auchter took office.[78]

"Generally we're very happy," says Steve Settle, who handles OSHA matters for the National Association of Manufacturers. "For most of our members, OSHA is not the dirty word it used to be."[79] That assessment is not shared by the victims of health and safety crimes in the workplace, who consider OSHA something of a four-letter word when it comes to law enforcement. "Anyone who believes employers in general like to spend money on safety and health hasn't spent much time in the workplace," notes Eric Frumin of the Amalgamated Clothing and Textile Workers Union. "But that's what Auchter believes."[80]

To Joe Velasquez, executive director of the Workers' Institute for Safety and Health, OSHA's least forgivable failure is that it has virtually abandoned any serious pretension of *deterring* violations. "The idea is that you've got to have an image of strong enforcement, because it's impossible to have a cop in every shop. The employer has got to know that he may be inspected and that if he doesn't comply with the rules, there will be heavy penalties. They're going into the worst places in the country, and what are they finding? Nothing."[81]

Safety Inspections

One of Auchter's rationales for changing OSHA's enforcement policies sounds unassailable. He announced, in October 1981, that he wanted to "insure the optimum use of our limited inspection resources to provide the greatest protection for workers most likely to be injured on the job."[82] Auchter's scheme is to target inspections in those industries with the highest hazards, which theoretically hold most of the risks.

It sounds like a good idea, but in actual practice it has resulted in the effective exemption of almost three-quarters of the most hazardous manufacturing industries from inspection. OSHA's new two-step process for general schedule safety inspections in the manufacturing industries has a deceptive appeal. First, only those companies whose injury rates for a "lost" workday exceed the national average for manufacturing industries are even considered for inspection. Consequently, many individual companies within these industries may go uninspected, even though they have injury rates higher-than-average for their industry. Second, for those industries that have the higher injury rates, the rigor of inspections has been greatly diluted. OSHA first inspects an employer's paper records of injuries, and if they show an injury rate below the national average, no inspection of that workplace is conducted. The inspector simply leaves the job site. The AFL-CIO calls this policy a "paper tiger."[83] Nearly 50 percent of the general schedule visits to manufacturing firms in fiscal year 1982 were merely reviews of paper records, not workplace inspections.[84]

Auchter's system of targeting high-risk industries has a number of serious deficiencies. First, as the AFL-CIO has pointed out,

"OSHA has never published any statistical study showing that an adequate relationship exists between lost-workday injury rates and the hazardous conditions at a workplace."[85]

Second, common health violations (excessive noise, dust, chemical exposures, etc.) that used to show up during the course of general schedule safety inspections are not found when the inspection consists of a simple review of file documents at the worksite office. The "lost workdays" statistics tell nothing about severe work-related illnesses that appear years later.

Third, the injury rates for each company include both white-collar and blue-collar injuries, thus reducing the average number of injuries for workers in high-hazard locations.

Fourth, companies have an incentive to fudge their statistics in order to avoid inspections.

Furthermore, as an AFL-CIO study points out:

> Average time spent on these paper inspections was 7.5 to 8 hours, compared to 12 to 13 hours to conduct an actual workplace safety inspection. Thus, in a "targeting" program, supposedly designed to focus inspection on hazardous conditions, 35 percent of the inspectors' time is spent looking at paper, not workplace hazards.[86]

The real failure of the new targeting system was pointed out by Peg Seminario, of the AFL-CIO, who asked, "If the agency is really inspecting more hazardous workplaces, why isn't OSHA finding more hazards?"[87]

Health Inspections

Auchter has attempted to exempt from inspections all but the industries using the most hazardous substances with high levels of risk and large numbers of employees exposed. The number of health inspections dropped 22 percent between 1980 and 1982, and health inspectors spent 25 percent fewer hours on each inspection in early 1983 compared to 1980. Budget cuts are a major reason. The number of health inspectors has dropped by 35 percent, according to the AFL-CIO, since 1980.[88]

A pilot program is being tested to further reduce health inspections by allowing a review of company records rather than on-site inspections. Since April 1982, OSHA does not reinspect companies if a "substantially complete health inspection" has been conducted within three years, and no serious violations have been found or a letter has documented "good faith" efforts to abate the serious hazards. Many companies have been declared exempt from inspections for three years under these formulas.[89]

On February 1, 1982, OSHA revised its procedures for handling complaints from workers about dangerous workplace conditions. Auchter decreed that immediate on-site inspections would be limited to "imminent dangers"—those hazards with a high likelihood of death or serious injury. The law requires OSHA to respond within twenty-four hours. Inspectors are allowed up to thirty days to respond to other complaints with on-site inspections, and may send the employer a request for voluntary compliance in cases where the complaint is filed with OSHA by telephone. Workers complain that OSHA will not make an on-site inspection in response to a complaint unless there is a catastrophe, although Auchter's staff contends the inspection is made in borderline cases. "I can't see what OSHA needs [before it] will go in and inspect a place," complains a health and safety expert in Philadelphia. "They want dead bodies. . . . It's back to square one."[90] From 1980 to 1983, the complaints from workers about health or safety problems dropped 50 percent.[91] Since there is no evidence of any massive voluntary improvement in workplace conditions, this reduction must reflect a general loss of faith in OSHA on the part of workers.

Ken Silver, formerly with the Massachusetts Coalition on Occupational Safety and Health, explains: "Workers have almost given up hope on OSHA effectiveness in helping solve their problems. They just don't feel OSHA can help them any longer."[92]

Follow-up Inspections

In early 1981 Auchter ordered that follow-ups be decreased to 5 percent or less of all inspections. "They don't pay off," he claimed.[93] OSHA had found that before the inspector returned, most of the violations had been remedied. But another survey for OSHA revealed that 32 percent of the follow-up visits produced more citations, and for the most egregious violations, the number of follow-up citations was even higher.

Dr. Eula Bingham disagrees: "If you don't have follow-ups,

people will not correct what they are supposed to correct."[94] Many OSHA inspectors also disagree. "Previously employers knew we were coming back. This played a large part in their correcting violations," explains a health inspector who has worked for OSHA for eight years.[95]

Penalties

There has been a precipitous drop in penalties paid by companies violating the law, from $25.5 million in FY 1980 to $5.5 million in FY 1982.[96] The fines have decreased because of the enormous reduction in serious, willful, and repeat citations, which carry larger fines. Penalties in excess of $10,000 must be cleared with Auchter before they are issued. Penalties are being reduced by 50–90 percent at informal conferences between OSHA area directors and companies in violation. In FY 1982, OSHA issued a total of only 181 citations for serious, willful, and repeat violations of the asbestos standard. The average penalty per violation was $216.35.[97]

Auchter sent a memo to his enforcement staff on October 31, 1981, instructing them to reduce the numbers of "contested" cases and to keep OSHA out of court.[98] During Dr. Bingham's term of office, companies were contesting 25 percent of the cases before the Occupational Safety and Health Review Commission. But in 1982, only 4 percent of the citations were contested by the companies.[99] This discrepancy has occurred not only because OSHA's citations are less severe, but because Auchter has made career advancement in the agency contingent on keeping down contested case rates. The number of informal settlements has increased by 20 percent, because area directors have agreed to drop charges and reduce penalties to settle cases informally.[100] Workers are excluded from these meetings or denied meaningful participation, although the law guarantees their involvement.

Auchter portrays his changes in enforcement policies as measures to make OSHA more efficient and effective. OSHA's goal, he claims, is to "make every one of its inspections count." Inspections are now "reaching the industries where the hazards are, not 'Mom and Pop' grocery stores." Follow-up inspections are being limited to "free our inspectors to visit other more hazardous workplaces."[101] The new policy of being less responsive to workers' complaints ensures that "OSHA inspections will reach the most hazardous workplaces and provide the greatest amount of protection for workers."[102] The new emphasis on settlement agreements "means our inspectors have more time for inspections instead of spending time in court."[103]

Auchter's logic for relieving corporations violating the law from most threats of enforcement is not generally accepted. "It was as if corporate America suddenly got healthy," says one former labor department solicitor.[104] Dr. Morton Corn, the former head of OSHA under President Ford and now director of the Environmental Health Engineering Department at Johns Hopkins University, wrote to Auchter: "I can certainly believe that you have well-intentioned goals for OSHA, but I must judge the outputs of your policies, not the intentions. . . . By every measure that is meaningful and important to me and to numerous other health and safety professionals, you have compromised the gains made at OSHA during the five years preceding your assumption of office."[105]

Auchter takes pride in having developed "voluntary compliance programs to give labor and management the chance to assume greater safety and health responsibilities at the worksite."[106] This "voluntary" philosophy was challenged by Representative George Miller, who stated: "This naive approach ignores the fact that every comprehensive health standard ever promulgated by OSHA has been challenged in the courts by the regulated industry."[107]

One of the most revealing symbols of how OSHA's approach to enforcement has changed is the new identification card that inspectors must present to the companies. The old card had sternly informed companies that the inspectors were authorized "to enter without delay, inspect and investigate during working hours and at other reasonable times . . . and to question privately any . . . employer, owner, operator, agent, or employee." The new OSHA calling card informs companies that OSHA inspectors are empowered "with the responsibility of carrying out in a courteous and professional manner inspections" outlined by the law. The card continues: "Your comments and suggestions on how we might be more effective in assisting employers and employees are welcomed."[108]

INFORMATION ON OCCUPATIONAL HAZARDS

Part of OSHA's past commitment to saving lives lies in educating people to become aware of dangers in the workplace. Auchter has all but abandoned that effort. He slashed funds for an educational program called New Directions, which gave grants to unions, universities, and companies, to run in-house training programs for workers. The budget was reduced from $13 million in 1981 to $6.8 million in 1983.[109]

Publications have been scrutinized for material irritating to industry. Days after taking charge of the agency, for example, Auchter removed from circulation and ordered destroyed one hundred thousand soon-to-be-published booklets describing the role of cotton dust in causing byssinosis (or brown lung). He said that the pamphlet was "offensive" and "biased," even while admitting that he had not read it. What he objected to most was the cover photo of textile worker Louis Harrell, looking forlorn and sickly. He was dressed simply, in workclothes, and wore a hat. The inscription inside the cover said that Louis Harrell had died of brown lung in 1978. Auchter first demanded that the pamphlet simply be destroyed. This action elicited such a public outcry that he agreed to release the book after it had been modified. Harrell's picture was dropped; the text was reprinted with a plain white cover and no accompanying illustrations. These silly changes were a waste of taxpayer money.[110]

Also removed from active circulation were two slide shows, one on acrylonitrile and one on cotton dust; an education pamphlet on cotton dust, designed for management, and one large poster; and three films about health and safety. One film was called *OSHA*, another *Worker to Worker*, the third *Can't Take No More*. All three were produced by OSHA before Auchter joined the agency. After public protest some were sent out on specific request, but none were advertised for circulation.

Then there was the matter of Current Intelligence Bulletins (CIBs)—small pamphlets produced jointly by OSHA and NIOSH to alert workers, plant managers, and labor unions about new scientific information. The CIB alters no rules and places no obligation on a manufacturer, but it is the major way for managers in small plants to keep up with new scientific research. The CIBs' chief purpose is educational. Nonetheless, Auchter has ordered OSHA to cease work on CIBs, leaving it up to its small sister agency, NIOSH, to carry the full load of preparing and disseminating future CIBs—a move to ensure that few, if any, CIBs will be issued in the future. Auchter, when questioned in a congressional hearing about dropping support for CIBs, stated that he was afraid that inspectors would use them to issue citations.[111]

The cuts in education and in training for workers are consistent with two other actions of Auchter's OSHA. Within weeks of taking office, Labor Secretary Donovan withdrew "for review" two proposed health standards worked out under the Carter administration but not yet final, both dealing with the release of information to workers.

One of these standards, requiring employers to carefully maintain medical records of employees, was extensively revised and restricted. Record-keeping is crucial both to workers and to their doctors, because of the long latency periods between exposure to a toxic substance and the discovery of disease. Without adequate medical records, it is not possible to trace cancer or other diseases back to their original source—a fact that some critics state is just what the employers want.

Employers must maintain medical records on those workers who have been exposed to certain hazardous chemicals listed by OSHA. Under Auchter's proposal, OSHA would eliminate 70 percent of the chemicals, justifying the reduction as a government-wide move to reduce the burden of paperwork on industry. The proposed rule concerning medical records would also remove the requirement that companies keep the medical records of their employees even after they leave.[112] This practice would help insulate companies from lawsuits by workers claiming that they were injured from exposure to hazardous chemicals while on the job.

The second proposal withdrawn by the Reagan administration was a strong "right-to-know" labeling standard that would require more than three hundred thousand companies that make, import, or process chemicals to tell employees which ones they are using and what hazardous properties they contain. Workers have wryly dubbed it the "right to know what's killing you" rule. It was developed by Eula Bingham, following recommendations from NIOSH, in 1974, and petitions and lawsuits by Public Citizen and others.

Auchter acknowledged that "it is vitally important that workers have access to information about the chemical hazards" they work with but criticized the Bingham proposal as "unwieldy, overly complicated, and extremely expensive."[113] In September 1981, he sent an alternative proposal to OMB for approval but could not get agreement to issue it. Auchter argued that his proposal would reduce deaths from cancer by four thousand a year. OMB called this estimate "wildly optimistic" and contended that only four hundred cases of cancer might be avoided.[114]

Determined to get the standard issued, Auchter decided to buck the system. He persuaded beer magnate Joseph A. Coors, a close ally of the Reagan administration, to complain to Vice-President Bush about the log jam. Two days later Auchter had OMB's permission to issue the proposal.[115]

Auchter was concerned about publishing the final "hazard communication" proposal before testifying at his March 1983 congressional appropriations hearings. At the hearings, he promised Congressman Obey he would move quickly in issuing the final standard.

"Let me give you an example why I hope you do," said Congressman Obey, who had a special reason to be interested in this particular standard:

My sister died of cancer a couple of weeks ago. When she was in the hospital, the doctor at first thought she had been experiencing an allergic reaction to a chemical, because her lungs filled up, and then the fluid disappeared. That doctor called the company involved where she worked [and] asked them what chemicals she was being exposed to. The company said, "I am sorry, we don't give out that information." I had to send somebody on that company floor, in order to get the information off the label. It happened to be trichloroethylene. I think that is just one little example of the helplessness that thousands of people feel in trying to deal with corporations who have information to which [those people] are entitled. . . .[116]

Auchter was proud of his proposal and of outfoxing the OMB. He boasted that he had simplified the requirements and had cut the price tag from $2.6 billion initially and $1.3 billion annually, to $582 million initially and $228 million per year, with new education and training provisions included.[117]

To cut the costs and industry's opposition to his "hazard communication" proposal, Auchter reduced record-keeping and labeling requirements and limited the scope to the manufacturing industries, thus exempting 80 percent of all the workers who are involved in some way with chemicals. Incredibly, he also allowed the manufacturer to decide if the substance is hazardous and therefore covered by the standard; allowed broad labeling exemptions (except for carcinogens, mutagens, and teratogens) in order to guard against the disclosure of trade secrets; and, most important, included a provision to fully preempt state laws concerning the labeling of chemicals in the workplace.[118]

Preemption of state laws is the key. It would allow Auchter to garner broad industrial support for his proposal by overriding a rapidly growing number of tough new city and state laws requiring labeling, which were passed with heavy lobbying by labor. Angry at Donovan's revocation of the proposed standard, the labor unions had succeeded in enacting seventeen state laws and dozens of city ordinances.[119]

In response, the chemical companies have shown their support for a weakened federal requirement that would nip the right-to-know movement in the bud. "Without a strong federal role, individual states will enact a variety of diverse labeling rules that would hamper interstate business operations and impede worker protection," complained the National Paint and Coatings Association, in written comments to the agency.[120]

But OMB still disagreed with Auchter's proposal. In its review, OMB had argued that it was "inappropriate . . . for the federal government to preclude states and localities from exercising their police powers, especially under the Reagan administration's policies of decentralization and renewed federalism."[121]

Labor and consumer groups disagreed for different reasons. While the Auchter proposal would cover the whole nation, it would not only preempt better state laws but give companies broad discretion to decide what to label and what to withhold as trade secrets. "It's really a very bad rule; it's full of loopholes," complained Michael J. Wright, of the United Steel Workers of America. Some OSHA officials agreed: "The information just goes from prince to prince," said one. "The data goes from the manufacturer [of the chemical] to the user, and not out to the public or the worker."[122]

On November 21, 1983, OSHA issued the final standard, which was similar in most respects to the proposal. Auchter boasted that it is "the most far-reaching action that OSHA has taken" since the agency was formed in 1971. He argued that it "strikes a very careful balance" between workers' need-to-know and manufacturers' need to protect trade secrets."[123] Citizen and labor groups immediately named it the "right-to-hide" standard because it allows employers to use their "professional judgment" in deciding which chemicals are not hazardous and thus need not be disclosed. Public Citizen and several labor organizations immediately challenged the standard in the US Court of Appeals, charging it is inconsistent with the law and fails to provide workers with adequate information relating to the hazards they are exposed to in the workplace.[124] Peg Seminario of the AFL-CIO complained particularly that sixty million workers in transportation, construction, and other industries would not be covered. And, she pointed out, "There was not one instance [in the record] where a trade secret was disclosed to a competitor. Yet the agency has bent over backward to protect manufacturers' so-called 'trade secrets.' "[125]

STAFFING CUTS

OSHA's mission to assure that "no employee will suffer material impairment of health or functional capacity even if such employee has regular exposure to the hazard dealt with by [the OSHA] standard for the period of his working life"[126] has been undermined in the Reagan administration not only by the revocation of standards and by the failure to issue and enforce them, but also by the dismissal of talented staff. In 1982 Auchter said, "When I arrived at the agency last spring, I quickly found that the myth of the OSHA bureaucrat—as an incompetent picker of nits—was exactly that: a myth, completely untrue. I have been consistently impressed and gratified by the high quality, competence, and dedication of the agency's employees."[127]

After the 1982 budget cuts, however, one-third of the agency's field offices were shut down. Further budget cuts forced 150 field inspectors to leave OSHA. About 30 other staff people left the agency between 1981 and 1982. Hundreds retired. Others got disgusted. In 1981 a federal inspector from California quit: "I got bored with the job, because the [enforcement] activity had slowed down and I was too young to vegetate. I felt I wasn't doing anything good anymore." He continued: "The people who were technically competent left; I joined [OSHA] to help people. . . . I guess I was a little naive."[128]

In April 1982, the *Washington Post* reported that all three of the staff physicians hired under the Carter administration by Dr. Bingham to increase the agency's expertise in occupational medicine—as well as Hays Bell, the director of the Technical Support Directorate—had resigned. OSHA employees, talking off the record, said that the resignations were triggered because "OSHA's medical staff feels Auchter had neither sought nor listened to its advice when making decisions about health."[129]

Patricia Sparks, former acting director of the Office of Occupational Medicine, explains why she left:

> We recommended that an emergency temporary standard be promulgated for EDB. We tried to give them a risk assessment, but that was ignored. The case of EDB is clear cut. It's a direct-acting carcinogen. That is, it doesn't have to mix with other chemicals or turn into something else in the body. It seems to damage DNA directly. There's also evidence that EDB has harmful effects on the reproductive system. I think they [OSHA administrators] understood the scientific data. But their priorities are in the political realm. Loyalty to the party that put them there—that's more their priority.[130]

Another doctor said: "Scientists and doctors are no longer being sought out for advice and have become uncomfortable with decisions being made here. They are concerned about [ruining] their reputations and what's being done by this administration."[131]

In the fall of 1982, the *Village Voice* investigated OSHA's handling of an oil-refinery explosion in Texas, which killed two workers and injured twenty-six more. OSHA managers initiated a search to uncover and reprimand the inspectors who spoke with reporter Norma Zanichow.[132] Firing a dissident voice fits the pattern of Auchter's OSHA.

Two months after Auchter's arrival as assistant secretary of labor, one of OSHA's top scientists, Dr. Peter Infante, publicly stated what was then the official OSHA position—that formaldehyde was a dangerous animal carcinogen and was a likely carcinogen in humans, too. The Formaldehyde Institute, a trade organization, complained. Auchter tried to fire Infante, but a congressional hearing into the muzzling of free speech and scientific independence cooled his ardor.[133]

Congressman Albert Gore, Jr. (Democrat-Tennessee) angrily charged: "To fire this scientist for expressing his scientific opinion on formaldehyde is a blatant effort to rid the government of a competent scientist whose well-founded views happened not to agree with an industry whose profits are at stake." A chastened Auchter ultimately backed away from the dismissal, and Dr. Infante stayed on. But staff intimidation continues.[134]

More than most Americans realize, OSHA is an agency that is meant to secure equal health rights for all Americans. A safe workplace should not be the result of coincidence or the exclusive right of white-collar executives. It is a right that belongs to all workers. The costs of job injuries and chronic diseases should not be displaced onto workers, at a considerable profit to the employer. Rather, with the help of OSHA, they should be borne by the companies that create them in the first place.

Dr. Sidney M. Wolfe, director of the Public Citizen Health Research Group, recently attacked the myth that deregulation is somehow a cost-saving move:

> We hear repeatedly from industry that it will cost millions to regulate carcinogens and other hazardous substances, but we have not focused on what it will cost *not* to regulate . . . or more accurately, what it will cost to allow industry to continue their damaging *private* regulation. Until OSHA was created, the cost of dangerous workplaces had been largely avoided by industry. It has

been borne by taxpayers through Social Security disability payments, to a small extent through worker compensation payments, and primarily through the death, disease, and disablement of workers themselves—a toll that can never be expressed in dollars, reversed, or compensated.[135]

Unable to muster a political backlash to the 1970 statute that created OSHA, the Reagan administration has resorted instead to backdoor administrative ploys and evasive rhetoric. Instead of heeding the dictates of science and the law, the agency has diligently rolled back what health and safety protections it could on behalf of its business allies. Except in isolated court cases, in which a stricter accounting is feasible, Thorne Auchter's lawlessness has gone largely unpunished. His legacy to the American workers of today and tomorrow is a sorry one indeed.

ENVIRONMENTAL PROTECTION

ENVIRONMENTAL QUALITY IMPROVEMENT ACT OF 1970:
"The Congress declares that there is a national policy for
the environment, which provides for the enhancement of
environmental quality."

The Environmental Protection Agency (EPA), whose administrator is the only regulatory chief reporting directly to the president, set the pace early in the Reagan administration for management abuses, violations of statutory mandates, conflicts of interest, political favoritism, and cover-up of its scandals. It inspired congressional investigations, front-page news, and public outrage. In the end the misdeeds of its Reagan appointees changed the political climate in Washington, DC, and across the nation, and crippled Ronald Reagan's deregulation of government health and safety standards. Reagan lost his miraculous control of Congress as he revealed his political vulnerabilities, and his credibility was permanently damaged. The harm done to the EPA and to the environment will take years to recoup. The harmful exposure of the citizenry to hazardous chemicals in the air, water, ground, and food products cannot be reversed.

The abuses at EPA were first exposed in late 1982, when the White House and Attorney General William French Smith instructed EPA administrator Anne Burford to resist disclosure to a congressional committee of "sensitive" documents about the agency's hazardous-waste enforcement program. Mrs. Burford was told to invoke executive privilege, a special authority reserved to the president for withholding information from Congress, usually in cases of national emergency, foreign entanglements, or military hostilities.

The White House at first ignored the burgeoning problems emerging from the congressional investigation. In December, the House of Representatives, for the first time in history, voted to hold a cabinet official in contempt of Congress. "My choice," said Burford, "was to faithfully carry out my job according to my best lights and in harmony with what the president had told me . . . to do and, at the other end of the scale, to spend a year in jail and pay a $1,000 fine. These choices aren't even in the same ballpark."[1]

As the story burst onto page one, congressional and media attention heightened, and disaffected agency employees were emboldened. They began to document how grants to clean up toxic waste had been announced to help re-elect Senator Richard Lugar (Republican-Indiana) and withheld to hurt ex-Governor Edmund G. (Jerry) Brown (Democrat-California) in his campaign for senator; how agency employees who had complained about the snail's pace of enforcement actions were harassed; how Rita Lavelle, Reagan's appointee in charge of the hazardous-waste program, lied about telling her former employer at Aerojet-General Corporation of potential EPA action involving its disposal of hazardous waste; how Lavelle's appointment calendar, listing meetings and high-priced meals, looked like a *Who's Who* of the chemical industry; and how advisors from the hazardous-waste industry were hired to help justify the failure to clean up dangerous hazardous-waste sites that were threatening not only the health of the population but also the environment. Hugh Kaufman, employed in the EPA's hazardous-waste division, got so aggravated at the abuses that he persistently blew the whistle on Lavelle and incited more congressional investigations. He accused Lavelle of delaying waste cleanup by engaging in lengthy negotiations and arranging "sweetheart" deals with industry, of using hazardous-waste cleanup money to buy fancy furniture and other perks, and finally of harassing him by investigating his outside activities and giving him an unfavorable reputation.[2]

Under the continuing pressure of six congressional committees investigating EPA's mismanagement, the White House told Mrs. Burford in early February 1983 to fire Rita Lavelle and several of her assistants. Mrs. Burford, in carrying out this instruction, cited a draft memorandum written in Ms. Lavelle's name, which complained that other agency personnel were "systematically alienating the primary constituents of this administration, the business community."[3]

With Watergate still fresh in the public memory, President Reagan ordered his aides and Justice Department officials to structure a compromise with the leading critics in Congress for disclosure or review of the documents requested. But it was too late. More conflicts of interest, involving regulated industries and EPA appointees, came to light daily. The public was entranced by the drama. Mrs. Burford hinted publicly that the White House was making a mistake by not disclosing all of the documents. Congress began to consider contempt charges against Ms. Lavelle and asked the Justice Department to review perjury charges. (She was subsequently acquitted of the contempt charge but convicted of perjury.) The White House then forced several other high-ranking EPA appointees to resign, in an effort to defuse the escalating political furor.

But the storm could not be contained. In mid-March Anne Burford resigned to end "the controversy and confusion," which, she said, prevented the agency from carrying out its job. President Reagan accepted her resignation "with deep regret" and praised "the progress we have made during your stewardship," saying, "You can walk out of the Environmental Protection Agency with your head held high."[4]

"Anne Burford wasn't rejected by the American public because she had friends who owned polluting industries," said a congressional aide who helped write several environmental laws. "That was why we were able to smile as we pushed her over the cliff. She was pushed because she was jeopardizing the health of the American people. And her policies were the policies of the Reagan administration, not Anne Burford's."[5]

The President then pledged that "Congress is not to be denied access to any documents" and quickly moved to control the political damage by appointing former EPA chief William D. Ruckelshaus to restore integrity to the agency.[6]

In the midst of the Burford battles, the human consequences of hazardous-waste contamination was imprinted on the public's consciousness when Times Beach, Missouri, was discovered to be contaminated with dioxin, one of the most hazardous toxins known to man. During the 1970s, waste oil containing dioxin was used by a contractor in Times Beach to control dust on nearby roads. In December 1982, a flood caused the dioxin-contaminated oil to spread throughout the entire town, depositing it on the properties of Times Beach's unsuspecting residents, who had to abandon their homes.

Meanwhile the political fallout continued. Environmental leaders issued reports detailing the destruction of environmental programs. "The Reagan administration's campaign to strip the American people of adequate environmental protection has penetrated every federal agency whose programs impact on our natural resources," complained Louise Dunlap, president of the Environmental Policy Center. William Turnage, executive director of the Wilderness Society, pointed out that Reagan had appointed staff who were "fundamentally, ideologically opposed" to the missions of the agencies.[7] And the public, increasingly aware of the Love Canal tragedy and of the consequences of hazardous-waste contamination, expressed indignation at the EPA's mismanagement and foot-dragging in cleaning up toxic waste dumps.

Support for Reagan's attacks on other health regulatory programs also disappeared. Enticed by the press's attention to the EPA scandals, members of Congress initiated investigations of other agencies likely to have inappropriately pandered to the regulated industry. Newspapers that had virtually ignored Reagan's regulatory policies set up teams of reporters to search for misdeeds.

ENVIRONMENTAL PROTECTION AND THE REAGAN PHILOSOPHY

The Environmental Protection Agency was created with the idea that pollution need not be the price of industrial progress. The same nation that put a man on the moon in 1969 formally acknowledged one year later that economic growth could be achieved without unhealthy air, polluted air and water, and an increase in premature deaths and disease. In 1970 Congress created the EPA to prod industry into doing what it would not do alone: clean up its waste.

The EPA spent the early 1970s establishing the regulatory framework to promote clean air and clean water, and to regulate pesticides and toxic pollutants. In 1976 and 1977 new laws were passed, empowering the EPA to regulate toxic substances, chemicals in the marketplace, and hazardous wastes "from cradle to grave."

It is an enormous task to oversee the 160 million tons of air pollution emitted annually, the 225 million tons of hazardous waste generated, the 4 million tons of toxic chemicals discharged into waterways and streams, and the 55,000 existing chemicals, plus the 600 to 1,000 new ones added each year.[8] Aided over the years by the development of a strong bipartisan consensus in Congress and the public's concern about environmental issues, the EPA has made some progress toward environmental cleanup during its short lifetime. Studies show that our air is significantly healthier than it was ten years ago, while numerous rivers that were pronounced "dead" twenty years ago are returning to life. Water-quality degradation has slowed down, despite increases in population and industrial production. With these success stories, and growing recognition of the relationship between environment and health, public support has remained strong. Ninety-one percent of the public supports a strong Clean Water Act, and 78 percent supports a strong Clean Air Act.[9]

But the election of Ronald Reagan, with his statements about "no-growth extremists," revived the concept that protecting the environment comes at the expense of growth. Since the days of his California governorship, Reagan has angered conservation groups. This is the man who summed up his views on conservation by remarking: "A tree is a tree—how many more do you need to look at?" During the 1980 campaign, Reagan asserted that the one eruption from Mount St. Helens created more pollution than all the cars in the US, that trees cause air pollution, and that oil slicks off Santa Barbara once purified the sea breezes.[10] This anticonservation viewpoint has reemerged during a decade in which it is estimated that the average American's exposure to toxic pollutants, by-products of the chemical revolution, will leap 50 to 100 percent within ten years.[11] According to former EPA assistant administrator William Drayton, the task of bringing toxins under control, while meeting air and water quality guidelines set by the Clean Air and Water Acts, will double the agency's workload in the 1980s.[12] Faced with this herculean task, the EPA could scarcely afford to fall under Reagan's ax. Nevertheless, in January 1981, the Reagan team began drastically cutting segments of the EPA's budget, dismissing staff, and terminating key environmental standards and proposals.

In the first month of his presidency, the EPA and other regulatory agencies were ordered by Reagan to perform cost-benefit analyses of proposed regulations under Executive Order 12291, which centralized within the White House's Office of Management and Budget (OMB) the authority to oversee all regulatory activities. The order showed contempt for the notion that health and safety benefits should supersede cost considerations in the setting of environmental standards. EO 12291 also meant that OMB budget director David Stockman could wield considerable control over environmental policy. Stockman was primed to take charge. In a 1980 speech to the National Association of Manufacturers (NAM) he had already prepared his "cost-benefit analysis" of the impact of acid rain in upstate New York lakes:

> [H]ow much are the fish worth in those 170 lakes that account for 4 percent of the lake area of New York? And does it make sense to spend billions of dollars controlling emissions from sources in Ohio and elsewhere if you're talking about a very marginal volume of dollar value, either in recreational terms or in commercial terms?[13]

After Stockman finished his speech, the NAM moderator remarked that it was "encouraging to know somebody who thinks like that is still in Washington and has something to say."[14]

Industry got just what it wanted from Stockman and his crew at OMB, as Burford's former chief of staff John Daniel finally made public in congressional testimony in September 1983. He told of how the OMB had leaked the EPA's proposed standards on high-level radioactive waste to industry before they were published, resulting in "tremendous pressure" on the EPA to modify them. He mentioned interference particularly with air and water quality standards and requirements for controlling uranium mill tailings. When Burford once tried to issue regulations over the OMB's objections, OMB official Jim Tozzi called to say that "there was a price to pay" for doing that and EPA "hadn't begun to pay."[15]

But Stockman was not unique. President Reagan filled the top-level positions at EPA with people "who think like that."

- Anne McGill Gorsuch Burford, EPA administrator, a former Colorado state legislator, who fiercely opposed any legislation regulating hazardous-waste disposal. In 1982 she married former Colorado house speaker Robert Burford (himself a Reagan appointee to the Interior Department), who had frequently assigned major regulatory bills to her legislative committee, which was known as "the killing ground." Mrs. Burford resigned from the EPA in March 1983.
- Dr. John W. Hernandez, Jr., from New Mexico, one of the persons initially considered for the position of administrator. Instead, he became the deputy administrator and later held the position of acting administrator after Mrs. Burford resigned. Two weeks after taking over as the EPA's temporary chief, Dr. Hernandez resigned, under fire from Congress, for his role in altering a draft report on dioxin.
- Colorado lawyer James Sanderson, Burford's choice to fill the EPA's number-three post. He was forced to withdraw from consideration. Sanderson did consulting work for the EPA for a year at the same time that he was representing Chemical Waste Management, a subsidiary of the nation's largest waste disposal firm, and the Denver Water Board, an industrial group concerned with relaxing water-quality standards. He has been the subject of a conflict-of-interest probe by the Justice Department, which has since been closed.
- Rita Lavelle, assistant administrator for Solid Waste and Emergency Response. Lavelle had been director of communications for the Aerojet Liquid Rocket Company, a subsidiary of the Aerojet-General Corporation. EPA records showed that Aerojet-General had the third worst pollution record in California. It was charged with improperly dumping up to twenty thousand gallons a day of carcinogens and other toxic wastes. Lavelle was fired by Burford in February 1983, amidst charges of

conflict of interest, mismanagement, and manipulation of the EPA's $1.6 billion hazardous-waste cleanup program. Lavelle was convicted on December 1, 1983, of lying to Congress about her management of EPA's hazardous-waste program. On January 9, 1984, she was given a six-month prison term and a $10,000 fine. She is filing an appeal.

- John A. Todhunter, chief of Toxic Substances and Pesticides. He previously served on the scientific advisory board of an industry-financed group that has continually downplayed the role of chemicals and pollution in causing cancer. Todhunter resigned in March 1983, amid reports that he ordered staff studies altered to make the toxic chemicals dioxin and formaldehyde appear less dangerous. In June 1983, it was learned that he also sought to influence the awarding of a government contract to his former firm.

- Robert Perry, a former Exxon trial lawyer. He was appointed as the EPA general counsel. Perry resigned after admitting that he was actively involved in a hazardous-waste-site cleanup settlement involving Exxon. Perry had earlier signed a statement saying that he would not involve himself in any matter related to Exxon's interests. He was under investigation for perjury, but his case has been dismissed.

- John Daniel, Burford's chief of staff. His previous job was as the Washington counsel for Johns-Manville, the nation's largest asbestos manufacturer.

So in 1981, the nation's environmental laws were in the hands of a president who accused the trees of causing air pollution, a budget director who bragged about his contempt for environmental laws, and a group of former employees and friends of polluting industries, whose previous jobs found them skirting or condemning the laws that they were now entrusted with executing.

When David Stockman scanned the EPA's agenda a few weeks after the 1980 election, he saw what William Drayton of the Carter EPA had seen: the EPA's workload was doubling. Stockman was alarmed. "Unless swift, comprehensive, and far-reaching regulatory policy corrections are undertaken immediately," Stockman wrote during the transition, "an unprecedented scale-up of the much discussed 'regulatory burden' will occur during the next eighteen to forty months."[16] A spate of laws regulating toxic pollutants was ready to be implemented, and unless the brakes were applied quickly, Reagan would find the EPA doing exactly what he had pledged in the campaign not to do—regulate industry.

The administration responded. In March 1981, Vice-President Bush's Task Force on Regulatory Relief announced that a number of major environmental regulations completed by the Carter administration—including rules governing hazardous-waste disposal, toxic effluent limits on industrial discharges into sewage treatment plants, and vehicle emissions—would undergo review.

These rules were subsequently suspended or canceled. In some cases no alternatives have been developed. A study by the Natural Resources Defense Council (NRDC) found that between January 1981 and October 1982, over half of the EPA's scheduled actions either had been canceled or had fallen behind schedule.[17]

With major rules delayed, the administration moved, in the words of James Watt, chairman of the cabinet's Council on Natural Resources and the Environment (CNRE), to "use the budget system as the excuse to make major policy decisions."[18] In 1981 and 1982, the budget for the EPA's four major programs (water, air, hazardous wastes, and pesticides) fell by 30 percent. An additional 19 percent cut was sought for 1983 but was stopped by Congress.[19] According to Senator Patrick Leahy (Democrat-Vermont), Reagan's proposals would have cut the operating budget of the EPA by 46 percent in the first three years.[20] Former interior secretary Stewart Udall, in a letter on behalf of the NRDC, noted that the cuts in both working capital and personnel added up to a total reduction of nearly 60 percent by the end of 1982—at a time when the EPA's workload was doubling.[21]

The budgets for three areas were particularly hard hit: research, aid to the states, and enforcement.

Research

"Our scientific evidence is the backbone of this agency," Anne Burford once asserted. By this definition, she left her agency spineless. The administration's 1984 budget request for EPA research was 53 percent below that of the Carter years.[22] Former EPA staffers charge that this research budget belies any commitment to sound science as the basis for regulations.

"If the Reagan administration wants to see good cost-benefit regulatory studies," commented Paul Portney, of Resources for the Future, "then these research budget cuts . . . make it virtually impossible to do it. I don't want to call the administration duplicitous, but you must consider the fact that you will not get the enhanced analysis the administration says it wants if at the same time it slashes the research budget needed to do it."[23]

A qualitative shift in the focus of research during the Reagan administration has been as important as the quantitative funding cut. The administration has sought to eliminate the invaluable exploratory research grants program, which helps identify emerging environmental trends. A few years ago this program produced a research plan for gathering information on acid rain and hazardous air pollutants, both of which have become important contemporary issues. The Reagan administration, however, does not acknowledge the importance of preparing forecasts of long-term environmental trends, and prefers to limit research to those activities that are more immediately useful to the regulatory program.[24]

The abandonment of long-term research left the administration free to seek scientific support for its relaxation of regulations. The Reagan EPA took no chances. It compiled a "hit list" of scientists with the agency and rated them on their willingness to support the administration's agenda. More than fifty scientists were removed from the science advisory boards during Reagan's first two years, based on lists describing some as "horrible," "a real activist," and "a Nader on toxics." The list also featured a candid evaluation of the EPA's research and development program: "Rhetorically, what have they done to earn their money? Is there need for any? They all seem to be invidious environmental extremists."[25]

Robert Sievers, a chemistry professor at the University of Colorado at Boulder, who got a thumbs down from industry, issued a two-page statement lamenting the implications of the hit list. "Many dedicated, highly competent EPA scientists are living in fear of losing their jobs," wrote Sievers. "We decry the situation

in Russia, where scientists of the wrong religion or political lean-
ing become nonpersons, unable to obtain support for their research or their livelihood. How can we ignore a similar trend in
our own bureaucracy?"[26]

Reagan-appointed administrators also attempted to block ongoing research within the EPA's regional offices. In 1981, Valdas
Adamkus, the EPA's regional administrator for Chicago, asked his
staff to prepare a public report on contamination of the Great Lakes
region by two toxic pesticides and herbicides, one of them being
dioxin. The report was instigated after a substantial concentration
of contaminants had been found in Michigan river fish, with the
highest concentration in fish from Saginaw Bay, on Lake Huron.

The findings of the report were of particular interest to the
Dow Chemical Company, whose Midland, Michigan, plant discharged wastes into rivers that pass into Saginaw Bay. When a
draft of the report was leaked to a Toronto newspaper in June 1981,
a Dow representative got in touch with Dr. John Hernandez, Jr.,
deputy administrator at the EPA, and asked for a copy of the
report, which had not been released. Hernandez gave it to Dow
to critique before EPA released it to the public.

Regional administrator Adamkus then received several calls
from Hernandez. "He angrily denounced the report," said Adamkus, "and called the work of our people 'trash.' " Hernandez also
said that Dow would get in touch with Adamkus. The first call
came from Ectyl Blair, Dow's vice-president for health and environmental sciences. "I listened to his comments, . . ." Adamkus
recalled, "and I realized that he was reviewing our document."[27]
Dow followed up with more calls, requesting a change in the
report's title, lowered estimates of the risks from exposure to
dioxin, deletion of references to miscarriages, to reduced fertility,
and to Dow's chemical agent orange, which contains toxic levels
of dioxin.

Meanwhile, the EPA staff in Washington was also on the
telephone. Messages from intermediaries were flowing to the authors of the report. Both Hernandez and John A. Todhunter,
EPA's assistant administrator for Toxic Substances and Pesticides,
were pressuring the authors to make drastic changes. Testifying
before the House Energy and Commerce Subcommittee on Oversight and Investigations, Dr. J. Milton Clark, a scientist in EPA's

Chicago office, said he was urged to soften the report's language by EPA scientists in Washington, one of whom told him "that some changes in the report had been dictated by Dr. Hernandez." And Adamkus testified that an aide to Todhunter had told Adamkus that her boss wanted to delete references to dioxin, miscarriages, and agent orange.[28]

As a result of the pressure from Dow and EPA administrators in Washington, a passage of six lines was deleted, which had indicated that Dow was "the major source, if not the only source," of dioxin contamination in the Saginaw Bay area.[29] Thus was the report issued. Dow has since dismissed the incident as a routine exercise in scientific peer review.

In 1983, the public found out more about the Dow Chemical Company's reasons for wanting the report altered. In a lawsuit filed on behalf of a group of Vietnam veterans, documents obtained from Dow showed that as early as 1965 the company had withheld information showing that dioxin could be "exceptionally toxic" to humans, and that one of its herbicides, agent orange, contained dangerous levels of dioxin. Correspondence between Dow and representatives of other chemical companies illustrates the extent to which they all knew of the hazards. A chemist for Hercules Powder Company wrote: "... liver damage [in tests on rabbits] is severe, and a no-effect level based on liver response has not yet been established. Even vigorous washing of the skin fifteen minutes after application will not prevent damage and may possibly enhance the absorption of the material. There is some evidence it is systemic."[30] That memo was written more than nineteen years ago.

But Dow still denies any liability. In early 1983, Paul F. Oreffice, the president of Dow, stated on NBC's "Today" show, "There is absolutely no evidence of dioxin doing any damage to humans except for something called chloracne. It's a rash." Dow, he said, had performed medical tests on individuals suffering from chloracne for "over twenty years"; and, he added, "There is no evidence of any damage other than this rash...."[31] Dioxin is now being linked by independent scientists to liver damage, to a rare soft-tissue cancer, and to birth defects in animals. And it is only one of the thousands of toxic chemicals that the EPA should be vigorously researching because they threaten our health and our environment.

Aid to the States

The Reagan administration justified the three-year, 46-percent cut in the EPA budget by asserting that more power would be delegated to the states. Current environmental laws, however, already burden the states with considerable responsibilities. The federal government writes the laws and sets the standards. The states help devise methods to meet those standards, and, with funding grants from the federal government, monitor, inspect for compliance, issue permits, and give technical assistance to industries.

A study made by the General Accounting Office (GAO) in 1982 warned that Reagan's funding cuts would contribute to "interstate inconsistency": "States that once lagged in their commitment to national environmental programs—and were persuaded by the incentive of federal aid—may find ample reason to relax environmental controls, thereby attracting industry and placing states with stronger environmental programs at an economic disadvantage.[32]

Delegating authority to the states to set their own standards undermines regulatory efficiency in three ways. First, it forces industry to comply with dozens of different air, water, and waste-disposal standards. Second, most states lack the funds to support the technical staff and research facilities needed to set high standards. Third, it puts states in conflict with their own interests in attracting industry. State-set standards permit competition among states, tempting them to attract business by weakening environmental laws, and possibly trading public health needs for corporate profits.

But the most serious problem with President Reagan's plan to delegate federal authority to the states is that he does not delegate the capital to carry out federal policies. Like most of his "new federalism" initiatives, increased state environmental responsibilities have been coupled, not with more but with fewer federal dollars—47 percent less over three years—to implement the rules.[33] "We're alarmed and disheartened that cuts of this nature are being proposed," said S. William Becker, of the State and Territorial Air Pollution Programs. "This [has] a totally negative effect on state programs.[34]

In 1982 a congressional study reported a similar reaction

from state officials to the claim that more could be done with less. Its results were summarized by a Utah environmental protection official: "If resources are cut, then programs will have to be cut. We are all making a mistake if we deceive ourselves into believing otherwise."[35]

As a consequence of the cuts in their grants, states will have to shrink the basic enforcement activities of monitoring, issuing permits, and conducting compliance inspections. Mississippi projected a 60 percent cut in air-quality monitoring and 26 percent fewer compliance inspections in 1983 because of decreased federal funding.[36] Tennessee projected that its hazardous-waste inspection frequency would drop by 27 percent in 1983, despite its attempt to accelerate enforcement activities. As of July 1982, only 11 percent of Tennessee's forty-three hundred hazardous-waste generators and disposers have been inspected.[37]

Enforcement

The Reagan EPA's enforcement activities further demonstrate the administration's lack of commitment to environmental protection:

- The president attempted to cut the EPA enforcement budget by 45 percent in his first two years.[38]
- The number of (general enforcement) civil cases referred by the EPA to the Department of Justice fell by 69 percent, from 252 to 78, in the first year of the Reagan administration.[39]
- In FY 1980, the last full year of the Carter administration, 131 air-enforcement actions were referred by the EPA to the Justice Department. In FY 1981, there were 52. As of mid-April 1982, there had been only three referrals for FY 1982.[40]
- In 1983, the EPA's regional offices were 1,000 to 1,600 employees short of the level needed to effectively enforce the law according to the agency's own studies.[41]
- Anne Burford told a small gas refiner, Thriftway Refinery Company, that she would not enforce the lead standard.[42]
- Large refiners were explicitly told that exceeding the

stricter lead standard, to a degree that would add an additional 10,000 tons of airborne lead, was acceptable to the EPA.[43]

A credible enforcement policy is vital if environmental laws are to be obeyed. If industry perceives that the EPA is not serious about enforcement, compliance will drop, because, as William Drayton says, "No one wants to be the sucker complying with the law."[44]

"It was a well-known fact that if a company didn't like what it was getting in negotiations with agency lawyers, it could go to the assistant administrator, the deputy administrator, or to Burford's office," says Anthony Roisman, who resigned in 1982 as chief of the Justice Department's Hazardous Wastes section. "They could just go all the way up the agency ladder to get what they wanted."[45]

Burford reorganized the EPA's enforcement office: it first was abolished, then reconstituted with a smaller staff; top officials were replaced, and all division responsibilities were redefined. According to an internal memo of April 29, 1982, the constant restructuring generated "considerable confusion in the regions about who in headquarters does what in the enforcement area and who to call to get something done." The memo also expressed concern that a perception of lax enforcement was causing industry to assume that it was in a "new ball game."[46] The agency listed 115 priority hazardous-waste sites and then sent the responsible parties a letter threatening enforcement action unless voluntary cleanup began. Only about 1 percent of the companies even bothered to respond. William Sullivan, EPA's enforcement counsel, conceded that "a one percent response was an indication of industry's perception that EPA is not as serious about enforcement as it should be."[47]

The reorganization of EPA's enforcement office was coupled with a drastic cut in enforcement funding. According to Jonathan Lash, of the NRDC, the administration has justified the cuts on the grounds that portions of the enforcement program have been transferred elsewhere or to the states. But a closer look at the budget indicates that this "diaspora of enforcement resources" has resulted in an overall reduction in the funds that are available for enforcement programs. In FY 1981, for example, the EPA spent $11.3 million for hazardous-waste enforcement. The FY 1983 request was $1.9 million. The budget document explains that portions of the program were transferred to the Office of Legal and Enforcement Counsel, the Regulatory Strategies Implementation Program (RSIP), and the states. For FY 1983, however, the administration also proposed heavy cuts for RSIP and state hazardous-waste grants. Only congressional intervention prevented all of these from being made.[48]

HAZARDOUS WASTE

Just at the state line in Anson County, North Carolina, is a grassy hill graced by trees, a Civil War farmhouse, and a herd of grazing cows. This is the hill on which the government plans to build a hazardous-waste landfill. It lies a few hundred feet from a small stream that runs into Jones Creek and then into the Pee Dee River, which crosses the state line and in a few miles flows past the town of Cheraw, South Carolina. Fifty-six hundred residents of Cheraw get their drinking water from the Pee Dee. They water their gardens with it, cook their food in it, bathe in it, wash their clothes and children with it. If contamination seeped into Jones Creek, it would reach the intake pumps for the city water supply in fifteen hours.

Clyde Wallace, an industrial engineer with the Stanley Tools plant in Cheraw, is shocked that the EPA would mark this 509-acre property a "secure" landfill, since it sits on a low hill bounded on three sides by small streams that flow into a major drinking-water supply. The bottoms of the waste pits would be no more than seven feet above the groundwater.

"I asked the EPA regional office in Atlanta," Wallace told a reporter for the *Washington Post*, "how a site seven feet above the water table could be considered safe. They answered, 'Hell, those regulations say you could build the site *in* the water table.' "[49]

North Carolina law forbids the state from imposing any regulations more stringent than the federal rules, and the governor, James B. Hunt, was under pressure from industry to provide a site for chemical waste. It was that pressure that led to the selection of the hillside in Anson County—sparsely populated,

largely black, and rural. Chem-Security Systems, which is building the landfill, has been owned since July 1982 by Waste Management, the nation's largest waste-disposal firm. It bought the
509-acre property under a John Doe assumed name. In a letter to
one protesting Cheraw resident, a lawyer for Chem-Security said
that the firm "has had no problems" complying with the laws and
regulations of another disposal site in Oregon. The letter neglected to mention that the water table at the Oregon site is six
hundred feet below the surface, in an area so dry that it gets nine
inches of rainfall a year and stands above a flood plain that would
carry the hazardous waste all the way to the ocean. But Landon
Scarborough, a hardware store owner in Anson County, who
heads a local group called CACTUS (Citizens Against Chemical
Toxins in Underground Storage), understands that the land in his
community is different. "If that thing overflowed" in Anson
County "thousands of acres could be contaminated."[50]

In 1982, citizens met with Anne Burford. At the least, they
argued, the distance between the bottom of the waste pit and the
groundwater table ought to be thirty feet, enough for a leak to be
detected and corrected before it might be too late. According to
Clyde Wallace, Mrs. Burford said such a rule would exclude more
than half of North and South Carolina and the entire state of
Florida. "Her position was that every state deserved [a waste fill],"
he said.[51] However, popular opposition to the landfill prevailed,
and in 1983 Chem-Security canceled building the site.

In 1983, the Office of Technology Assessment reported that
one ton of hazardous waste is generated yearly for every person
in the United States. The waste is classified in the following
categories: radioactives, inflammables, heavy metals, asbestos,
acids and bases, and synthetic organic chemicals. Hazardous waste
is disposed of in different ways. Among the methods used are
surface impoundments (pits, ponds, and lagoons), landfill or
burial, pretreatment, incineration, resource recovery, and deep-
well injection.

While garbage and human waste can be broken down in the
soil, most hazardous waste remains poisonous for centuries. Heavy
metals remain a hazard forever. In most cases, the disposal of such
waste has been undertaken by industry in the cheapest and most

convenient manner possible. Consequently, disposal sites have not been adequately safeguarded for the public's health and safety.

"The short-term and long-term dangers from improper disposal of hazardous wastes is one of the most crucial health and safety issues confronting the United States in this century," says Anthony Roisman.[52] Already it has been necessary to evacuate two communities, Love Canal, New York, and Times Beach, Missouri. Many other communities suffer from a high incidence of cancer, birth defects, and other health problems, because of hazardous-waste contamination of the water and soil.

Congress finally addressed the issue of hazardous waste in 1976 by enacting the Resource Conservation and Recovery Act (RCRA). The RCRA directs the EPA to set standards for hazardous-waste sites. These standards determine which sites are safe and which must be closed "to protect human health and the environment." To finance the cleanup of existing and abandoned hazardous-waste sites, Congress in 1980 enacted the Superfund law—the Comprehensive Environmental Response, Compensation, and Disability Act. "Thus when Reagan was elected," observes Roisman, "the statutes, regulations, and enforcement programs adopted by the Carter administration to control future hazardous-waste disposal and cleanup past hazardous-waste problems were in place and ready to operate."[53]

But after Reagan took office, his appointees organized an all-out attack on the regulations established under the RCRA. Reagan's EPA has followed a course of action that emphasizes deregulation and cost savings to industry at the expense of adequate protection of public health and the environment. Urged on by David Stockman, director of the OMB, and by Vice-President Bush's Task Force on Regulatory Relief, Anne Burford either suspended or weakened most hazardous-waste regulations shortly after taking office in 1981.

The most graphic illustration of the prevailing attitude in the EPA was its suspension of the ban on storing drums of liquid hazardous waste in landfills—four months after the ban had gone into effect. Khristine Hall of the Environmental Defense Fund explains:

The ban was promulgated by the Carter EPA for compel-
ling health and environmental reasons: all landfills leak,
and placing drums of liquid waste in landfills encourages
the leakage. The drums degrade, releasing their contents,
and the crushing down of drums creates subsidence [sink-
ing] and cracks in the covers of landfills. Although it
acknowledged that drummed liquids in landfills present
significant health problems, EPA suspended the ban
without giving notice or allowing the public to comment.[54]

Public outcry at the suspension forced the EPA to reimpose the
ban one month later, but not before the agency had lost its credibility.

Landfills and surface impoundments constitute the domi-
nant methods of hazardous waste disposal. Both have been plagued
with structural and operational problems. An EPA assessment of
surface impoundments released in 1980 indicated that of the
twenty-six thousand known impoundments, 70 percent allowed
contaminants to infiltrate into the ground unimpeded.[55] In a report to the California assembly, in February 1982, on hazardous
waste, Dr. Peter Skinner, an engineer with the New York State
Environmental Protection Bureau, noted that "secure" landfills
are really just "inverted mud huts" or "clay barges filled with toxic
chemicals, floating on a sea of groundwater." Dr. Skinner supplied
a few examples of the problems caused by storing hazardous waste
in landfills:

- In 1972, Chemtrol, Inc., opened and filled six landfills near
  Lewiston, New York. By 1981, there were substantial
  leaks and the New York State Department of Environmental Conservation required 300,000 gallons of leachate
  a month to be pumped out and detoxified on site—at a
  cost of over $1 million.
- As of 1981, according to a study by Princeton University
  scientist Peter Montague, four of New Jersey's five "secure" landfills had failed to work properly before being
  filled and closed.
- As of 1982, the state of Kentucky had spent more than $7
  million in maintenance of hazardous-waste sites.[56]

"The fundamental problem with landfilling," says William Sanjour, chief of hazardous-waste implementation for the EPA, "is that no one knows how to do it. All the research we've done indicates that when we put stuff in the ground, it's going to come out."[57] Hugh Kaufman, an official in the EPA's hazardous-waste division, agrees: "There isn't an engineer or scientist in the country who doesn't recognize that nobody has designed a landfill that will not leak. It just doesn't exist."[58] And says Dr. Peter Skinner, "All the alluring scale models and colored graphics cannot hide the fact that these quasi-engineered pits are no more than in-site repository experiments, backed up by neither scientific proof nor laboratory testing."[59]

It is clear from Dr. Skinner's testimony and the evidence available to the public that landfills and surface impoundments are not equipped with sufficient safeguards to protect the public's health and the environment. Individually, the safeguards available —synthetic liners, leachate collection and treatment systems, leachate detection systems, and groundwater monitoring systems* —do not provide adequate protection against leaching and contamination. If combined, however, they can minimize the threat.

On July 13, 1982, the Reagan EPA issued standards requiring all existing and new landfills and surface impoundments to install groundwater monitoring systems, with several exceptions. Monitoring is not required at sites where the potential for groundwater contamination is low, or where a double liner and a leachate

---

* *Leachate collection and treatment systems:* located underneath landfills and surface impoundments, but within the liner or walls, the systems consist of gravel channels that collect leachate and lead it to pipes. Once in the pipes, the leachate is pumped out of the landfill or surface impoundment and treated (detoxified) on site.

    Leachate detection systems: used only in conjunction with double liners, these electrical moisture detection systems are located in between the two liners and alert the operator that leachate has penetrated the first layer of lining.

    Groundwater monitoring systems: these consist of wells dug near the landfill or surface impoundment. Dug at levels approximating the top and bottom of the site, the wells allow the operator of the site to judge whether it has begun to leak into the surrounding land.

    Synthetic liners: generally, these are plastic membrane liners, approximately thirty millimeters thick, which are chemically treated so that they are resistant to the wastes contained within the site.

detection system have been installed. In addition, companies are required to demonstrate their ability to finance the future maintenance of their landfills and impoundments, and to handle possible decontamination in emergency situations, as well as provide liability coverage for injury or damage to other parties resulting from site operations. The EPA also required that new landfills and impoundments be equipped with a synthetic liner, as well as a leachate collection and treatment system. Existing sites are exempt.[60]

The Reagan standards do not take into account the importance of combining safeguards in order to reduce the possibility of leaching and contamination. By exempting groundwater monitoring requirements at sites where the potential for contamination is low, the EPA eliminates one of the few available mechanisms to detect leakage. Such an exemption does not provide an incentive for good management. Instead, it allows a company to bypass the best available monitoring technology if it selects the proper site for waste disposal. Furthermore, the exemption disregards the inevitability of leakage—and thus jeopardizes the public's health and the environment in the long term.[61] "You're talking about holding out millions of tons of hazardous waste with material not much thicker than the cuffs of your sleeves," says the EPA's William Sanjour. "The seams leak. When they're installed, they get cuts in them. The waste material eats away at them. When the land settles, you get cracks. You get roots growing through them, you get animals burrowing."[62]

By exempting companies from installing liners and leachate collection systems in existing sites, the EPA abandoned the notion of preventive action to control pollution at these sites. The EPA's approach poses significant problems. First, the public health and safety in regions with existing sites is entirely dependent upon the detection of contamination by groundwater monitoring systems, a technically complex—and on its own unreliable—process. Second, corrective action in the absence of liners and leachate collection systems is absurdly expensive and insufficient. Though the operator of the site may be able to clean up the contaminated water, the toxins will continue to leak into the ground.[63] Such drainage is particularly alarming considering that a quarter-inch-hole in a one-acre liner can discharge one thousand gallons of leachate a day.[64] Third, industry cannot be relied on to comply with monitoring requirements. In September 1983, the GAO issued a report on hazardous-waste facilities, showing that 78 percent of the facilities inspected did not comply with the federal groundwater monitoring requirements.[65] This statistic supports a recent EPA study, carried out by the agency's regional offices, which found that 74 percent of the hazardous-waste facilities do not comply with groundwater monitoring requirements.[66]

To be even minimally effective, the EPA standards must be enforced. In a June 18, 1982, memorandum, assistant administrator Rita Lavelle articulated her standard for a "vigorous" monitoring and enforcement program: the EPA or the states must visit a major disposal site once a year, other sites once every four years, and generators and respirators once every twenty-five years.[67]

According to Khristine Hall, of the Environmental Defense Fund:

> A credible compliance monitoring program would consist of annual visits to all major facilities, annual visits to half of the nonmajor facilities, and annual visits to 20 percent of the generators and transporters. Since there are estimated to be about 2,136 land disposal facilities, 7,858 treatment and storage facilities, and 63,318 generators and transporters, over 18,000 inspections should be made each year. EPA and the states will perform only about half that number in 1983 and slightly over one-third of the number in 1984. This is not a "rigorous inspection and enforcement effort."[68]

The 1983 GAO report also supports the claim that EPA has not done an adequate job in delegating inspection and enforcement authority to the states. The report indicates that as of December 31, 1982, an average of 45 percent of the total number of facilities in the states that were reviewed had been inspected. The percentage of facilities inspected, however, varied widely—between 18 and 88 percent—from state to state.[69]

Much of the blame for the states' poor performance must be put on Mrs. Burford and her Washington administrators. She increased state responsibility without allocating sufficient funds for those tasks. She constantly reorganized the central and regional enforcement offices, so that the delineation of responsibility was not clear. The GAO study reports that state inspectors have ceased giving evaluations of an individual site's contingency plans for emergency decontamination and for providing liability coverage. State officials point to the "lack of EPA procedures and guidance" and "limited inspections resources" as reasons for not providing such evaluations.[70]

Ironically, the risks to health and the environment arising from 75 percent of the waste stored in landfills could be significantly controlled through technologies that are already known: recycling, treatment, or incineration. Not only would these methods help protect human health and the environment, but they could "lead to economic benefits to the waste generator."[71] But, according to William Sanjour, "the Reagan administration is more interested in protecting its clients' industry than in reducing costs." Dumping is popular, because it is simple and cheap to a select group. "The real cost of dumping is not borne by the producer of the waste or by the disposer, but by the people whose health and property values are destroyed when the waste migrates onto their land and by the taxpayers who pay to clean it up."[72]

Rita Lavelle defended landfill disposal by arguing that "it is not the responsibility of the regulatory agencies to create or change economic incentives. We have to leave the marketplace alone."[73] She added that if you make disposal too expensive, "companies will dump their waste on the roadside."[74] Rigorous laws reinforced by strict enforcement to deter such behavior was not part of her vocabulary.

SUPERFUND

In 1978, in Niagara Falls, New York, state officials evacuated 240 families in the area known as Love Canal, after dangerous concentrations of highly toxic and carcinogenic chemicals had been discovered leaking from a sixteen-acre landfill.

And in Shepardsville, Kentucky, in the "Valley of the Drums," between 17,000 and 100,000 drums of waste were dumped illegally, allowing their contents to spill into a local creek.

In the wake of Love Canal and the "Valley of the Drums," Congress enacted the Superfund law, in 1980. Financed by a tax on chemical and oil companies, the $1.6 billion Superfund was intended to provide resources for the speedy cleanup of the most dangerous abandoned hazardous-waste sites. It would enable cleanup to begin quickly, while the EPA searched for the responsible parties and negotiated or litigated with them for reimbursement. Polluting companies refusing to pay their fair share of cleanup costs would face fines that were triple the amount of their liability for damages at a particular site.

In Anne Burford's first year in office, only two Superfund cases were referred to the Justice Department. In 1981 and 1982, the Reagan EPA spent or obligated barely one-tenth of the money available, and as of September 1982, actual cleanup work had started at only 19 out of 413 identified sites.[75] A lawsuit won by EDF in 1983 forced a reluctant HHS to set up a registry listing those who have been exposed to toxic substances and a special agency to deal with illnesses and injuries resulting from toxins, because of the explicit requirement in the Superfund law that it do so.[76]

When the Reagan administration came to Washington, the spirit of the Superfund law changed dramatically. "The Reagan EPA politicized the Superfund program, delayed needed expenditures for site cleanup, and signed deals with hazardous-waste dumpers," says Anthony Roisman. "In short, the effort to get on top of the hazardous-waste problem before it got out of hand was totally frustrated by Ronald Reagan."[77]

From the outset, both Burford and Lavelle indicated that agency-industry negotiations would precede, rather than coincide with, the cleanup of abandoned dumpsites. William Hedeman, who directed EPA's Office of Emergency and Remedial Response, testified that there was an "implicit policy at EPA to slow down Superfund money."[78] There also seemed to be an explicit policy to squander it. EPA's inspector general found that one-third of the $180 million slated for cleanup of Superfund sites was not spent on its intended purposes.[79] According to outspoken EPA staffer Hugh Kaufman, Superfund money was used to buy "fancy furniture, bigger offices, and other perks" for Reagan appointees.[80]

The first use of the Superfund authority came after a toxic site in Santa Fe Springs, California, caught fire in July 1981. Reagan had been in office only six months. But the EPA quickly negotiated an extraordinary settlement with one of the responsible parties. Rather than requiring it to finance complete removal of the hazard, the EPA limited the company's cleanup responsibility. The settlement also included a remarkable commitment. The EPA agreed to testify on behalf of the company in any subsequent lawsuit brought by injured citizens.[81] This early settlement set a clear precedent for future administration negotiations with industry.

Delay and red tape, constantly derided by Reagan when he was a candidate for the presidency, were skillfully employed by his political appointees to slow down the use of Superfund. "During the Burford-Lavelle reign," said Hugh Kaufman, "it would take as many as forty-nine signatures just for the bureaucracy to make a decision about thinking about making a decision about cleaning up a toxic waste site sometime in the future."[82] These delays created a deep sense of frustration among the EPA's regional managers, who felt handcuffed in their cleanup efforts. But the state officials were even more aggrieved than anyone else. Consider the following:

More than half of the Chem-Dyne waste dump near Cincinnati, Ohio, had been cleared by the state when local authorities ran out of money and asked the federal government for Superfund assistance. It took almost a year for the EPA to agree to an additional $2.4 million for a cleanup. Six months later the cleanup was still not under way. "We repeatedly told them that if they didn't come up with some money, we'd lose momentum on the cleanup," said Cincinnati official John Garretson. "Barrels are rusting and deteriorating out there, chemicals are leaching into the soil and the groundwater. And they've let it happen for political and bureaucratic reasons." Garretson also indicated that the $2.4 million would not be enough to clean up the site.[83]

If some state officials were frustrated by the turtle pace at the EPA, others found their appeals rejected entirely. In October 1982, Rita Lavelle refused the request of the state of Arkansas for funds to remove oil-laden dirt contaminated by PCB (polychlorinated biphenyl) from a public alley in Fort Smith. Concentrations reached 133,000 ppm of soil, or 13 percent by weight. In rejecting Arkansas' request for $8,000 to erect a temporary fence around the site, Lavelle argued that "in order for a child to consume the actual lethal dose of PCB, the child would have to eat about one hundred fifty grams of oil-laden dirt, the equivalent of about three large candy bars."[84]

Reagan appointees also manipulated Superfund for political advantage. The Stringfellow Acid Pits, fifty miles east of Los Angeles, is a twenty-two-acre dump, known as the Love Canal of the West. From 1956 through 1972, 34 million gallons of toxic industrial wastes were deposited at this site. It is listed as one of the top priorities for cleanup among 413 selected hazardous-waste dumps. Few people complained about the legal dump until heavy rains in 1978 caused an overflow of chromium, acid residues, lead, arsenic, nickel, cadmium, trichloroethylene, and dichlorometane. According to one lawsuit, chemicals have contaminated ground-water in the area and threatened a groundwater basin that provides drinking water for nearby communities.[85]

In the spring of 1982, the EPA negotiated to pay $6.1 million from Superfund to help clean up the dump. But in late July, the Stringfellow cleanup was put on hold. Some agency officials had charged that Burford did not want to do anything that might have helped then Governor Edmund G. (Jerry) Brown, a Democrat, win election to the US Senate. One former aide to Brown said that a distraught EPA aide telephoned, saying that orders had been given to delay funding for a cleanup of Stringfellow and other dumps in California until after the November congressional elections.[86]

On the other hand, congressional investigators acquired documents indicating that dumps in several Republican districts were approved in 1982 for pre-election cleanup announcements, despite warnings from EPA officials that the projects had not been adequately studied. The $7.7 million cleanup at Seymour, Indiana, for instance, was accelerated, according to Hugh Kaufman, to help re-elect GOP Senator Richard Lugar.[87]

The Seymour settlement has generated considerable controversy, because a company that had helped create the hazard in the first place was awarded the EPA cleanup contract. Chemical Waste Management, a subsidiary of Waste Management, Inc., ended up making money both ways: first by dumping industrial waste, and then by receiving the $7.7 million contract to clean it up. The firm already had four government cleanup contracts worth $1.1 million, despite the fact that it has violated federal and state laws at half a dozen waste sites around the country. Only a month before getting the Seymour contract, violations were found at another one of Chem Waste's sites, prompting the EPA to propose a $48,500 fine. The company is represented by Denver lawyer James Sanderson, who was Burford's first choice for the EPA's number-three post. He was harshly criticized by congressional investigators for working part time as an EPA consultant while continuing to represent the firm.[88]

The Seymour settlement also stipulates that some waste will be burned at sea, aboard *Vulcanus I*, Chem Waste's incinerator ship. The EPA and scientists know very little about the environmental effects of burning wastes at sea, and *Vulcanus I* is the first ship built for what is expected to be a very lucrative market. The EPA went out of its way to help Chem Waste get a head start on ocean incineration and initially granted *Vulcanus I* a research permit, allowing millions of gallons of PCB and other toxins to be burned in the Gulf of Mexico, with little public notice and no requirement for research, evaluation, or monitoring of the pyre.[89]

Less than six months after Burford's resignation, the EPA announced that it was expanding its list of the nation's most hazardous abandoned chemical dumping sites. The agency has proposed to add 133 sites to the current list of 413 that are eligible for top-priority cleanup. At the same time, agency officials estimate that without increased resources, permanent cleanup work would start at only half a dozen more sites during the next year, bringing the total number of sites undergoing cleanup to 26.[90]

Lee Thomas, the EPA's assistant administrator for Hazardous Waste Cleanup, told a press conference in September 1983, that adding additional sites to the priority list "doesn't mean that bulldozers will be pulling up at the new sites tomorrow." There is no "quick fix to the problems of this magnitude and complexity," Mr. Thomas said, noting that there may be more than twenty thousand abandoned chemical dump sites around the country that pose a threat to the public's health and to the environment. The EPA estimates that the Superfund list will grow to 2,200 sites, at a cost of $16 billion for cleanup.[91]

Under Ruckelshaus, the EPA had sought to develop a comprehensive strategy to diminish the threat to public health posed by dioxin. The agency originally proposed cleaning up hundreds of dioxin-contaminated sites by establishing an assessment and cleanup program separate from Superfund, with separate financing as well. Alarmed by the "budgetary implications" of the EPA's draft proposal, the OMB opposed the agency's initial dioxin strategy. A revised strategy was subsequently announced to the public. In January 1984, the EPA stated that it would systematically investigate potential sites for cleanup and assess the extent of dioxin contamination and the risk to public health. Designated sites would then be placed within the Superfund's cleanup schedule but would not be given priority status. The Superfund would receive no additional funds to compensate for the new sites added to its schedule.[92]

CLEAN AIR

First enacted in 1967 and substantially amended in 1970 and 1977, the Clean Air Act is one of the most successful pieces of environmental legislation ever enacted. Under the act, the EPA must set health standards for six conventional pollutants—carbon monoxide, sulfur dioxide, hydrocarbons, nitrogen dioxide, lead, and ozone (smog)—that emanate from both mobile sources (cars, trucks, and buses) and stationary sources (industrial plants and factories). The act is a classic example of federal-state partnership: the federal government does the research, writes the National Ambient Air Quality Standards, and provides grants to the states. The states monitor and inspect for compliance, but this local enforcement activity is backed by a strong federal enforcement presence at the regional level. The EPA has concurrent authority to enforce the law to protect against nonenforcement.

The National Ambient Air Quality Standards ensure the

right of Americans to breathe clean, healthier air. The standards are set at levels needed to protect the health of the public generally, as well as such sensitive groups as asthmatics, children, and senior citizens, with an adequate margin of safety.

The Clean Air Act is unusual in its specificity and its inclusion of deadlines for the reduction and control of dirty air. Because the act tightly controls administrative discretion, the Reagan administration sought to convince Congress to amend the law and remove many of its particular requirements. In May 1981, conservative members of the House Energy and Commerce Committee, with the support of the administration, unveiled a bill proposing more than seventy changes that would, as the members of the National Clean Air Coalition so aptly put it, "maul the Clean Air Act." Introduced by Congressman James T. Broyhill (Republican-North Carolina), the bill would have crippled existing air quality standards, extended cleanup deadlines by five to eight years, and repealed conservation programs for clean air regions. The auto-industry lobbyists teamed up with House Energy and Commerce Committee chairman John Dingell, from Dearborn, Michigan, to lead the battle for the bill. After eighteen months of intensive lobbying and bitter wrangling in the committee, it was stopped by one vote, primarily because of the determination and persistence of Health subcommittee chairman Henry Waxman, of Los Angeles, a prime area in need of clean air controls.

New Source Performance Standards (NSPS)

In addition to establishing air quality regulations, the 1970 Clean Air Act requires the EPA to set technology guidelines, called New Source Performance Standards (NSPS), to ensure that new industrial plants use the best pollution control technologies available. The EPA analyzes the pollutants that a particular industrial process generates, and examines the technology designed to reduce such emissions. Performance standards require the best pollution controls that are available and practical, taking costs and possible side effects into account.

In FY 1982, the EPA promised to issue sixteen proposals and fourteen final rules for New Source Performance Standards. In fact it issued only one of each,[93] and they are extremely weak. One regulation, for example, was proposed for industrial boilers, a growing source of sulfur dioxide, which is a major component in the formation of acid rain. The EPA guideline would permit more pollution than most current boilers now emit.[94] At the existing pollution rate, given our growing dependence on coal, sulfur dioxide emissions will triple in the next twenty-five years. This rule would permit even more emissions under the guise of controlling such pollution.

Prevention of Significant Deterioration (PSD)

The 1977 amendments to the Clean Air Act wrote into law a crucial air pollution control program, to assure that air quality in clean air regions around the country does not deteriorate rapidly because of industrial expansion. The program, known as Prevention of Significant Deterioration (PSD), establishes limits on the total amount of pollution increase that may be permitted in clean air regions. It prevents states from competing to degrade their air quality standards to lure businesses, and it establishes the priority that clean air is something more than a reservoir for industrial pollution. Industries constructing facilities in those areas must obtain a permit that ensures that they are using the Best Available Control Technology (BACT) and not exceeding the pollution budget for that region.

The Reagan administration sought to abolish clean air budgets in these areas, and to legalize pollution in national parks and wildernesses at the same levels that are permitted in major cities.[95]

Polluted Areas

States in which pollution levels exceed federal health standards (called nonattainment areas) must undertake a program to clean up existing pollution sources. They must also regulate the construction of new facilities to ensure that the air quality improves.

In the past, the building of a new blast furnace, an organic-chemical-producing facility, or other major new sources of pollution in such an area has been seen as an opportunity to make progress toward a healthier future for the area's residents. The Clean Air Act requires that the builder of any new facility that might be a source of pollution install the best available pollution controls, in order to minimize emissions. The law also requires the builder to obtain pollution reductions in existing sources at sufficient levels to offset the pollution added to the area by the new sources.[96] If this assurance were not required, the quality of air might never improve in cities experiencing industrial expansion or modernization.

But the Reagan administration sought to change this progressive strategy, without even consulting Congress, by a seemingly minor revision in the federal regulations. By changing the definition of a new "source" of pollution, the EPA exempted 90 percent of new, heavy-industrial facilities from the Clean Air Act's requirements. A "source" was exempt unless it caused a *net increase* of more than a hundred tons per year in pollution. A new blast furnace replacing an old outdated one, in other words, could be built with pollution controls even less effective than those of the old one. Instead of upgrading the quality of the nation's healthful air, Mrs. Burford offered industrial interests perpetual easements from upholding clean air standards.[97]

Responding to a lawsuit against this new interpretation filed by the NRDC, a federal Court of Appeals called the redefinition of "source" impermissible. The government has appealed the case to the Supreme Court.

Hazardous Air Pollutants

The Clean Air Act instructs the EPA to regulate air pollutants that "may reasonably be anticipated" to cause death or disease. There are dozens of such pollutants, but in ten years the EPA brought only four under control—asbestos, mercury, beryllium, and vinyl chloride. The Reagan administration has ignored an inventory of thirty-seven toxic pollutants, listed by the Carter administration, which had not taken action on them. Reagan has also cut the budget for their regulation so sharply that action may be delayed until the end of the decade.[98]

Auto Emissions

Under Reagan, the EPA has also pushed for a relaxation of carbon monoxide auto standards, from 3.4 grams to 7 grams per mile. The EPA maintains that stricter pollution control devices on cars create higher levels of pollution, because they are likely to malfunction. General Motors agrees with that point. According to a GM spokesman, the company hopes to save between $50 and $300 a car by eliminating certain pollution control devices.[99]

The National Clean Air Coalition, however, says it has not seen sufficient evidence to show that the present technology is not working, or that air quality will not be affected by relaxing carbon monoxide emission standards. Currently 161 counties exceed the health standard for carbon monoxide, which at low levels slows reflexes, causes brain dysfunction, and creates stress for individuals suffering from coronary disease.

Diesel Emissions

In November 1982, the EPA proposed a two-year delay for the 1985 standards requiring a reduction of diesel emissions in automobiles, from 0.6 to 0.2 grams per mile. This action disregards serious questions about the long-term health hazard posed by the increased presence of diesel emissions. A fine particulate is emitted when diesel fuel is combusted, which contains up to ten thousand chemicals, dozens of which are known or suspected to cause cancer. The health impact of such a complex particle has worried EPA scientists. In a December 1981 memo to Mrs. Burford, they cautioned, "If diesel emissions are not prudently controlled," the ensuing health effects "may well be significant."[100]

The proposed delay is now considered a *fait accompli*, since the EPA has not taken any subsequent action. The Reagan administration may also try to weaken the standards by allowing the 1987 emissions to be increased from 0.2 to 0.3 grams per mile.

The proposed delay also stalls any action on setting tougher emission standards for trucks and buses, which constitute a large share of diesel-powered vehicles. David Doniger, an attorney for the Natural Resources Defense Council, compares the administration's response to the reaction against the struggle to get catalytic converters in gasoline-powered cars ten years ago. "What EPA has done is to reward the auto companies for stonewalling."[101] Meanwhile, the cost of these delays will be borne by the public, who will continue to breathe increasing quantities of the unhealthy emissions.

Acid Rain

Acid rain is the name given to man-made pollution, largely composed of sulfur and nitrogen oxides, that is transformed chemically in the atmosphere and falls back to earth as acidic rain, snow, or dry particles. Its impact may be felt thousands of miles from its original polluting source. Acid rain destroys life in freshwater lakes and streams, especially in the northeast. There is evidence that it damages forests. But the worst long-range effect may be its impact on microorganisms that fix carbon and nitrogen in the soil.

Acid rain damage is both an environmental and a financial issue. In Maine, for example, acid rain damage threatens the $32 million sport fishing industry. Twenty-one percent of Maine's streams and 29 percent of its lakes have been acidified. Many can no longer sustain a trout fishery. At least five of the state's salmon rivers are so acidic that they endanger young fish, disturbing the food chain upon which plant, animals, and humans depend.[102]

Five billion dollars' worth of damage annually is sustained in the eastern United States alone from acid rain. Thousands of lakes are threatened with extinction by rain and snow routinely falling with acidity levels closer to vinegar than to water. The congressional Office of Technology Assessment reported that in northern and central Wisconsin and the neighboring Michigan highlands, close to half of the twenty-two hundred lakes are already becoming acidified, jeopardizing the state's $6 billion annual tourist industry.[103]

Acid rain has become a major irritant in US relations with Canada. About 50 percent of the acid rain affecting Canadian lakes originates in the United States. Only 10 percent of the acid rain falling in the northeastern United States is of Canadian origin. In Canada's most frequented tourist and recreation areas, as much as 75 percent of the acid rain originates in the United States. Compared with the United States, Canada has made major progress in reducing sulfur emissions. Between 1970 and 1980, Canada reduced sulfur dioxide emissions by 27 percent. As a result of the Canadian program, there are no regions in Canada that do not meet the US Clean Air Act standards for either sulfur dioxide or nitrous oxide. In the United States, as of December 31, 1982, twenty-four regions failed to attain these standards.[104]

Harrison Wellford, a former Carter administration official and now a Washington attorney representing the Canadian government on acid rain, points out that further Canadian reductions may be contingent upon reciprocal action in the United States. "In 1982, Canada embarked on a mandatory program to reduce sulfur emissions an additional 25 percent by 1990. Canada has offered to reduce emissions an additional 25 percent (for a total reduction of 50 percent from 1980 levels), if the United States were to adopt a parallel program. Up to now, the Canadians have made all the sacrifices; the US has only talked."[105]

The Reagan administration has taken no action on acid rain. Instead it promised to do more research and analysis, while simultaneously easing restrictions on the industrial boilers that emit sulfur dioxide. Until recently the EPA refused even to call acid rain by that name. It preferred "nonbuffered precipitation." The administration, however, was finally forced to acknowledge what everyone else knew: acid rain exists, it is caused by sulfur dioxide emissions, and it wreaks severe economic and environmental damage. This belated acknowledgment "is a step in the right direction, but it's like the Neanderthal finally coming out of the cave," comments NRDC's Elizabeth Barratt-Brown. The Reagan administration had acknowledged only what "has been the scientific consensus for years."[106]

In July 1983, after William D. Ruckelshaus had succeeded Anne Burford as administrator, the National Academy of Sciences issued a report concluding that a reduction in pollution from industrial sources would reduce acid rain. The report recommended a cut of 50 percent in sulfur dioxide emissions from coal-burning power plants and other industrial sources in the eastern part of the country. David Schindler, a biologist at the Freshwater Institute in Winnipeg, whose research supported the report's findings, stated that a reduction of sulfur emissions by half would shrink the area currently affected by acid rain by three-quarters.[107] While Ruckelshaus promised to have a recommendation on acid rain for the president by September 1983, he stated in October that no such recommendation would be forthcoming, and that no time-table had been set for one. The delay is believed to be the result of strong opposition from high-level members of the White House staff, including OMB director Stockman.[108]

CLEAN WATER

"If the fish are dying, the people are not far behind," commented the head of the American Public Health Association in the early 1970s, reflecting the alarm over the condition of our nation's waters. In the 1960s, Lake Erie degenerated into a dead and stagnant body of water, unable to sustain fish and plant life. The spectacle of flames playing on the surface of Ohio's Cuyahoga River dramatized the need to control pollution that is being discharged into lakes and rivers from industry disposal systems, sewers, and other sources. With the resources and controls guaranteed by the 1972 Clean Water Act, the Cuyahoga has since been revived, and Lake Erie is once again usable by sport fishermen.

The objective of the Clean Water Act is to restore and maintain the chemical, physical, and biological integrity of the nation's water. A key interim goal is to achieve fishable-swimmable waters by 1983. Today a majority of the nation's waters meet this goal for nontoxic pollutants. And many industrial and municipal facilities, including organic chemical plants, soap and detergent manufacturers, pulp mills, and food processing plants, already meet the 1985 goal of zero discharge of pollutants. The accelerated degradation of our nation's waters has been solved, despite a rising population and industrial expansion.

Water degradation did not begin to subside until after 1972, when Congress ordered a shift to uniform technology-based controls. "The right to pollute was repealed," says Thomas Jorling, a Senate aide who helped write the act and later served as an EPA official.[109] The act ordered the EPA to set minimum, uniform technology standards for municipal sewage facilities, to provide federal funds to localities for new sewage treatment plants (Publicly Owned Treatment Works, or POTW), and to establish discharge limits for each of the major polluting industries. The act was amended in 1977, to order industries discharging pollutants directly into rivers to install the Best Conventional Technology (BCT) for conventional pollutants and the Best Available Technology (BAT) for toxic pollutants by 1984. The move to uniform technology-based controls symbolized both the commitment to cleanup and the recognition that scientists cannot yet determine what constitutes safe levels of exposure to toxic water pollution for human, animal, or aquatic life.

Reviving the "Right to Pollute"

The Reagan administration has proposed changing the law so that industries can escape their obligation to install the Best Available Technology to control toxic pollutants if they can demonstrate that water quality standards can be met without BAT. Congress previously rejected this approach to pollution control as unworkable. Standards based on water quality alone are inadequate for controlling toxic pollutants, because no one knows how much exposure to toxins is allowable before it is considered dangerous. The administration has also tried to delay compliance with BAT until 1988.[110]

Industry groups argue that BAT requirements are far too expensive for them to implement, but the Clean Water Act requires only the "Best Available Technology [that is] *economically achievable*" (emphasis added). Moreover, BAT is not hypothetical; it is based on what some firms within an industry are currently using. Still, industry groups, reluctant to make new investments in pollution-control technology, have protested, and the Reagan EPA has tried to accommodate them.

The Reagan administration had advocated moving from uniform technology-based controls to site-specific, water-quality-based controls. Pressured by the OMB, the EPA under Anne Burford proposed reversing the cleanup momentum by allowing states greater freedom to downgrade rivers currently designated as fishable or swimmable to navigable, industrial, or other statuses that would make a river less protected against pollution. A utility or chemical company would have been able to pressure state authorities into downgrading a river by arguing that the costs to industry outweigh the benefits of a fishable-swimmable river. Additionally, high-quality waters, like those in national parks, would have been downgraded as well under the Reagan proposal.[111]

Robert Flacke, New York's commissioner of environmental conservation, worries that his state's stringent water pollution controls could be an economic liability if the federal government shifts cleanup responsibility to the states. "The temptation to lure industry by reducing environmental requirements is obvious," said Flacke. "This is the real problem with the 'New Federalism' as it applies to the environment: it forces states to choose between short-term economic gain and protection of irreplaceable resources."[112] Financially strapped states are certainly not capable of developing the technical resources and personnel that are needed to help local officials prepare both guidelines and an acceptable schedule to follow to preserve the quality of their water. The two-year, 70-percent cut in water-quality research and development sought by Reagan indicates that the EPA would not provide any assistance. In addition, the president sought to shrink general support for state water-pollution-control programs by 56 percent in 1983.[113]

"It's unconscionable from our perspective," says Dan Barolo, a state water pollution official. "Unfortunately, the partnership seems to be a one-way street at this point. We welcome the opportunity to share resources and knowledge. What we don't welcome is the continuing transfer of responsibilities without the resources to carry them out."[114]

Congress, however, is unlikely to accept the Reagan proposals. Under pressure for more than two years from environmental organizations and the public, who value the benefits of the nation's progress toward cleaning up its polluted waters, members of Congress pushed Ruckelshaus to withdraw the proposal and replace it with sound regulations supported by environmental groups. In November 1983, Ruckelshaus introduced new water-quality rules that require states to provide a more comprehensive and formal analysis explaining why, in specific instances, the goals of the Clean Water Act cannot be met. At the same time, the EPA renewed its support for the agency's "non-degradation" policy, which protects pristine waters, such as lakes and streams in national parks.[115]

Pretreatment

Although the majority of polluting firms use municipal sewage treatment facilities, which effectively remove common or degradable organic wastes, toxic pollutants frequently pass through these plants and are discharged into the public water supply. In other instances, toxic pollutants corrode pipes and filters or upset the delicate bacterial processes at work, undermining the federal investment in a treatment plant, and diminishing the facility's capacity to treat conventional waste. Moreover, toxins contaminate the sludge wastes from the plant, creating new waste disposal problems and severely restricting the sludge recycling capacity. To prevent these problems, the Clean Water Act requires industrial firms to remove toxins from their waste water by "pretreatment," before discharging them into a municipal sewage treatment plant.[116]

Upon taking office, the Reagan administration suspended implementation of these critical pretreatment regulations indefinitely by placing a moratorium on such requirements. The Natural Resources Defense Council sued. A federal court held that the EPA's action was illegal and ordered the agency to reinstate the regulations. "President Reagan's record on cleaning up toxic water pollution is a disgrace," claims Fran Dubrowski, senior attorney and a director of NRDC's Clean Water project. "His administration has repeatedly tried to stall or gut the pretreatment program, one of the nation's most important activities for controlling toxic industrial wastes. Were it not for vigorous citizen oversight, litigation, and strong congressional support for this program, it would not be on track today."[117]

Nonpoint Source Pollution

Nonpoint source pollution consists of contaminants in water that cannot be traced to a single, discrete source. It includes fertilizers and pesticides used for agricultural purposes; acid residues from mines; and soil erosion from construction sites, logging areas, and farms. Rainfall washes these pollutants into lakes, rivers, and streams, and the resulting chemical brew deteriorates water quality. Nonpoint source pollution is estimated to account for nearly half of all conventional water pollution in the country.[118] The present Clean Water Act does not require controls on nonpoint source pollution, and environmental organizations have been working to amend the law to require Best Management Practices (BMP). These include soil conservation efforts, controlled application of agrichemicals, buffer strips, catchment basins, and other such common-sense, readily available measures. The Reagan administration, however, has shown little interest in assuming federal leadership to control such pollution.

Safe Drinking Water

According to figures assembled by state agencies in 1980, more than 2,894 wells in eighteen states had been discovered to be contaminated by volatile organic compounds.[119] The Michigan Department of Natural Resources, which conducted one of the most comprehensive state-wide studies, identified 268 sites where groundwater contamination was known, 381 sites where contamination was suspected, and more than 50,000 sites where the potential for contamination was high. For the 268 known cases of contamination, the cost of determining the extent of contamination was estimated at $12.9 to 46.1 million.[120]

After a scandal-ridden period at the EPA, the entry of Ruckelshaus has brought some hope. Agency officials have said that there is no longer discussion of legislative amendments to ease the standards that are imposed under the Safe Drinking Water Act, or to weaken the protection provided by the Resource, Conservation and Recovery Act, the Clean Water Act of 1972, or other statutes. But Ruckelshaus has stated that he does not believe that the severity of the issue demands a concerted federal groundwater policy.[121] Others, however, disagree and argue that the contamination of the nation's drinking water is a growing problem whose impact needs to be better understood.

Dr. Irving Selikoff, director of the Environmental Sciences Laboratory at the Mount Sinai School of Medicine in New York, is one who is alarmed over the growing presence of chemical contaminants in the environment and their impact on public health. Testifying before a House subcommittee investigating dioxin, Dr. Selikoff warned that physicians "have literally no idea of what to look for" in establishing a correlation between exposure to certain types of chemicals and specific diseases. As an example, Dr. Selikoff referred to a *New York Times* article which stated that one-third of the American public is drinking contaminated water, and pointed out that physicians "have very little or no knowledge of what to expect as a result of the contamination of public water supplies. . . ."[122]

Environmental groups and concerned citizens are hoping that Ruckelshaus' decision not to weaken current water-quality standards is an indication that the EPA will give its groundwater policy more serious consideration. The agency is presently reviewing a groundwater policy and is expected to present its decision later in 1984.

PESTICIDES

The 1972 Federal Insecticide, Fungicide, and Rodenticide Act requires the EPA to regulate pesticides used for controlling insects, rodents, weeds, and various diseases. A pesticide can be marketed only after it has been registered with the EPA, and after that agency has undertaken a scientific review of its potential hazards, set residue tolerances for human food or animal feeds, and determined that it has no "unreasonable adverse effects."

Closing the Doors to the Public

We might expect "safety first" to be the guiding principle of the EPA's Office of Pesticide Programs (OPP), but the Reagan pesticide policy outlined in an agency memo issued in June 1981 reflects a different approach: "We intend to assure that the introduction of new pesticides into commerce is not impeded by delays in processing. Regulations will be reviewed and revised to facilitate registration and reduce the time required."[123]

The remarkable speed with which the EPA has processed registration applications for the use of pesticides contrasts sharply with its foot-dragging on the Superfund, clean air, and clean water regulations. Negotiating directly with pesticide manufacturers while bypassing public discussion was one of the "streamlining" procedures intended to shrink the "resource burden" on the EPA and provide "regulatory relief" to industry.

By mid-1981, pesticide manufacturers were involved "early and throughout the [registration standards] process," according to an internal memo.[124] While the EPA viewed the comments of pesticide producers and users as essential, public participation in the development of the standards themselves was thought to "only add delays to the system."[125] Accordingly, efforts were undertaken to exclude the public from pesticide regulation. Throughout 1981, the EPA ignored a law, passed in 1978, that requires the agency to make public the health and safety information pertaining to registered pesticides.

A Texas lawyer discovered the EPA's new policy when he requested information on the pesticide Carbofuran in July 1981. He needed the information because he was suing the pesticide's manufacturer, the FMC Corporation, on behalf of three farmworkers who had become ill after working in a field sprayed with the pesticide. The law gives the manufacturer thirty days to prove that revealing information about the product would involve disclosure of a trade secret, and if there is no response, the EPA is required to release the data. FMC asserted no claim of confidentiality, but the EPA withheld the data. When the lawyer sued the EPA for release of the information, the agency contacted FMC and gave the company a second chance to assert a confidentiality claim. The company finally replied, long after its right to do so had expired. When the EPA then asked for further delay, a southern Texas court ordered a halt to the stalling. FMC settled the lawsuit out of court immediately after the data were ordered released.[126]

While the Reagan administration withheld health and safety data past the legal time limit, pesticide manufacturers went to Congress to try to get the disclosure requirements changed. Unsuccessful, they returned to the EPA and persuaded the agency to issue regulations adopting the legislative changes that they had been seeking. Today scientists at the EPA cannot publish pesticide information except in brief excerpts or summaries. But because scientists must analyze data in detail in order to prove or disprove it, the restrictions have a "chilling effect" on criticism by independent scientists, according to Jay Feldman, of the National Coalition Against the Misuse of Pesticides.[127]

In May 1983, a coalition of environmental and labor groups sued in the federal Court of Appeals to rescind virtually every pesticide regulation issued by the EPA between March 1982 and May 1983, on the grounds that they were reached in closed-door negotiations with industry. The suit alleges that 60 percent or more of all pesticides in use have not been tested for carcinogenicity, that 90 percent have not been evaluated for mutagenicity, and that 60 percent have not been tested for their capacity to cause birth defects.[128] The suit is still pending.

Shortcuts on Safety

The lawsuit reflects a concern that the close relationship between the agency and industry was compromising standards for pesticide registration. Pesticide manufacturers, of course, were quite happy with the EPA's actions. "There's a much more positive atmosphere at EPA," remarked the the National Agriculture Chemicals Association's Luther Shaw in 1983. "They are very cooperative, willing to work out problems. . . . There don't seem to be many complaints from our members now."[129]

Environmentalists have a different view. "We have gone from a rather neutral Carter administration, which did no affirmative harm, to a period of gross malfeasance at EPA," said Al Meyerhoff, of NRDC. "EPA is simply looking at the needs of industry and getting as many new products on the market as quickly as it can."[130]

The EPA's policy of reducing its backlog severely affects its scientists who review pesticide registration applications. They are pressured to permit the marketing of the pesticide without necessary independent research. With such a decline in professional standards and ethics there is a lowering of staff morale and commitment. The scientists at the EPA complain that their colleagues in industry frequently ignore or dismiss potential toxic effects that are evident in the experimental data, questions that independent scientists are more likely to probe. They also complain that industry has begun to employ new levels of "ingenuity and cleverness" in their submissions to the agency, forcing EPA scientists to respond to specious analyses and to identical arguments presented in dozens of different cases. This volume of diversionary material also prevents the EPA from exploring all but a handful of the incomplete analyses submitted by pesticide manufacturers.[131]

"Strong pressures are being placed on agency scientists," according to a congressional staff report, "reinforced by explicit ties to performance ratings and salary adjustment, to reduce the backlog of reviews, to shorten turnaround times, and to be more responsive to the concerns and scientific arguments expressed by the pesticide industry and users."[132] An EPA scientist concurs:

"There is an emphasis on numbers. Science is becoming an assembly line. It is only a matter of time before errors start showing up in the reviews and on the registrations."[133]

What now shows up on EPA reviews, in several dozen instances, according to congressional investigators, are verbatim copies of summary statements submitted by industry. In at least one instance, both the manufacturer and the EPA reviewer overlooked strong evidence of the pesticide's toxicity.[134] In another case, the Uniroyal Chemical Company submitted a lab report on its pesticide Harvade, which the EPA reviewer then used as his own. The Harvade incident was uncovered by Dr. Adrian Gross, a scientist who had been demoted in May 1982, after writing a forty-eight-page memo to his superiors, charging them with illegally aiding two large chemical companies in registering another dangerous insecticide. Gross' audit of the Uniroyal data suggests that Harvade could be a serious health threat. As of August 1983, it was still on the market.[135]

EPA's attitude toward its pesticide regulatory duties is revealed in its response to the recent discovery that there are one hundred forty pesticides currently on the market whose registration hinges totally or partially on fraudulent tests conducted in 1976 by Industrial Bio-Test Laboratories, who were held criminally liable in federal court on several counts. The case is now on appeal. Yet instead of removing these pesticides until new testing is complete, the EPA is simply requiring manufacturers of thirty-five of these pesticides to agree to new tests. According to OPP Chief Edwin Johnson, few, if any, of those thirty-five pesticides would qualify for registration with the present data, and retesting will probably show additional "health effects we didn't know about."[136] In addition, some new tests may take up to four years to complete. Despite all this, the manufacturers are being allowed to keep these questionable pesticides on the market as long as they agree to retest. "If the EPA is registering a product, the public assumes that that product is safe," says Jay Feldman, of the National Coalition Against Misuse of Pesticides. "At the least, the EPA has to go on an aggressive . . . program of informing the public whether the particular product has been registered with faulty data."[137]

Emergency Exemptions

Section 18 of the present pesticide law permits only "emergency" use of banned or unregistered pesticides. In the last three years, the number of Section 18 exemptions granted has skyrocketed. An observer might conclude that the election of Ronald Reagan had sparked a nationwide insect outbreak. In its first full year, the Reagan EPA approved 505 emergency exemptions, compared to 198 in the last full year of the Carter administration.[138] The ratio of emergency exemptions granted to those denied was 10 to 1, compared with Carter's final-year ratio of 6 granted, 5 denied.

Pesticide manufacturers use Section 18 to skirt the normal registration process or to dump backlogs of banned pesticides on the market. "Section Eighteens are quick," says Maureen Hinkle, a pesticide expert for the National Audubon Society. "You say 'Here's an emergency,' and EPA gives you an exemption. . . ."[139]

EPA officials defend Section 18 exemptions with the lame excuse that consumer and environmental groups have not tried to stop them. Yet these very officials neglect to notify the public either when an emergency exemption is being sought, or when one is granted. Take, for example, the ban on the pesticide dibromochloropropane (DBCP). When the EPA approved the emergency use of the banned pesticide on twenty thousand acres of South Carolina peach orchards, it was news to Brett Bursey, head of one state environmental group. "We learned about this after the public comment period had expired," he said. "Nobody knew about it."[140]

DBCP was banned in the United States in 1979, because alarming numbers of workers manufacturing the pesticide had become sterile. The public became aware of new evidence linking the pesticide with cancer when the California Department of Health released a study showing high rates of leukemia and stomach cancer in areas where DBCP was found in the drinking water. DBCP, one of a handful of chemicals removed from general use by the EPA, was banned after two years of hearings and nine thousand pages of testimony.

Dr. John Todhunter, the Reagan EPA's former chief of toxic substances and pesticides, was apparently more impressed with a study by Clemson University scientist Dr. George Carter, which concluded that DBCP could be used safely if it was sprayed in the fall, before the peach trees bloomed. It turned out that research on DBCP given by Dr. Carter to the EPA in 1982 was funded by the pesticide's sole remaining manufacturer, the Amvac Chemical Company. Under the EPA exemption Amvac would have supplied more than nine hundred thousand pounds of DBCP to South Carolina growers at a price of $1.8 million. Amvac will not release the study to the public.[141] While basing its decision, at least in part, on this study, EPA granted an exemption for DBCP.

"There is no way on earth I know of that you can assure the objectivity and integrity of a study when it is paid for by a company," said Dr. Robert Jackson, the North Carolina health commissioner. "Companies hire the institutions and, as soon as the money goes there, it becomes to the researcher's advantage to tell them what they want to hear. EPA pulled a real fast one," he said. "They okay it and then make us enforce it. . . . Our data confirms the presence of DBCP in groundwater. It is heavy in some of our peach-growing areas." Only a court order prevented the use of the pesticide in South Carolina.[142]

Toxaphene and EDB

Just before the 1982 congressional elections, the EPA announced a ban on the pesticide toxaphene, a suspected carcinogen. The Reagan administration's environmental record had been attacked throughout the campaign. At the press conference announcing the ban, EPA's Dr. Todhunter could not resist a little pre-election crowing. "In contrast to our predecessors," said Todhunter, "we don't sit around and talk about our commitment to the health and welfare of the country. We're much too busy doing our job for the taxpayers of this country."[143] The EPA's job, in this instance, consisted of banning a pesticide that the chemical industry was no longer producing. Toxaphene's use hovered around 100 million pounds a year in the early seventies but had dropped to 16 million pounds by the time of the ban because the pests had developed an immunity.[144]

While the agency tried to score political points with the toxaphene ban, pesticides like ethylene dibromide (EDB) remained on the market. National Cancer Institute studies show EDB to be a potent carcinogen. Dr. Adrian Gross at the EPA concluded that the federal EDB exposure level of 20 ppm was unsafe. "I do not know of any registered chemical which has produced as many malignant tumors of a very unusual variety," said Gross.[145] But EPA's Todhunter claimed that the risk from a single exposure to EDB was less than the risk of smoking one cigarette in your life.[146] This view is questionable. It has been documented that two California workers were overcome in seconds and died within a few days after being exposed to what state health official Dr. Richard Wade called "a pretty weak solution of EDB" (200 ppm per million). "Every organ in their body decayed," said Dr. Wade. "They turned bright green. Their skin fell off. . . . They were rotting before they died."[147] After television exposés and highly publicized congressional hearings in September 1983, the EPA banned the use of EDB as a soil fumigant on September 30.[148] (For more on EDB, see pages 92–96.)

Since then, the EPA has felt increased pressure to set a safety standard for EDB. In December 1983, Florida state health officials halted the sale of national brand-name, grain-based products after they were found to contain traces of EDB. Other states, including California, were quick to follow suit and began testing products for contamination. Alarmed by such state initiatives, the EPA in February 1984 recommended safety levels to the states for raw grains and ready-to-eat foods already in supermarkets. The agency also announced an immediate ban on the use of EDB as a grain fumigant and is considering a ban on its use as a fumigant on citrus and other fruit.[149]

Courting Cancer

Todhunter's cavalier attitude toward safety reflects the Reagan administration's philosophy that pesticides and chemicals are presumed safe until proven dangerous. Years ago the Congress decided that conservatism is a virtue when evaluating the safety of pesticides and toxic chemicals. To justify their relaxed safety standards, the Reagan EPA is trying to make new distinctions between benign tumors (those that do not spread and invade other cells) and malignant tumors (those that do metastasize and spread to other parts of the body). Most important, Reagan's regulators are challenging the accepted scientific convention that substances that have carcinogenic effects on animals pose carcinogenic risks to humans.

The federal government's policy on cancer research has long accepted animal data as a necessary and valid basis for regulation. Appropriately, it does not rely on mortality statistics as the sole regulatory stimulus. The Reagan administration, however, has revised this scientific principle, and the OPP may now determine that humans may face no hazard even when a chemical causes cancer in laboratory animals. The predominant view of the scientific community is that such a judgment cannot be made. I. Bernard Weinstein, a respected scientist at Columbia University's Institute for Cancer Research, dubs the scientific foundation of the Reagan EPA's new approach to cancer "largely theoretical and [without] factual basis in terms of current knowledge."[150] Norton Nelson, the chairman of the board of National Counselors of the Toxicology Program, told a congressional panel in the spring of 1983 that the Reagan administration was "covertly" scuttling traditional scientific bases for cancer regulation.[151]

The future of the multimillion-dollar pesticides market depends to a great degree on the EPA's scientific assumption about carcinogenicity. The EPA's "chemical revolution" will bequeath an epidemic of cancer to the next generation if it continues to weaken the scientific basis of pesticide regulation. The Reagan administration has stretched the law to the limit in the management of pesticides—issuing exemptions, changing standards, and ignoring violations. To lock in these actions, the chemical manufacturers and the White House have lobbied Congress hard to change the law, but have failed. Congress is more inclined to listen to the scientific community, the environmental experts, and the voting public.

THE EPA UNDER WILLIAM D. RUCKELSHAUS

Two months into his tenure at the EPA, William D. Ruckelshaus told an interviewer that he had succeeded in getting the agency "out of the headlines."[152] The remark indicates the importance of one of his roles: to politically neutralize the environmental issue.

When Reagan was asked whether he would modify his environmental policies in light of the mismanagement, conflicts of interest, political manipulation, and industry-agency collusion that was revealed, his response was simply, "I'm too old to change."[153]

Why did the president choose Ruckelshaus? he was asked. Ruckelshaus was "the right man for the right job at the right time," said the president.[154] As so often happens, a seemingly harmless and shallow platitude uttered by Reagan reveals the substance of his policy. Ruckelshaus was the first director of the EPA, from 1970 to 1973, and thus could project an image of incorruptibility and commitment to environmental protection. He was the deputy attorney general who refused, during Watergate, to fire Archibald Cox at President Nixon's request. He was also the man who, after leaving the government, became a consultant to the vinyl chloride industry, trying to push a weaker regulation of that highly toxic plastic through the EPA. He then became a top executive at Weyerhaeuser Corporation, a huge timber company, which has been ranked by the Environmental Action Foundation as one of the five worst polluters of 1981. This "right man" may not, therefore, be out of step with this administration. "They had to go with pragmatism. They did not have the luxury of going with ideology anymore" a conservative House Republican leader commented.[155] The "right job" for such a man would be to confer respectability and credibility on an agency torn by several years of public scandal. Whether the job is to be more than that and whether Ruckelshaus will repair the damage from the early Reagan years remains to be seen.

It took President Reagan two years to realize that public support for environmental laws is so strong that it is politically necessary to at least *appear* to be protecting the environment. The administration was "confused," says Ruckelshaus, about public support for environmental laws.[156]

Ruckelshaus has said that he will enforce the law; he encourages public participation; he decries political "hit" lists and "sweetheart deals"; he praises his agency's staff and tries to bolster their morale; he meets with environmentalists and consults with Congress. Certainly these changes represent a major shift in style from that practiced by Burford. But the fact that Ruckelshaus is lauded for his actions tells us more about how little we expect from Reagan regulators than it does about the rigor of Ruckelshaus' environmental protection.

Ruckelshaus' stylistic changes may actually prove most useful in obtaining the "regulatory reforms" desired by Reagan. Ruckelshaus admits that he has changed since his first devoted tenure as administrator of the EPA in the early 1970s. Now he believes that the "EPA must abandon or at least modify its traditional role as an advocate for a cleaner environment and instead adopt the role of educator."[157] One of Ruckelshaus' messages is that "there must be a clear up-front recognition that attempting to cope with air pollution by measuring health or environmental effects is inherently impossible."[158] Yet this is exactly what the Clean Air Act mandated—and has accomplished—since 1970.

Ruckelshaus' belief in the inherent impossibility of meeting clean air health standards suggests a reluctance to get tougher in fighting hazardous air pollutants. Standards for toxic air pollutants require an "ample margin of safety to protect public health," but most scientists believe that no safe level of exposure to carcinogens can be determined. Ruckelshaus favors a regulatory approach that would make such a judgmental determination the cornerstone of toxic pollutant control, rather than requiring installation of the best available technology (BAT) and then determining whether any residual health risk requires further controls. In a major address to the National Academy of Sciences, Ruckelshaus decried the country's "emotionalism" about toxic substances and urged that environmental protection be founded on "risk assessment."[159] But without the "emotionalism" of victims and reformers, most of the laws that today protect the public's health and the environment would not be on the books. It is too easy for officials to find ways to manipulate results and minimize the plight of victims. During the summer of 1982 the EPA decided to change the phrase "potential lives saved" to "collective reduction in mortality risk to the population as embodied in the estimate of statistical lives saved" when measuring the benefits of regulation.[160] Who understands this?

Ruckelshaus disappointed many who thought that he might use the first few months of his tenure to regain some of the ground lost during Burford's reign. Consider a few of his early actions:

- Ruckelshaus initially supported the administration's three-year, 46-percent cut in the EPA's budget. When Congress took the initiative to restore the EPA's budget, Ruckelshaus was prompted to follow.[161]
- Ruckelshaus told a congressional panel that there was no need for a federal groundwater policy, even though the EPA estimates that 90 percent of the over eighty thousand hazardous-waste sites in the country threaten to contaminate groundwater.[162]
- Ruckelshaus, under pressure from the OMB, withheld endorsement of a $150 million federal matching grant program to control nonpoint source pollution.[163]
- Ruckelshaus indicated opposition to stricter controls on hazardous-waste disposal in landfills and small generators of toxic waste.[164]

Finally, Ruckelshaus will continue to face pressure not only from within the White House, but also from the OMB in its attempts to get the EPA to relax its guidelines in interpreting environmental regulations. In a November 7, 1983, letter to Ruckelshaus, OMB's Christopher DeMuth criticized EPA's policy of approving new chemicals for entry into the market, arguing that the agency should tolerate a greater margin of risk in assessing these chemicals. Such attempts by OMB to control agency policy confirm Reagan's determination to pursue his deregulation policies through exerting pressure on Ruckelshaus.[165]

OMB's stranglehold over the EPA is most apparent in its control over the agency's purse strings. Ruckelshaus has been persistent in trying to restore the EPA's budget to a level of $1.35 billion for FY 1985, but faces strong opposition from OMB's Stockman, who has approved a $1.21 billion EPA budget for that year. While Ruckelshaus could appeal directly to the president, he knows that his request greatly exceeds the president's 1985 limit and that the gap, as one budget official has stated, is unlikely to be closed.[166]

Much of the increase in funds requested by the EPA would go to programs dealing with hazardous waste and pesticides, two issues that Ruckelshaus considers priorities for FY 1985. Other EPA-requested increases are earmarked for programs that the

Reagan administration had cut heavily in previous years: state grants, enforcement, and health effects and environmental monitoring. These programs will most likely continue to receive minimum funding.[167]

William Drayton, former EPA assistant administrator for policy under the Carter administration, continues to be concerned about the Reagan administration's neglect of the agency's crucial health and safety programs. "The central point is no one is asking for the resources that are actually needed for the new programs, including the hazardous-waste program, the Superfund, and the toxic substances program. . . . The White House is still making it impossible for the agency to carry out its mandate."[168]

The unrestrained assault on environmental policy that occurred under Burford has stopped under Ruckelshaus. But the agency continues to defer to industry pressures and is failing to fully implement the newer environmental laws. The Reagan administration now knows that wholesale dismantling of environmental laws, which are supported by 80 to 90 percent of Americans, is not the way to get re-elected. But it is clear that the president sees Ruckelshaus' chief function as protecting the administration from political damage, rather than protecting the nation from environmental damage.

TRANSPORTATION SAFETY

NATIONAL TRAFFIC AND MOTOR VEHICLE SAFETY ACT OF 1966: ". . . To reduce traffic accidents and deaths and injuries . . . resulting from traffic accidents."

It was the morning of April 21, 1981. Mrs. Lawana Hansen was driving her eighty-one-year-old mother from her home in Sandy, Utah, to Twin Falls, Idaho. Heading north on I-15, in Salt Lake City, their 1975 Oldsmobile was suddenly sideswiped by another vehicle. Mrs. Hansen lost control as the car swerved violently across the median, striking a loaded gasoline tanker almost head on. It was all so sudden, so unexpected. Shattering glass and crushing metal, the car was totally demolished, the front end completely crushed.

Lawana Hansen and her mother were seriously injured— but not killed—in the accident. Mrs. Hansen suffered a ruptured spleen and a broken leg. Her mother broke a leg. But the accident was so severe that investigators were amazed both women lived. How did they survive?

Totally unknown to the two women at the time, their Olds was equipped with air bags. On impact, they filled up with air, cushioning the women from the full force of the crash. After seeing the mangled car, Mr. Hansen explained, "It's a miracle my wife and her mother lived. The steering wheel was pushed back to within inches of the seat back. The brake was pushed to within two inches of the seat. Neither woman had any cuts or marks above their knees—the bags protected them from broken glass."

The Hansens had purchased the Olds as a used car and were unaware that the vehicle was equipped with air bags hidden in the steering column and dashboard. The car was one of about ten thousand such vehicles built by General Motors during the 1970s.

"I've always been against air bags, because I thought they would ruin the looks of the car, but you really can't tell they're in there," explained Mr. Hansen. "What amazed me is that the thing was six years old and usually after six years you can't get the windshield wipers to work." The future is of particular concern to Mrs. Hansen. "Where will we find another car with air bags? We'll never be satisfied riding in a car without air bags."[1] But with the exception of the 1984 Mercedes, which can be bought with optional air bags on the driver's side in some models, new cars are not equipped with this feature. None have been available since 1976, when General Motors discontinued offering them as an option.

MAKING CARS SAFE:
THE STORY OF SAFETY-STANDARD 208

Although the first attempts to make automobiles safer to drive were somewhat crude, auto companies have understood for decades the need for built-in crash protection. An advertisement for a 1940 Dodge enticed buyers with its safety virtues: "Instrument panel is smooth and flush. Back of front seat is heavily tufted to protect rear-seat passengers in case of an emergency stop. Door handles are smooth, rounded, and curve inward for safety!"[2]

"Crashworthiness" design—the science of packaging people in automobiles—has progressed dramatically since then. "[I]n the fourteen years between 1942 and 1956, a new engineering field has been created, namely, that of crash-survival design engineering," explained Dr. William Haddon, in 1964.[3] Haddon helped sensitize the engineering and medical professions, and later, the US Congress, to the vehicle-design precautions that can minimize the damage to car occupants in crashes. The basic idea of crashworthy engineering resembles carefully wrapping fragile china plates in thick paper, and encasing them in a sturdy cardboard box. With breakage a strong likelihood, we design the packaging to lessen the risks.

In 1966, Ralph Nader's *Unsafe at Any Speed* exposed the design hazards of the General Motors Corvair and Detroit's indifference to safety. This work induced Congress to require that automobiles be designed to protect the occupants. Alarmed at the rising death toll on the highways, Congress passed a landmark auto safety law, creating the National Highway Traffic Safety Administration (NHTSA) and placing it in the new Department of Transportation (DOT), to find ways to counteract the epidemic of highway crashes. Haddon was appointed as the agency's first administrator. Within weeks he set about issuing rudimentary federal standards that have made cars safer ever since: laminated windshields, collapsible steering assemblies, dashboard padding, improved door locks, dual braking systems, and many other automatic safety features. According to DOT, cars are 25 percent safer today because of the required installation of these innovations, which have resulted in more than eighty thousand lives saved since 1968.[4] The price tag is negligible. Approximately twenty-seven fatalities are avoided for each $1.00 invested in new car purchases by consumers.[5]

The value of these standards was discovered in 1981 by a former critic of the government's auto-safety actions. Larry Givens, editor of *Automotive Engineering* magazine, changed his views after his own son was involved in, and survived, a severe three-car crash. Givens admitted, in the pages of his magazine, that "very probably, each of the three drivers would have been impaled on his steering column, the other occupants would have been mangled in various ways, and all seven could easily have perished in flames from ruptured fuel systems. Suddenly [the crash safety standards] became very real concepts to me, instead of just abstract rules on pieces of paper."[6]

No crashworthy engineering design, however, can begin to approach the lifesaving potential of "inflatable restraints," an aerospace-inspired safety technology perfected in the late 1960s. The device, which has come to be known as the air bag, has the remarkable ability to inflate from the dashboard and steering column, in 1/25 of a second, to cushion car occupants from the unforgiving, rigid interior surfaces of the vehicle. To absorb the energy of the crash and protect the fragile limbs and torsos of occupants in a soft pillow of air, the device immediately begins to inflate. It works automatically to protect occupants in frontal crashes, the type of crash in which 55 percent of highway deaths occur.

What is so amazing about this unique "technological vaccine" is not its superb and reliable performance, but the industry-generated political opposition that has withheld it from widespread use today. While people not as lucky as Mrs. Lawana Hansen are killed daily on the highways—one hundred twenty each day of the year, on the average—the auto industry continually resisted efforts by the NHTSA to require installation of air bags in cars. Just as the industry had nearly exhausted its interminable line of excuses, legal appeals, political subterfuges, and public relations ploys, the Reagan administration stepped in to relieve manufacturers of their obligation to implement standard 208, which requires the installation of air bags or automatic safety belts in all new cars.

Safety standard 208 was first proposed in 1969 and was formally issued in 1971 by Transportation Secretary John Volpe. At the request of Henry Ford II, the Nixon White House postponed the standard in 1972, and four years later Transportation Secretary William Coleman rescinded the standard outright. Coleman instead pushed several manufacturers to sign an unenforceable contract to supply at least forty thousand (and up to four hundred thousand) air bag–equipped cars in the early 1980s, but there was much skepticism that they would voluntarily do so.

It might have been the end of this impressive safety technology had not President Carter's transportation secretary, Brock Adams, issued a new, revised standard 208, in June 1977. Hoping to accommodate the industry's complaints about inadequate "lead" time once and for all, Secretary Adams gave auto manufacturers four to six years to meet the performance requirements for automatic occupant protection in 30 mph frontal crashes. The manufacturers were given the choice of supplying air bags or automatic seat belts. Larger-model vehicles had to comply by 1982, and all cars by 1984. After more than a decade of exhaustive testing and public debate, standard 208 was poised to go into effect. When fully implemented, the standard would prevent an estimated nine thousand deaths and sixty-five thousand injuries each year, making it one of the most important public health actions ever taken by the U.S. government.[7]

Mortgaged as it is to business interests, however, the Reagan administration lost no time in rescinding standard 208. Within three weeks of taking office on January 21, 1981, Reagan's new secretary of transportation, Drew Lewis, proposed delaying the standard. Eight months later, on October 23, 1981, he revoked the standard completely. Because previous administrations had rebutted the many diverse objections of industry to standard 208—its cost, its reliability, its effectiveness, its public acceptability—the incoming administration had to search hard for a rationale for the rescission. Lewis decided to claim that manufacturers would choose to install detachable automatic belts instead of air bags; car occupants would not use the belts but would detach them instead; and the standard, therefore, would cost money but save few, if any, lives.[8] This contorted reasoning, arrived at after overruling the recommendations of the agency's top scientific and engineering staff to retain the standard, was the triumph of the administration's deregulatory ideology over scientific facts. The proven effectiveness of air bags was skirted by theorizing, without evidence, that manufacturers would install the automatic belts—an alternative technological choice allowed by the standard to help automakers comply with, rather than evade, the requirements.

In announcing the revocation of the standard, NHTSA administrator Raymond Peck argued that "only by rescinding the standard" will car buyers be offered this advanced technology. With perplexing logic and characteristic doublespeak, Peck asserted:

> It is time to stop the uncertainty about this standard. It is only by rescinding the standard and proceeding with what I have called this morning . . . "a full court press" on technology, that we will be able to make material, substantial impact on reducing death on the highway."[9]

Revocation of the crash protection standard enraged members of Congress. Representative Timothy Wirth (Democrat-Colorado) whose subcommittee oversees the NHTSA, charged that Peck had "signed the death warrant for thousands of Americans, while sentencing millions more to a life of serious disability and injury." He noted that "the tragedy is that the technology exists to save these lives cheaply, but the auto industry refuses to use it."[10] Senator John Danforth (Republican-Missouri), chairman of the Senate transportation subcommittee, subsequently complained that the administration was stalling implementation of "a technology proven over and over again to save human lives—thousands of lives."[11]

More than two years after the 1981 revocation, General Motors still refused to offer air bags on a voluntary basis or even to supply air bag–equipped vehicles to the government for its fleet of cars. The Ford Motor Company offered to develop "a practical program" if ways were found "to simplify the effort"—code words for paring down specifications for air bag–equipped vehicles, so that the devices would be installed only on the driver's side of the car and would not be tested for compliance with the standard. Ford finally agreed in 1984 to equip five thousand, 1985-model Topaz cars, with driver-side air bags, for the General Services Administration (GSA), which manages the government's fleet of cars, for a demonstration program under NHTSA's auspices.[12] But the grand proclamation that NHTSA would pressure and negotiate with the auto industry to voluntarily "adopt the newest safety technology" for sale to the public was forgotten, an expedient political excuse at the time and a stale piece of last year's news.

Safety Standard 208 Goes to the Supreme Court

Despite angry public rumblings about the revocation, the Reagan administration had hoped that standard 208 had been disposed of once and for all. Unable to achieve its goals from the outside, through lobbying, bogus objections, and pleas for more time, the auto manufacturers calculated that with their clout inside the Reagan White House, they could banish forever the standard for automatic crash protection. A broad coalition of consumers, physicians, insurance companies, and victims' groups, however, rallied to fight the NHTSA's flimsy rationale for rescinding standard 208. Led by State Farm Insurance Company, a challenge was filed in the US Court of Appeals for the District of Columbia.

On June 1, 1982, the US Court of Appeals overturned the department's revocation of standard 208, chastising the Department of Transportation for failing to "heed the goals that Congress asked it to meet." Calling the revocation arbitrary and capricious, the court said that the agency had not mustered "one iota of evidence" and had "wasted administrative and judicial resources" in fighting the standard."[13]

In upholding standard 208, the court was impressed by the safety and economic merits of implementing it. William Nordhaus, a Yale economics professor and a former member of the president's Council of Economic Advisors, had prepared a detailed analysis of the automatic crash-protection standard for the insurance industry. Rescinding the standard, concluded Nordhaus, "would be extremely costly to the nation." He added:

> It would cost approximately $2.4 billion for every year of the delay and a total and indefinite rescission would impose costs on society of more than $30 billion for a steady state 1984 fleet. The costs of a rescission are 3 ½ times the benefits.

Moreover, Nordhaus calculated that rescission of the standard would result in approximately 6,400 more highway deaths and at least 120,000 more moderate-to-critical injuries per year.[14]

Despite the growing body of evidence of the desirability of air cushions accumulated over twelve years, the White House refused to concede. It decided to appeal the Court of Appeals decision to the US Supreme Court, where it expected to have a friendly audience, particularly among Justices Burger, Powell, Rehnquist, and O'Connor. But the Burger court surprised everybody. On June 24, 1983, in a landmark case, the Supreme Court ruled *unanimously* that the Reagan administration had failed to present an adequate basis and explanation for rescinding the standard. It instructed the Department of Transportation to reconsider its actions and make them consistent with the court's directives. "The first and most obvious reason for finding the rescission arbitrary and capricious," said the Court, "is that NHTSA apparently gave no consideration whatever to modifying the standard to require that air-bag technology be utilized." The Supreme Court also recognized the obstructionist role played by automobile manufacturers with respect to standard 208. "For nearly a decade the automobile industry waged the regulatory equivalent of war against the air bag and lost—the inflatable restraint was proven sufficiently effective."[15]

Chrysler called the decision "surprising and disappointing."

Other automakers said that safety belts are enough to do the job of saving lives.[16] GM's chairman of the board, Roger B. Smith, offered only another delaying tactic. He proposed that the government "retain one, or preferably two, private consulting firms to conduct studies and report their conclusions . . . as to the air bag and alternatives . . . to address the engineering adequacy . . . and the cost of various systems."[17]

But the Senate Appropriations Subcommittee on Transportation, headed by Mark Andrews (Republican-North Dakota), told the agency, "In view of the Supreme Court opinion, the committee urges the department to resolve this matter so that passive restraints can be made available to the American public at the earliest practicable date."[18] His Republican colleague, Senator John Danforth (Missouri), has expressed anger for more than three years over the delays and obfuscations about getting air bags into cars. On September 20, 1983, he finally gathered enough bipartisan support in the Senate Commerce, Science, and Transportation Committee to send to the full Senate his bill requiring air bags in some lines of cars. His frustration is evident. "I've given up on the administration. . . . [It] cares only about one thing and one thing only, and that's money . . . I really believe that there is a philosophical objection to safety regulation by the Reagan administration."[19] At his oversight hearings on NHTSA in the same month Danforth was even tougher: "According to DOT's own data, each year of delay has meant thousands of avoidable deaths and tens of thousands of needless injuries. 'Arbitrary and capricious?' Those are lawyers' words. 'Insane,' 'unconscionable,' 'wrong'—these words are closer to the truth."[20]

What Next?

In February 1983, four months before the Supreme Court acted, Secretary of Transportation Drew Lewis resigned, and the president appointed Elizabeth Dole to succeed him. She had been a commissioner at the Federal Trade Commission in the 1970s, with a reputation for moderation, and had served quietly in the Reagan White House in charge of public liaison. Her husband, Senator Robert Dole (Republican-Kansas), is chairman of the powerful Senate Finance Committee.

Dole made it clear that she wanted to take highway safety initiatives. Within two months of taking office, Dole forced NHTSA administrator Peck to resign. He made numerous gaffes during Dole's first months on the job and earned a reputation on Capitol Hill for verbosity and disdain for safety. In April, Dole very carefully spoke out in favor of air bags. While refusing to comment on the challenge to the standard pending in the Supreme Court, she said that the air bag "is a good safety device," and that the department intended to "encourage market incentives to promote it in coming months." The DOT would finance air bags in the five thousand government-purchased (GSA), 1985 Ford Topaz cars and would retrofit air bags for five hundred state-police vehicles, both on the driver's side only.[21]

Dole was latching onto a GSA project, recommended several years earlier by Ralph Nader, to get some air bag–equipped cars into production. But her purpose was muddied by statements in Dole's announcement suggesting that this tiny fleet could document the fatality- and injury-reducing effectiveness of air bags.[22] While it sounds sensible, to be statistically valid, at least five hundred thousand such vehicles would have to be on the highway for at least three years. Advocates of standard 208 rightly saw this argument as a potential delaying tactic. Besides, the technology has been tested successfully for years in laboratories, on proving grounds, and on the highways.

Shortly after the Supreme Court's decision, an automotive trade magazine quoted one "high-ranking aide to President Reagan" as boasting, "The administration plans to fight this challenge [the Supreme Court mandate] all the way. If we lose, the worst the carmakers should expect might be an automatic seat-belt requirement some years down the road."

Dole's sympathetic interest in air bags may not be sufficient to result in any significant government action. Ronald Reagan had spoken out against air bags in 1974 and 1975, and during the 1980 campaign had repeated, "The US auto industry is virtually being regulated to death. . . . It simply needs the freedom to compete, unhindered by whimsical bureaucratic changes in energy, environmental, and safety regulations."[23]

As to who will make the decision, the "high-ranking aide"

explained, "Mrs. Dole's marching orders on this one will be cut by" the White House.[24]

Evidence of this was revealed in Dole's Notice of Proposed Rulemaking for Standard 208, released on October 18, 1983, to comply with the Supreme Court's order. Like apple pie and motherhood, it is all things to all people. It also keeps the administration's options wide open for as long as possible. It proposes to retain the standard, with a new compliance date set for 1987 models; or to amend the standard (perhaps to require only air bags or to prohibit detachable belts); or to rescind the standard (with a better rationale). It also suggests the Department might conduct a demonstration program, seek enactment of mandatory safety belt use laws, or even propose legislation requiring the auto companies to provide a variety of restraint systems for sale, including air bags. Secretary Dole, in her announcement, emphasized her safety orientation. She reiterated "I have no mandate higher than safety" and stressed "I want to determine this as quickly and expeditiously as we can" with a final decision by April 12, 1984.[25]

Congressional reaction to Secretary Dole's decision was swift and unequivocal. Representative Timothy Wirth of Colorado characterized the failure to implement standard 208 as more "stonewalling and more unconscionable delay." In reciting the years of protracted rulemaking, Wirth stated, "We have been on this merry-go-round for over 15 years, and the Reagan administration is once again showing its callous disregard for the safety of Americans. . . ."[26] Senator Jack Danforth of Missouri likened the administration's decision to a four-corner offense in basketball that could keep the ball in play while running down the game clock: "The ball passes from player to player. But nothing ever happens. It's the ultimate stall, the deep freeze."[27] Dole's decision on standard 208, however it turns out, will be the one associated with her tenure as secretary and recorded in history. But at best, Dole is expected to get permission to enlarge the meager government fleet project to emulate former Secretary Coleman's plan for an air-bag demonstration to test public acceptance of air bags. However, such a demonstration project makes little sense today.

Since Coleman left office in 1976, numerous marketing studies from General Motors have been revealed, public opinion surveys published, and assessments made of the reactions of the three hundred GM owners who have survived air-bag crashes. All of the studies found strong public endorsement of air bags. In addition, a new DOT study has found that GM did not try to market its air bag–equipped vehicles effectively in 1974–76, thus resulting in sales of only ten thousand cars.[28]

Recognizing that the government might once again stall and avoid reinstating standard 208, in September 1983 a broad array of organizations, including medical, consumer, worker, and insurance groups, geared up once again to press for it. They formed the National Coalition to Reduce Car Crash Injuries, fearful that yet another fleet "test" would spell delay and would be no substitute for a standard affecting the crash design of all cars.[29]

Regulations that necessitate the development of technology, unlike simpler government requirements, depend for effectiveness on at least some degree of good-faith compliance by the regulated companies. If the new technology is defect-ridden or annoying to use, it will be rejected by the public. Amazingly, the auto manufacturers have touted safety belts as sufficient, even though the vast majority of car occupants (more than 85 percent) refuse to use them, and less than 9 percent of accident-involved occupants wear them.[30] In addition, Detroit has persistently resisted installation of air bags, whose inobtrusiveness and effectiveness would likely make it the most popular safety restraint. Air bags provide exceptional protection in two-thirds of all serious crashes,[31] and require no action by the user. They are also far less complex or costly than air conditioners or automatic transmissions. In mass production, air bag suppliers say a price tag of $200 would be profitable for the industry, which is about the same price as a vinyl roof and exterior trim package.[32] Furthermore, the additional cost of installing air bags would be more than offset by the fuel savings resulting from automotive fuel economy standards issued in 1977. A 1981 DOT report to Congress stated that, assuming a gas price of $1.52, the average purchaser of a 1985 model car could obtain a saving of $3,300 in gasoline costs compared to the purchaser of a 1977 car. Since fuel savings increase with the purchase of smaller cars, which are in most need of air bags, the DOT issued the fuel economy and automatic safety standards at the same time in 1977.[33]

Inside the industry itself there are, of course, many advocates of air bags and other safety designs that still have not been installed because of management preoccupation with cutting costs and indifference to trauma. But in the tightly controlled bureaucracy of the mammoth auto companies, neither the engineering experts nor management executives are willing to risk their careers to fight for lifesaving, safety design improvements.

There is something even more unsettling about why air bags are not in most cars today. The air bag is a space age safety system developed by the genius of the US automotive scientific community. It has been advocated by the industry's most talented leadership, including former GM president Edward N. Cole, who told the *Washington Post*, in 1976: "I am very much in favor of it for a couple of reasons. It's passive, you don't need to do anything. Particularly for the most severe [injuries] to the head . . . it protects the head and neck, the most vulnerable part of your body. The shoulder belt does not."[34] In 1977, Cole also shared his view that "the only way passive restraints are going to get to first base is [by] making them mandatory."[35] Despite their origins in Detroit, past enthusiasm, and the humanitarian need, air bag–equipped cars have not been offered for sale by American manufacturers since 1976.

Air bags are the most tested vehicle-safety device, with a billion miles of actual on-road use, five thousand crash tests, and evaluation by industry and government showing them to be far more effective than equivalent manual-belted cars. But while the scientists and engineers at GM and Ford have prevailed technologically to perfect the air bag, their chief executives and legal counsel have prevailed politically to defeat it. For more than a decade, air bag technology has been resisted and overriden by corporate managers, who apparently place a greater priority on demonstrating that the government cannot tell them what to do than on the lives of their customers. They have misstated its effectiveness, maligned the technology, recklessly exaggerated the price, and dismantled their air bag scientific and production teams.[36] These actions show an absence of moral and ethical leadership in our nation's largest businesses. And in the Reagan administration, these companies have found their ultimate allies—in government—to endorse further delays and postpone the availability of the air-bag technology.

Despite these trends, one foreign automotive manufacturer, with a deserved reputation for independent thinking, is offering air bags in some 1984 models. Mercedes-Benz began offering driver-side air bags in cars sold in Europe and the Far East in January 1981 and within less than three years, 17 percent of the buyers ordered the air bag with its gold-plated $1,000 price tag.[37] Mercedes has advertised and promoted the system and has air bag–equipped cars available at dealerships, two key steps GM failed to take in 1974. Mercedes is now importing the technology to the land where it was invented. Having waited out the worst of the Reagan deregulation mania, it decided to offer the system, after "favorable acceptance of the system in Europe."[38]

The Trauma

Submerged underneath all the rhetoric about regulation and costs are the people affected by the manufacturers' decisions. The manufacturers, in effect, regulate the consumer by what they offer or refuse to offer in the marketplace. The consuming public rarely has any say about whether safety features are built into cars (or other products), but they are victimized by decisions such as cutting down on safety provisions to curtail costs in the hopes of increasing sales. In the saga of the air bag, we can meet a few crash survivors (there are about 300) who lived to tell how the air bag saved their lives, and why they have spoken out publicly to push car manufacturers to once again include this option in their products.

There is Dr. Arnold Arms, the elderly doctor who fell asleep while driving home in the late afternoon from his grueling rounds of visiting patients. His 1975 Oldsmobile 98 Regency hit a large transit bus head-on, at about twenty-five miles per hour. But as he later exclaimed, with surprise still in his voice, "My car was completely demolished; however I was able to get out . . . without any injuries, due solely to the effective use of my air bags, as I was not using my seat belt. Nearly all my friends . . . have been begging for air bags since they saw what happened to me in the accident, and we have all been disappointed and distressed that we have been unable to procure them." [39]

The severity of Dr. Arms' type of crash is revealed by another head-on, car–metro bus crash in Washington, DC, eight years later, in which one occupant was killed and two hospitalized. [40]

And there is Chris Burns, sixteen and a new driver, who in August 1975 rounded a curve too rapidly in the middle of the day: "I didn't know it at the time that I was going too fast. . . . I grazed off a rock and then saw this tree—all of a sudden it was getting bigger, and then 'boom.' I realized how bad it was—the car was totaled. I was in such a state of shock. At that time I was wishing I wasn't alive, because I was afraid of what my father would say." The air cushion inflated and held Chris in place so that he didn't smash into the steering column, dashboard, and windshield. Chris is now twenty-three years old. [41]

The stories go on and on. But there are millions more—tragic ones, about children, teen-agers, and adults, who will never recover from their crashes. Unlike Chris Burns, Bryan Wicks and his girlfriend, Laura Toombs, both sixteen, died after their 1980 Pontiac failed to negotiate a curve and struck a utility pole in Aurora, Illinois, in July 1983. [42]

Each year for twenty-five years, 44,000 to 54,000 Americans have been killed in highway crashes—almost the number of Americans in our armed forces killed in the entire Vietnam War. Auto crashes are the major cause of death for Americans under the age of thirty-four. They are the largest single cause of paraplegia and quadriplegia, a major source of epilepsy, and a primary cause of serious head injuries. Brain and spinal-cord injuries account for almost 60 percent of all fatalities. [43]

Motor vehicle crashes cost the nation more than $57 billion in quantifiable losses each year. [44] Every ten minutes, twenty-four hours a day, 365 days a year, another American is killed in a motor vehicle crash, and every ten seconds another person is injured, more than the casualties of a major airline crash every day of the year. President Reagan condemned the Russian attack on the Korean airline in September 1983 as a "massacre" and an "act of barbarism." Surely the question must be asked whether revocation of the automatic crash-protection standard 208 is anything less. The Reagan administration's three-year delay thus far in implementing standard 208 will result in as many as 25,000 needless auto-crash deaths and 200,000 needless injuries.

Unquantified and often unseen are the heartbreak, emotional trauma, and strain on the family following the severe injury or sudden, unexpected death of a beloved relative or friend. Stories like the one about Suzie and Mark Aldrich, who were hit by a drunk driver, are the routine, not the exception. A two-paycheck family, with two young daughters, they lost their credit and telephone and had to drastically cut their food budget to avoid mortgage foreclosure, while Mark recuperated for three months in the hospital from severe multiple injuries. They faced at least $10,000 in medical bills, not paid by disability insurance. The financial strain, the long separation, and the impact of Mark's injuries overwhelmed the family.[45]

Although much of the government's work to delineate or characterize the reasons that we need automotive safety regulation has been discontinued or submerged by Reagan appointees, a NHTSA study of the effects of auto crashes on American families, begun in 1980, was finally published in 1983. It found that:

> In some families, financial costs paled in comparison to victims' continuing pain, disability, and psychological stress and other family members' emotional strain and added burdens of care. In others, economic hardship blighted the victims' convalescence and rehabilitation and deepened the entire family's misery. In all families, the quality of life deteriorated markedly for at least a year, and in some, accident-related problems have persisted for much longer periods and may affect succeeding generations.[46]

As one mother commented to NHTSA researchers, "When you lose a parent you lose your past. When you lose a child, you lose your future."[47]

A NHTSA staff study of the economic costs of motor vehicle crashes published in 1983 connects these findings to the governments actions: "If the focus of policy decisions were purely the economic consequences of motor vehicle accidents, the most tragic, and in both individual and societal terms, possibly the most costly, aspect of the toll of such accidents would be overlooked."[48]

THE RUSH TO DEREGULATE

The Reagan administration's distaste for standard 208 is not an isolated example of antiregulatory zeal. Removal of that standard is only the centerpiece of the administration's broader attack on crucial safety standards to improve the crashworthiness of cars. In a defiant speech to the National Automobile Dealers Association, Reagan's first transportation secretary, Drew Lewis, was blunt about his contempt for safety regulations: "If I could do it, there would be a four-year moratorium [on new regulations]. I know four years is unrealistic, but my point is that this administration opposes regulations."[49]

In fact, Secretary Lewis went much further. After the 1980 election, based on a list prepared by General Motors, Ford, and Chrysler, Secretary Lewis and Vice-President George Bush issued a report calling for a thirty-four-point agenda of "Actions to Help the US Auto Industry." On April 6, with great fanfare, the vice-president announced the program as part of the administration's Economic Recovery Program of initiatives to assist the US auto industry. The plan included not only spending cuts and tax "reforms," but "general regulatory relief." The safety standards targeted by Bush were characterized as items that could be "relaxed or rescinded, with little or no cost to worthwhile regulatory goals." The recommendations proposed delaying standard 208 and other crash-protection standards, lowering the 5 mph bumper standard, rescinding a requirement for clear visibility in cars, and cutting back on safety standards for heavy trucks.

The new proposals marked a major departure in the conception of the federal auto safety program. Safety improvements in cars, the very heart of the NHTSA's mission, were now redefined as economic burdens to be avoided. This shift flouted the agency's statutes, scientific evidence, and even the economic realities of auto safety regulation. According to the White House, the seventeen safety standards targeted by the vice-president for elimination would save the industry $556 million in capital investment, and consumers $4.9 billion in sticker prices, over five years.[50] Bush claimed that repealing the regulations would "address directly the immediate problems of depressed sales, record losses, and severe unemployment." The vice-president even boasted that the "relief measures" would return two hundred thousand unemployed auto workers to work by the end of 1982.[51] Even city officials in Detroit, suffering through their worst recession, were skeptical. "If I thought this proposal would create a hundred more jobs, I'd give it very careful consideration," said Esther Shapiro, director of consumer affairs. "But I don't believe it will create more jobs."[52]

The chairman of the board of General Motors, Roger B. Smith, whose company had urged even greater regulatory rollbacks, was happy but not entirely satisfied with Bush's announcement. While the proposals represented "a sensible step toward making regulation more cost effective," Chairman Smith complained that they covered only a small percentage of the standards affecting the auto industry.

While publicly proclaiming the necessity for rigorous cost and benefit analyses before initiating government action, the Bush proposals were based largely on the intensity of the industry's complaints and its unsubstantiated price information. GM's Smith, for example, while blaming regulations for declining auto sales, failed to acknowledge the role of Japanese competition, high interest rates, and dramatic new-car price increases (31 percent between 1978 and 1983). Nor did he offer any hard data to support his assertions. Given the fashionable deregulatory climate, it was far more convenient for Smith and other Detroit executives to blame regulation for layoffs and lagging car sales than the industry's own mismanagement, inefficiencies, and financial miscalculations. Independent auto industry experts, such as Walter Adams, a renowned Michigan State University economist, were more realistic. "The US auto companies had operated in an essentially non-competitive environment in which they played follow-the-leader imitating each other's mistakes," he told the *Detroit News* in 1980.

The alleged "savings" from deregulation, claimed by Bush and Lewis, are refuted by the transportation department's own studies. The economic cost of auto crashes is $700 per household each year, a figure that does not even count the *human* benefits of saving lives and reducing injury. Vehicle standards save money by lowering insurance costs ($3 billion less because of the existing safety standards)[53] and by eliminating the myriad costs associated with disabling crashes—unemployment, welfare, social security, and disability payments; lost federal and state taxes; hospitalization, long-term health care, and rehabilitation costs; and enduring psychological trauma and family disruption.

The administration's cheerleaders for deregulation assiduously failed to mention the considerable benefits (economic and human) of vehicle safety standards. Indeed, the Department of Transportation's figures show that existing auto safety standards save more than ten thousand lives per year, and that for each dollar consumers pay for safety features (a total of $370 per car), twenty-seven lives are saved. (The $370 figure represents the *price* charged to consumers, not the lower *cost* incurred by manufacturers, who normally reap a profit on safety features.)[54] Congressman Timothy Wirth, of Colorado, who scrutinized Reagan's attacks on NHTSA, calculated that the alleged savings from the Bush deregulation package amounted to only $9 per car buyer.[55] Moreover, most automakers are not passing on these savings to consumers (although the Ford Motor Company had promised to), so the net result for consumers is less quality in the car, with no reduction in price.

The facts surrounding the economic cost of "regulatory relief," which never received a full airing in the press, are actually secondary to another consideration: the law. Clarence Ditlow, director of the Center for Auto Safety, the only full-time public interest group overseeing the auto safety program, pointed out that in 1966 Congress decided economic factors would take the back seat:

> The [auto safety] statute specifically requires the development of safety standards "to reduce traffic accidents and deaths and injuries." It requires that standards be practicable and stated in objective terms. But there is no authority to issue or revoke vehicle safety standards based on the economic conditions facing the manufacturers. To the contrary, the Senate Committee when enacting the law authorizing NHTSA expressly stated "that safety will be the overriding consideration."[56]

The law and order that the Reagan administration has urged in other spheres of government are conspicuously absent in his government's auto safety program.

And, of course, the political climate plays a role. With Reagan at the helm decrying regulations, the manufacturers are seizing an opportunity to get rid of "bothersome" requirements. Never mind the payoff or the justification. Only two years earlier, for example, Ford's chairman of the board, Philip Caldwell (he then served as Ford's president) expressed a different view. In a January 16, 1979, news release, he said:

> There's been a lot of moaning and groaning about the burdens of government regulation on the industry and a lot of people say Washington is killing the business and taking the fun out of it. I don't think so. On the contrary, I think the revolutionary changes in automotive design that the regulations have initiated are creating a great new market for our products.[57]

A Lack of Purpose

The man President Reagan appointed to head the NHTSA was a lawyer for the coal industry, with no knowledge of, or sympathy for, health and safety programs, let alone auto safety programs. Shortly after his appointment was announced, however, Raymond Peck boasted to the agency staff that he was "the best deregulation lawyer in town."[58]

With the enthusiastic backing of DOT's Secretary Lewis, Peck set out to systematically dismantle established NHTSA programs, willfully ignore the law, flout nonpartisan traditions at the agency, and override the agency's own staff recommendations. Motivated by ideology and contemptuous of scientific fact, he openly attacked or covertly neglected the three major lifesaving programs under the agency's aegis: motor vehicle safety standards, motorcycle safety, and the 55 mph speed limit. Each program has been scientifically shown to save thousands of lives and mitigate hundreds of thousands of injuries each year. Even die-hard skeptics of NHTSA programs like Henry Ford II conceded that the government's efforts had been beneficial. Ford acknowledged on "Meet the Press," in October 1977, "We wouldn't have safety without the federal law, we wouldn't have emission controls without the federal law, and we wouldn't have as much fuel economy without the federal law."[59]

Perhaps the best exposition of Peck's grasp of his agency's mission came in his testimony before the consumer subcommittee in the House of Representatives, in March 1982. Congressman Timothy Wirth, chairman of the subcommittee, questioned Peck about his activities at NHTSA:

> MR. WIRTH: Could you tell me and the subcommittee in summary form what it is you are doing for safety?
>
> MR. PECK: Yes, we are continuing with not only our regulatory reform efforts, but our regulatory priorities.
>
> CONGRESSMAN WIRTH: Let us go ahead with safety. We have heard about the new federalism and regulatory reform and all that mind control stuff that goes on in this administration. What are you doing for safety?
>
> MR. PECK: Let me give you a specific example:
>
> CONGRESSMAN WIRTH: That is what I want. Let us have some specifics, one, two, three, four, five, no filibusters—specifics.
>
> MR. PECK: One, we have approved an internal order to assure that petitions for rulemaking are classified within seven days, handled within thirty days, and depending upon the actual complexity of the issue, finally resolved.
>
> CONGRESSMAN WIRTH: Let us talk about safety, not internal bureaucracy at NHTSA. What are you doing for the American people in terms of safety on the highways?
>
> MR. PECK: Mr. Chairman, this is the heart of our rulemaking responsibilities. When we get a petition for a rulemaking, it is the most direct, most immediate calling to our attention by the public, by an organized interest group, by whomever it may be.
>
> CONGRESSMAN WIRTH: I would like to know for the record right now, what have you done? One, two, three, four, five. I have cited you what you have not done. I have cited to you what the legislation says you are supposed to do. I have gotten no response yet in terms of what this administration has done about highway safety in the United States.
>
> MR. PECK: Now, Mr. Chairman, that is neither a fair nor an appropriate question.
>
> CONGRESSMAN WIRTH: I cited the start, the intent and the pur-

pose of the act. And you agreed that that was what the legislative authority says.

MR. PECK: The legislative authority also imposes, and the courts have reaffirmed over and over again, additional responsibilities which I would be remiss in my sworn duties to ignore. And those responsibilities include a determination that a specific standard is reasonable, appropriate, and leads to highway safety.

Now, with that kind of a background, I will tell you specifically what I have done. I have found that the 208 standard would not have led to highway safety and would not have satisfied that congressional mandate. I have found that several other specific standards were adopted either in advance of technology or because of changed circumstances, fully documented in the record, no longer met the congressional test for what a motor vehicle safety standard can and must be.

CONGRESSMAN WIRTH: I hear already, Mr. Peck, what you are not doing, all right. What I would like to know again, if I could repose the question, all right, is what you are doing for safety.

You have eliminated the 208 standard, the automatic crash protection standard, right? Now what have you done?

MR. PECK: Mr. Chairman, I have already introduced into the record the three management processes whereby we will make research and development priority decisions, rulemaking priority decisions, and rulemaking evaluation decisions. Those documents speak for themselves and fully answer your question.[60]

Administrator Peck had difficulty articulating the agency's safety priorities under his administration, because they indeed have been meager. He finally remembered to mention two promotion programs, against drunk driving and encouraging safety belt use, which are the only safety "initiatives" of the Reagan administration. Clearly stung by Congressman Wirth's grilling, three weeks later the Department of Transportation formally announced the initiation of a new three-year, $9.6 million campaign to increase safety belt usage.[61]

The safety belt program was politically acceptable to the

Reagan administration, and it passed muster with Detroit; it did not involve any regulations, was voluntary, had a modest price tag, and would take at least three or four years to find out if it did not work.

Increasing seat belt usage is, of course, extremely important. And government support for child-restraint usage laws has continued from the Carter administration to the Reagan administration. Unfortunately, however, there is massive public resistance to adult safety belt usage; since their introduction fifteen years ago, only about 12 percent to 14 percent of the driving population wear them today. The Insurance Institute for Highway Safety has studied more than a dozen voluntary seat belt campaigns worldwide since 1968 and found efforts to increase belt usage do not work. Both government and private industry have inaugurated expensive public information programs, which have had no long-term effect on belt usage. In some foreign countries, particularly Australia, mandatory belt usage laws have dramatically increased belt usage, up to 85 percent.[62] Research reveals, however, that drivers most likely to be involved in crashes are least likely to wear their belts. In other countries, such as parts of Canada, even with the mandatory laws, usage has barely exceeded 50 percent.[63]

The fact is, the American public has resisted efforts to change their behavior, to buckle up—some 100 billion times a year if all occupants wore their belts. In contrast, they have been very accepting of invisible, built-in safety devices in automobiles, such as collapsible steering assemblies, laminated windshields, dual braking systems, head restraints, side door protection, and other similar systems. Similarly, air cushion restraints are buried in the dashboard and the steering column. They do not interfere with the driving function, nor do they require the occupant to take any action to be fully effective. Seat belt usage in the United States exceeded 15 percent only when the 1974 models contained ignition interlocks, which prevented car users from starting the engine until their seat belts were fastened. This requirement, suggested by the Ford Motor Company, was revoked by Congress in late 1974 because of the public outcry. In the same vein, it is not likely that mandatory seat belt usage laws will be either enacted or found acceptable by the public, in large measure because of strong objections to the discomfort and inconvenience of existing belt systems.[64]

In revoking the automatic crash protection standard, the Department of Transportation witnesses before Congress frequently claim that increasing belt usage is a much faster way to assure the protection of car occupants because all vehicles are currently equipped with belt systems. However, in response to questions from Representative William Lehman (Democrat-Florida) in appropriations hearings in 1983, departmental witnesses acknowledged that the seat belt promotion program goal for the next three years is only 25 percent.[65]

Under the automatic crash protection standard, after the first year 10 percent of the vehicles (all new cars) would contain the automatic safety technology, either air bags or automatic belts; in the second year, 20 percent would; in the third year, 30 percent; and so on. Standard 208 was scheduled to take effect on a phase-in basis, between 1982 and 1984. Thus, had Reagan not revoked it, at least 35 percent of the cars on the road would have contained the crash protection technology by 1986. No scientific studies or prior experience in any way suggests that the administration's belt usage goal of 25 percent is achievable. Congress has been particularly skeptical about the efficacy of the $9.6 million expenditure for the belt program. The House Appropriations Subcommittee on Transportation, in its August 19, 1982, report, stated that it had "deep reservations about the ultimate effectiveness of the current seat belt usage programs."[66]

Improved Side-Impact Protection

Approximately sixty-six hundred people are killed each year in side-impact automobile crashes. To reduce the harm done from these types of crashes (representing about 20 percent of all occupant crash casualties), the NHTSA proposed development of a standard in December 1979, to require stronger side protection in cars. A specific proposal was due to be issued in the spring of 1981.[67] After delays of more than a year, however, the Reagan administration, on July 12, 1982, summarily rescinded the pending proposal. It claimed that the agency's research

has demonstrated that there are many questions remaining concerning the most appropriate test methodology
and performance criteria and levels. Many complex issues
have arisen which will require considerable time to resolve.[68]

Only a year later, the agency acknowledged that "significant improvements are possible in side crash protection . . . by strengthening the door beams, strengthening the vehicle frame, and by
making other structural improvements to more effectively absorb
the energy of a severe crash." The benefit would result in fifteen
hundred to two thousand fewer deaths per year at a price to
consumers of $10 to $50 per car.[69] Despite these findings, the
agency still has no plans for translating this knowledge into new
safety requirements. And the auto companies have not taken any
steps to voluntarily make improvements.

The Perils of Steering Columns

The largest single source of automotive crash casualties resulting
from accidents is the steering column, which is the cause of one
in four occupant deaths or serious injuries.[70] At a cost of less than
$10 per car, the current federal standard requiring collapsible steer-
ing assemblies has reduced injuries (serious to fatal) to the driver
by 38 percent in post-1968 vehicles.[71] Impressive as this statistic
may be, NHTSA discovered, after an extensive crash-testing program in 1979 and 1980, that even further improvements could be
achieved in the crash performance of steering columns, particularly in front-wheel-drive vehicles.[72] Yet in 1981, in response to a
petition by General Motors, the NHTSA saw fit to *weaken* the
existing standard for steering columns, because GM wants to build
five degrees' more tilt into its "tilt and telescoping" columns. The
agency had denied a similar petition in 1976, but in 1981 under the
Reagan administration it found a justification for reversing itself:
GM's tests alleged that abrupt, short-duration forces "apparently
do not transmit potential injuries to the driver."[73]

The agency reiterated the urgent need for improved steering
columns in a 1983 report, which called for reducing the size of the
steering wheel and column, and increasing the padding of the

steering wheel hub. At a consumer price of between \$20 and \$30 per car, these design changes could save five hundred to one thousand lives a year and prevent at least twenty thousand severe injuries.[74] Despite this knowledge, the agency's formal agenda calls only for more research.

Forgotten Pedestrians

About eight thousand pedestrians, mostly children and the elderly, are killed each year by automobiles. A proposal made by NHTSA in 1980 to require smooth surfaces and other energy-absorbing designs for the fronts of vehicles—due to be issued in late 1981—has never been developed into a final safety standard.

The agency did report in 1983 that "research is near completion, and final testing will verify the relationship between the crash-force characteristics of a more forgiving bumper and the extent and severity of human injury."[75] But the agency then projected that another year's work—until the summer of 1984—would be needed just to produce a final report, let alone a safety standard. Equally disturbing, no further work was under way on the second stage of the pedestrian standard for grills, hoods, and fenders, which are associated with 69 percent of all pedestrian casualties. Research to prepare this standard has barely begun.[76]

PROVEN PROGRAMS LEFT TO WITHER

Numerous other vehicle safety standards that were once planned or in progress before the Reagan administration came to office are now stalled, with no deadlines for completion. Standards that should have been issued during the first year of the Reagan term include:

- heavy vehicle conspicuity and braking capability (to reduce the risks of truck collisions)
- tether anchorages in passenger cars (to allow child-restraint systems to be securely fastened)
- rear underride protection (to prevent cars from riding under trucks in emergency stops), and
- lower dashboard impact protection (to reduce injuries to small children and the lower extremities of adults).

In addition, pending standards for occupant visibility and improved seat-belt design for comfort and convenience were rescinded by the Reagan administration in early 1981 before they had a chance to take effect. Other lifesaving proposals to upgrade roof, rail, and pillar structures; prevent door and side window ejection; improve the instrument panel; and prevent lacerations by glove compartment doors have been allowed to languish.[77] The only mandatory new safety standard issued during Reagan's first three years in office requires high-mounted stop lamps for passenger cars to reduce rear-end collisions.

The 55 mph speed limit, which has saved 4,000 to 5,000 lives a year since its enactment in 1974, is no longer vigorously supported by the federal government. Consistent with the 1980 Republican Party platform, the NHTSA has pared back its research and enforcement assistance for 55 mph, despite continued strong support for the law by the American public.[78]

The Motorcycle Scandal

Motorcycle and moped fatalities have climbed dramatically since 1976, when Congress revoked the authority of the Transportation Department to withhold grant-in-aid highway funds to states that fail to enact motorcycle helmet-use laws. As state after state revoked its helmet laws—twenty-eight states between 1976 and 1980—motorcycle deaths increased drastically. Even though the motorcycle population is only 3.5 percent of all vehicles, motorcycle deaths increased from 7.2 percent to 10 percent of all traffic fatalities. Nationwide, the 4,400 Americans, mostly young males, who are killed in motorcycle crashes represents an increase of 1,200 motorcycle deaths, or 27 percent, compared to 1975.[79]

The dimensions of this growing tragedy were documented by the Carter administration, in 1980, in a comprehensive report detailing several years of research on the enormous increase in head injuries that correlated with revocation of state helmet-use laws. As a result, states stopped revoking the laws, and proposals to re-enact helmet laws were introduced in several states. Louisiana even succeeded in re-enacting its law. Besides the helmet laws, the report recommended more accurate testing to determine the skills necessary for motorcycle operation, improved conspicuity for motorcyclists, and more reliable front and rear brakes.[80]

In the face of the extensive research into motorcycle crashes, the response of the Reagan NHTSA has been astonishingly feeble. Over the vigorous objections of the agency's professional staff, virtually all programs concerned with motorcycle safety have been abandoned and funding reallocated to other activities. No rationale has been expressed for this inaction. Perhaps it is a reaction to the complaints of a vocal minority of motorcycling enthusiasts who oppose the most basic reforms. But even the ultraconservative Loeb newspapers in Manchester, New Hampshire, have acknowledged, "We must say that we're having second thoughts" about earlier opposition to motorcycle helmet-use laws, because "increasing numbers of head, spinal, and other injuries to helmetless riders are being reported at local hospitals."[81]

THE HIDDEN STRATEGY: CRIPPLING NHTSA'S INSTITUTIONAL STRENGTH

What is least visible but most unfortunate about the Reagan reign at NHTSA is the destruction of the agency's institutional resources. The scientific staff, research capabilities, publications, educational materials, data systems, and other in-house programs play an indispensable role not only in the agency's life but also in the public policies developed to reduce death and injury on the highway. Yet few of these assets have escaped attack by the administration, which means that it will take years for the agency to fully recover its former capabilities.

The Brain Drain

The scientific and engineering expertise of the NHTSA has been seriously weakened, demoralized, and misdirected. Internal reorganizations, reassignments, reductions in force (layoffs), and forced retirements have resulted in the loss of more than two hundred NHTSA staff—a quarter of its work force. More than forty highly trained professional engineers and scientists, with master's degrees and PhDs, have prematurely retired or resigned.[82]

The House Appropriations Subcommittee on Transportation in 1983 refused to grant the administration's request to further reduce personnel at the NHTSA. The committee told the agency that it was "not convinced that NHTSA can carry out its statutory responsibilities at [a further reduced] level without posing additional risks to the American public."[83]

New Restrictions on Information

The agency no longer conducts its work in an open, accessible manner, as befits a federal agency. Instead, it has pulled a veil of secrecy over many of its enforcement actions, defect investigations, technical data files, and communications with the auto industry—a process that keeps the public out and the corporate procrastinators in. Delays in carrying out the law have become legion. Reports required by law to be submitted to Congress annually on July 1 have consistently been late, sometimes a year or more.

Publications have been recalled with an energy not applied to the recall of dangerous cars. Citizens' access to research documents, publications, films, and simple answers to questions have become costlier, more difficult, or flatly impossible. The NHTSA's Office of Consumer Affairs is moribund. *The Car Book,* a unique guide published in December 1980, listing crash test results, fuel economy, insurance discounts, and defect recalls by make and model of car, was not reissued in subsequent years, and distribution of the first edition was discouraged in numerous bureaucratic ways. Distributed by the government's Consumer Information Center, in Pueblo, Colorado, more than 1.5 million copies of the first edition of *The Car Book* were requested by the public—the single most requested publication in the history of the center. In addition, the agency has canceled distribution of most of the free auto and highway safety publications previously available through the center. Press releases informing the public of the agency's actions are issued infrequently, and those that are merely promote minor projects rather than announce news.

Budget cuts have forced the technical reference librarians at the NHTSA to cancel subscriptions, cut acquisitions programs, reduce hours and personnel, and discontinue computer information-retrieval services. A monthly publication listing highway safety literature produced around the world is now published only occasionally, in a truncated form, by the Transportation Research Board, and subject bibliographies on specific areas of highway safety research have been discontinued, thus hindering research in the field and tying up reference librarians in lengthy and repetitious searches. Computer indices of correspondence from consumers, compiled by subject, are no longer readily available for research by interested citizens. These letters are vital barometers of trends in defects and supply early-warning signals to the public. In addition, restrictive policies have hampered the flow of information from the agency's researchers, and the public has been kept in the dark about NHTSA's research activities and findings: research reports are not printed until one or two years after completion, public announcements about this work are not issued,* and findings are not widely disseminated. In mid-1981, the OMB directed all agencies, in violation of the Freedom of Information Act (FOIA), to place a moratorium on the distribution of its technical reports. The moratorium was removed when publicly challenged.[84] In short, hundreds of millions of dollars of valuable research has become virtually inaccessible to the public, researchers, congressional committees, and the General Accounting Office.

Even more insidious, in early 1982 the agency secretly initiated a so-called cooperative automotive research project with the Motor Vehicle Manufacturers Association, the trade association representing the major US manufacturers. When this secret project was discovered, the agency was roundly criticized by public interest groups, academic leaders, and members of Congress. The meetings were held in private, without any prior public announcement or any invitations to other interested persons. No other organizations or entities were allowed to participate, either in defining the subjects to be investigated or in the actual research activity itself. An elaborate research program concerning future motor-vehicle safety standards was developed but not disclosed, until demands were made under the FOIA. In essence, this group was a secret, hand-picked, advisory committee established by the

---

* In mid-1983, one enterprising research office recognized the need to disseminate its findings and started preparing summaries of recent research for distribution to interested experts.

agency, which, acting as a liaison with industry, would receive advice and recommendations regarding the allocation of scarce research funds. It was clearly illegal under the Federal Advisory Committee Act, which requires a public charter, balanced representation, public notice of all meetings, and transcripts or minutes of each meeting's discussions.[85]

With even more duplicity, Administrator Peck revoked the agency's most important pending rulemaking action—for side-impact protection—so that the industry "cooperative" group could "research" side-impact protection issues. But the secret research was really aimed at delaying any new standard without justifying the delay. And, in fact, when withdrawing the rulemaking notice for the side-impact protection, the agency did not disclose its actual reasons.[86] Despite the public fuss, the agency refused to discontinue the "cooperative" project with industry until it was sued in the federal district court by Public Citizen.[87] The Justice Department, representing the agency, quickly settled the case by agreeing to dissolve the group.[88]

Although the Reagan administration claims that the marketplace should govern consumer behavior, it has aggressively moved to undermine the consumer's knowledge in marketplace transactions. It revoked a portion of the standard concerned with grading the quality of tires, which required manufacturers to tell consumers, according to government-specified tests, how their tires performed in terms of treadwear, a measure of tire durability. The standard, which took effect in 1979, for the first time gave consumers reliable and unbiased comparative information on tire performance.[89] In addition, the Reagan administration has refused to put into effect a pending proposal that would require automotive manufacturers to print ratings of a car's safety performance in protecting its occupants in a crash, with the price listing on the windows of new cars. This program would give consumers information about safety performance in the dealer's showroom and would encourage manufacturers to compete in building crash safety features into cars.[90] In short, the administration has subverted one of the NHTSA's chief responsibilities—to disseminate information to the public, to Congress, and to the scientific community.

Safety Defects—Failure to Enforce the Law

During the first two years of the Reagan administration, the NHTSA's investigative activities concerning defects and safety enforcement suffered from improper secrecy and enormous delays. A number of investigations were terminated, complaints by consumers remained unanswered, a serious defect was covered up, testing programs were cut, and fines remained uncollected.

Since the auto safety law was enacted in 1966, more than a hundred million cars have been recalled in order to correct safety defects. Many of these defects have resulted in unexpected and unnecessary injury and death to car owners. Some of the more famous recalls required by the agency include the Firestone 500 tire, the Ford Pinto fuel tank, and the Chevrolet engine mount. During the Reagan administration, however, the NHTSA avoided its enforcement responsibilities until it was severely criticized for failure to carry out the law. During the first nine months of 1981, for example, as part of the Reagan focus on cooperating with the auto industry, the NHTSA did not issue any notices or press releases to alert the public about vehicles that were recalled because of NHTSA's investigations or manufacturers' decisions. In August 1981, the *Detroit Free Press* discovered that this information was being withheld from the public. When a reporter asked the Ford Motor Company why it had not announced several recalls of the Escort, Roger Maugh, Ford's director of automotive safety, acknowledged that Ford formerly put out news releases on all recalls because "the federal government was making announcements of them on a routine basis." Ford wanted to make sure its views got across. Maugh explained that Ford no longer issued releases routinely because "to my knowledge" the Reagan administration wasn't making routine announcements.[91] After a storm of protest, Ford and Chrysler regularly began issuing releases on defect recalls, and the agency started putting out releases occasionally.

But the major blowup occurred when it was discovered that the agency had been covering up a brake recall on the GM X-body cars. On January 5, 1983, the *New York Times* published a front-page story revealing that for eighteen months the NHTSA had not disclosed that the General Motors recall in August 1981 of 47,000 1980 GM X-body cars, to correct a brake defect, was totally insufficient. The story revealed that the NHTSA had conducted proving-ground tests in 1981 and 1982, showing that the brake linings were too aggressive, and that many more X-body cars needed to be fixed.[92] The agency was stunned by the disclosure and the critique. Nine days later, on January 14, 1983, the NHTSA announced an initial safety recall of 320,000 X-body cars, to correct the brake lockup defect.[93]

While NHTSA and General Motors were dragging their feet for more than three years, X-car owners were being injured and killed in tragic highway crashes. Reporter Jack Anderson has assembled a partial chronology of the events surrounding the brake lockup incident, and of the deaths caused by the delay:

- July 1, 1981: NHTSA safety engineers decided to begin an investigation after receiving 212 owner complaints of brake lockups, involving fifty-eight accidents. GM was notified privately; no press release was written, though that is customary.

     A week later, initial tests gave evidence that "gripping" brake linings were causing lockups. GM was notified; the public was not.

- August 2, 1981: Kim Sutton, eighteen, of Maryville, Tennessee, lost control of her Buick Skylark after applying the brakes on a rain-slick road, spun into the opposite lane, and was hit by an oncoming vehicle. She died twelve days later.

     Robert Olive, the Sutton family's attorney, told my associate, Tony Capaccio, that the accident "sure looked like brake lockup."

- August 5, 1981: GM voluntarily recalled forty-seven thousand X-cars (though not the model that Kim Sutton had been driving). The NHTSA had evidence linking the linings to the brake lockups, yet the agency allowed GM to replace only the valves that control the rear-brake hydraulic pressure.

- November 1981 to June 1982: Further NHTSA tests confirmed that the brake linings, not the hydraulic valves, were at fault. The raw data lay in the files for seven months before being collated, and even then were not made public. During those months, three more people died and one person was crippled in X-cars suspected of brake lockup.

- June 1982 to December 1982: After the report was prepared, the NHTSA inexplicably sat on it.

- December 15, 1982: Kathryn Tapp, seventeen, of Teton, Wyoming, was driving her Citation in a light snow when its front end went into a slight fishtail. According to witnesses, when Tapp put on the brakes, the car swerved violently into an oncoming vehicle. She died of her injuries.

    Robert Tapp, Kathryn's father, said he "didn't know about the X-car problem," and added, "Had we known about it, my wife would have taken the car in, or she would not have allowed it to be driven until it was fixed."

- December 17, 1982: The NHTSA sent GM a stern letter demanding more information about the brake problem and implying that a recall might be necessary.

- January 12, 1983: Dorothy Belt, of Elmhurst, Illinois, while driving her Phoenix on a slippery road, applied the brakes and spun across the center line into the path of an oncoming car. She and a passenger died.

- January 13, 1983: NHTSA safety engineers recommended a formal "defect finding."[94]

GM at first refused to cooperate, but on February 9, just before the NHTSA's public hearing, GM said that it would conduct a new recall. GM then haggled with the agency over the corrections to be made, but finally announced on March 30 that the second recall was under way.[95]

Representative Timothy Wirth immediately asked the

GAO to investigate the cause of the delay. After searching the agency's files and interviewing its engineers and managers, the GAO "found serious problems in the Safety Administration's [the NHTSA's] handling" of the investigation. It discovered that the current administrator of the agency had conducted no regular review that would lead to the discovery of defects and enforcement of regulations to correct them; and thus, cases sat for months with no action.[96] By mid-1983, fifteen Americans had died in crashes involving the brake lockup problem, 1,740 owners had complained about experiencing sudden locking of the rear brakes, and 71 drivers and occupants of these vehicles had been injured.[97]

In April 1983, Administrator Peck was removed from office by the new secretary of transportation, Elizabeth Dole. On August 3, 1983, several days before a major congressional hearing to review the GAO findings and the reasons for the coverup of the X-body defect, the Department of Justice filed a stunning $4 million lawsuit against General Motors, demanding the recall of all 1980 GM X-body cars—totaling about 1.1 million vehicles—in order to correct yet another problem that was causing brake lockup; and seeking penalties for false statements, withholding of information from the government, and knowledge of the brake defect problem beginning in the winter of 1978, long before the car was ever sold to the public. The combination of congressional and public criticism, the adverse public reaction to the misbehavior at the EPA, and the enormity of the evidence against General Motors finally persuaded the Reagan administration to perform its assigned duties under the statute and to enforce the law. Secretary Dole called the lawsuit "one of the most serious ever filed by the NHTSA."[98] GM said that the government's action was "unwarranted": "We categorically deny the government's assertion of misrepresentation. Accordingly, we will vigorously defend [against] the lawsuit."[99]

In filing suit against General Motors, the Reagan administration finally took on the responsibility of enforcing auto safety requirements. But given President Reagan's distaste for regulation —even life-saving regulation—and his past track record, there are few expectations that the auto safety mission will ever be carried out faithfully under his aegis.

THE FEDERAL AVIATION ADMINISTRATION

The Federal Aviation Administration (FAA), the other major agency in the Department of Transportation concerned with the safety of passengers in transit, mirrors the NHTSA in its incestuous relationship with the industry that it regulates under the Reagan administration. The FAA has always had a close working relationship with the airline manufacturers and carriers. In airline travel the industry bears the full brunt of the liability for any crash resulting in injuries to passengers. Thus, it has always valued the protective relationship that the FAA supplies through its standards and its licensing of pilots.

The FAA administrator for Reagan's first three years, J. Lynn Helms, is a former industry executive. He served as head of the Piper Aircraft Corporation, and he boasted about his ties with industry. He resigned in late 1983 after revelations of unsavory business dealings conducted even after he came to the FAA. In a 1981 meeting with airline industry executives, he told them what they wanted to hear:

> Unless I get fired, we're going to take the FAA down a different path, and I'd rather we go with it where you fellows want to go . . . what you want to do. . . . We don't have to talk about safety. Hell, everybody in this room is dedicated to safety. We wouldn't be in this business, but we do have to keep the business going, and keep the industry going.[100]

To carry out his pledge, Helms withdrew safety regulations proposed by his predecessor but not issued in final form; moved to eliminate existing regulations; turned down recommendations for safety improvements from the National Transportation Safety Board; and encouraged voluntary, instead of mandatory, safety improvements for the future.

For example, the FAA withdrew its proposal to require that aircraft designs be periodically reviewed, to ensure that they provide an up-to-date level of safety. Under current regulations, once a particular type of aircraft has been approved, it can be manufactured that way indefinitely. The FAA also withdrew its proposal to require installation of more fail-safe tires by the end of 1983, so that the airlines could use up old tire inventories. An FAA proposal—merely to increase the reporting of malfunctions in doors, emergency exits, escape slides, and other equipment, which can mean the difference between life and death for airline passengers —was also withdrawn.

The FAA also rejected ideas from outside experts. It turned down a petition, for instance, from the Aviation Consumer Action Project to upgrade the seat-strength standard, issued in 1952, which now allows aircraft seats to be one-third as strong as car seats. Current airplane seat structures have led to numerous deaths and injuries when passengers in low-impact crashes have been propelled around the cabin by seats that tore loose. The FAA even turned down a modest request from Public Citizen to require modern first-aid kits on airlines to assist passengers who become ill. About fifty people die in flight each year, and countless others are afflicted with life-threatening illnesses, which would respond dramatically to treatment, if it were available. Doctors ride on about 75 percent of all long-distance flights, and 90 percent of the doctors surveyed have indicated a willingness to help if asked.

The FAA has also turned down recommendations from its sister agency, which investigates aircraft crashes, the National Transportation Safety Board. The board, for instance, had been in favor of setting up procedures to prevent the ice formation that caused the Air Florida crash at Washington National Airport in 1982.

One of the disturbing features of Helm's FAA was its downgrading of air safety enforcement. Helms followed a "don't rock the boat" attitude and in three years he chopped the number of airline safety inspectors by 23 percent, even though airline deregulation had increased the number of new airlines. The dangers inherent in this policy were brought home in late 1983 by a fatal Air Illinois crash and the grounding of several small airlines for safety reasons. Led by Rep. Norman Mineta (Dem.-Calif.), chairman of the House Aviation Subcommittee, key congressmen and private safety groups asked the FAA how safety could be maintained with fewer inspectors. The FAA never had a good answer. Faced with mounting public reaction, in February 1984 Transportation secretary Dole announced a 25 percent increase in the number of inspectors. It remains to be seen how long it will take before they are in the field and whether there will be a new "get tough" policy.

While the regulatory decisions at both the FAA and the NHTSA have made travel more risky, the impact on vehicle safety is more significant for several reasons. First, many more people are killed and injured in car crashes each year than in aircraft accidents. The equivalent of a plane crash—120 deaths—occurs on the highways *every day*. Second, auto manufacturers can often avoid responsibility for their design errors or manufacturing defects because drivers are frequently blamed for crash and injury factors beyond their control, such as defective brakes and unforgiving vehicle interiors. By contrast, airline makers and transporters are more likely to be held liable by a court for harm to passengers, and, therefore, they are much more safety oriented than automakers.

During the Reagan years, the death rate on the highway has dropped dramatically from fifty thousand deaths per year in 1980 to forty-four thousand in 1982. The White House and the OMB have suggested that their programs promoting belt use and discouraging drunk driving have produced this result. But in 1983, NHTSA scientists did a thorough analysis of the death rate phenomenon and found that the economic effects of the recession caused 8 to 10 percent of the 14-percent drop; demographic factors, such as a decline in the number of young people in the population, was responsible for 2 to 3 percent of the drop; a reduction in drinking while driving, prompted by enactment of a number of tough state laws and a new federal law, caused 2 to 3 percent of the drop. Increased restraint usage, said NHTSA scientists, accounted for less than 1 percent of the 14-percent drop.[101]

Thus, the need for improved vehicle safety design is not only critically important; with smaller cars becoming more common, it is more important than ever. If the Reagan administration would heed its scientists rather than its political advisors, perhaps the interests of the public, as reflected in the agency's statutory mandates, would prevail.

ENERGY

DEPARTMENT OF ENERGY ORGANIZATION ACT OF 1977: "The establishment of a Department of Energy is in the public interest, to promote the general welfare by assuring coordinated and effective administration of federal energy policies and programs."

Eileen Choiniere, of Pittsfield, Massachusetts, is thirty-nine years old, is disabled, and receives $407 a month in Supplemental Security Income (SSI) benefits. Her gas bills are currently averaging between 40 and 50 percent of her SSI check. Rent consumes another 45 percent of her income, leaving 5 to 15 percent for food, clothing, and medical needs. "I'm handicapped, not working, and my heating bills are already high. If the cost of gas goes up, I'll probably starve to death."

Two caseworkers visited an eighty-year-old woman living alone in a remote, rural area, in a run-down house with broken windows and two barely functional coal stoves. The house was so cold that water dripping from a tap in the kitchen sink froze, even though there was a small fire in the kitchen stove. The rest of the house was no warmer than 45° F. The woman refused to acknowledge that she was cold and stated that she always lived with very little heat.

An elderly man was found to have turned off the gas heater to his water. He takes cold baths to save energy and higher gas bills, despite the fact that these baths only make him sick, requiring him to buy medicine he cannot afford.

Another elderly man was found in a frozen coma, with his

temperature down to 64.4° F. He survived, but his gangrenous limbs had to be amputated.

These are just a few of the "cold facts" collected by the National Consumer Law Center (NCLC) on the plight of the poor, the disabled, and the elderly in this nation as a result of spiraling energy costs.[1] Although energy costs and availability are no longer page-one stories, the cost of energy is a major concern for the twenty million poor in this nation, including six million older Americans, and another eleven million unemployed individuals.

Senator John Heinz (Republican-Pennsylvania), chairman of the Senate Special Committee on Aging, held hearings in the winter of 1982 on "Energy and the Elderly: the Widening Gap."[2] He said that in 1977 nearly a thousand people died as a direct result of excessive cold. According to figures from the National Institute for Aging, that is just the tip of the iceberg.[3] Hypothermia (insufficient body heat) may be the root cause of death for as many as twenty-five thousand older Americans each year. A study by the Brookdale Center on Aging at Hunter College[4] suggests that the number of deaths in which hypothermia is a contributing factor may be as high as two million annually.

Hyperthermia (excess body heat) is an equally severe threat for many. In 1979, two thousand individuals died during record temperatures in July and August. Senator Lawton Chiles of Florida noted at a hearing in 1980 that during that summer volunteers found elderly persons who were mortally afflicted by the heat—yet, they had unplugged window units or fans in the same room. "To think that people died from heat prostration because of the overwhelming fear of an electric bill is simply shocking," Chiles proclaimed.[5]

The Reagan administration sees things in a different light. The cornerstone of Reagan's energy policy is the revival of nuclear power and the withdrawal of government involvement in conservation and renewable energy production. Most members of Congress oppose dropping conservation programs. Reagan's major piece of legislation, the Economic Recovery Plan, called for doing away with almost all forms of financial assistance and information outreach to citizens.

The administration has proposed axing both the Low-Income Home Energy Assistance Program (LIHEAP) and the low-income weatherization program. Reagan proposed that states use Health and Human Services funds and block grants to deal with low-income energy problems, although these programs were also cut by 50 percent. Consumer information, so essential in a market that disguises which energy purchases cost the least, was zeroed out supposedly because Reagan's executive order accelerating the deregulation of oil provided sufficient incentives for conservation.

Previously free publications from the Department of Energy are no longer available, or obtainable only at a high cost. The Reagan administration essentially disbanded or severely undermined three information clearinghouses: the DOE Office of Consumer Affairs, the Solar Energy Research Institute's outreach program, and the newly created state Energy Extension Service. The administration also abandoned all plans to set appliance and building standards, despite the fact that setting such standards would reap consumer savings of billions of dollars in annual fuel bills.

At the same time President Reagan pursued these drastic cuts in consumer aid and assistance, his administration was pushing for lavish increases in subsidies and government contracts for the major energy corporations. He abandoned his pre-election promise to shut down a colossal pork-barrel project, the $88 billion Synthetic Fuels Corporation. In fact, the first $15 billion was authorized for expenditure by President Reagan. Nuclear power corporations, in particular, received special tax exemptions worth billions of dollars under the Economic Recovery Plan. The DOE budget also has shifted markedly toward nuclear power subsidies —in fiscal year 1984, 60 percent of the $11.3 billion DOE budget went to the fabrication of nuclear warheads, and 84 percent of the remaining $4.5 billion went to civilian nuclear development.[6]

Overall, President Reagan has wreaked havoc on nearly a decade's worth of bipartisan effort to seek the most environmentally sound and economical energy strategy for US consumers. Many members of Congress have strived to salvage some of the conservation and solar programs from complete elimination. Representatives from the president's own party documented how he could save $15 billion per year in obvious Pentagon waste, which could be used to weatherize every low-income household in America and thereby annually save taxpayers $2 billion in low-income energy assistance payments.[7] The president steadfastly refused to act on the information. Instead, the Reagan administration succeeded in largely replacing federal support of America's least costly energy sources for support of the most costly ones.

Speaking out against President Reagan's decision to cut the FY 1982 budget for the Low-Income Home Energy Assistance Program by 50 percent, in the face of anticipated 25-percent increases in fuel costs, Senator William Cohen (Republican-Maine) said: "When Americans must choose among basic necessities—food, clothing, health and shelter—there is a crisis. It is a crisis measured not only in budgets for this or that fiscal year. It is measured by the fears of the elderly. I, for one, will not measure austerity in terms of human life. In my judgment, that is rather a measure of public dispossession."[8]

High energy prices are driving more and more Americans, particularly older ones, into poverty. According to the National Council on the Aging, the incidence of poverty among older Americans increased by four hundred thousand in 1979, from 5.4 to 5.9 million—with energy playing a significant part in the decline of older Americans' economic welfare.[9]

The elderly have borne the burden of spiraling energy costs in another way as well. The price of heating or cooling their senior centers is rising. The cost of delivering meals to the home has skyrocketed. The vast network of nutrition sites are forced to pay increasing costs for energy and for the delivery of food to the elderly. The availability of volunteers has diminished because of rising energy costs of transportation. There is a clear pattern of reduced services to older people by institutions that once provided a lifeline for them.

Another factor that limits access to energy is that many elderly live on fixed incomes. They find their ability to survive reduced each month. As one observer put it, "Discretionary income to them is becoming, like their youth, only a memory."

Fifty percent of the elderly in the United States live in the regions hardest hit by energy cost increases. The Northeast-Midwest Coalition, a bipartisan congressional group, indicates that from 1970 to 1980 the average annual cost of heating a home in New England increased from $386 to $1,325, and in the Midwest from $367 to $1,150.[10] Homeowners must now spend $285 for heating fuel during the single coldest months, while the maximum monthly SSI payment is $248. During the five years preceding 1982, Social Security benefits increased 42.7 percent, and SSI benefits about 24 percent. These increases did not keep pace with fuel costs, which rose 337 percent during that same period.

The poor and unemployed are another segment of the population deeply affected by energy prices. Over the last decade, energy prices have increased three times as fast as the overall Consumer Price Index, whose increases were largely influenced by energy price increases. These rising energy prices have dealt a crushing blow to the nation's poor. During this period, heating oil prices have risen approximately six-fold, natural gas prices have increased roughly four-fold, and the price of electricity has tripled. By contrast, the consumer price index has little more than doubled. Natural gas continues to increase at an annual rate of roughly 20 percent, much higher than other products.

According to a 1983 study by the National Consumer Law Center (NCLC), *Out in the Cold,* the hardships that followed the oil price shocks of the 1970s are now being duplicated by the natural gas price shocks of the 1980s. The problem, the study says, is likely to be much more severe than the oil crisis and have a severer impact on the poor. First, 55 percent of the American poor heat with gas, while less than 20 percent heat with oil; hence, many more indigent Americans will be affected by rising gas prices. Second, unlike the Carter administration, which fought for a crude oil windfall profits tax to aid the poor, the Reagan administration is adamantly opposed to both a gas windfall tax and any substantial low-income energy assistance program. Third, the current administration has proposed deregulation of the natural gas industry, which would be likely to double current gas prices.[11]

The NCLC study found that in thirty-eight states the families of unemployed workers will have less than $100 per week remaining from the average benefits check to cover food, shelter, medicine bills, and other necessities after paying for natural gas. In twenty-three states, there will be less than $75 per week left from the average unemployment check for the month; in seven states, there will be less than $50 per week; and in three states, less than $25 per week will be left. Even these figures, the report notes, reflect the problem only as it is faced by those unemployed who are receiving benefits. Of the 11 million unemployed in October 1982, only 47.6 percent were receiving unemployment benefits. More than 5.7 million received no benefits; and as unemployment persists and the benefits of more individuals expire, that number is bound to grow.

Another NCLC study, *Energy Debts: The Coming Crisis for the Poor*, showed just how severe this problem already is by looking at the rising number of utility shut-offs. The number of households with overdue utility bills and the average size of those bills have both risen dramatically since 1980.[12] According to public utility commissions in eleven cities in which natural gas is the primary heating fuel, the NCLC study reported, natural gas prices increased an average of 92.5 percent from 1980 to 1982. The number of households in arrears increased by 25 percent. The number of households sixty days or more in arrears jumped by 35 percent during the same period, and the level of debt owed by those in arrears jumped by more than 80 percent. Shut-offs mirrored the figures—45 percent greater frequency over the same two-year period.

"There appears no way out," concludes the report. "The level of past debt, when coupled with reasonable projections of future costs, simply renders a deferred or extended payment plan inapplicable. Indebtedness and current costs have just outstripped the ability to pay."

By 1982, twenty-nine states had established some form of restriction on cold-weather shut-offs. Yet Representative Louis Stokes (Democrat-Ohio) could say on the House floor in March 1983, "In the state of Ohio alone, we have seen natural gas prices rise seven hundred percent over the past ten years. . . . The enormity of the crisis is reflected by the fact that over forty-five thousand Ohioans were shut off without heat in November because of their inability to pay their bills."[13]

According to the Ohio Action Coalition, in April 1983 the number of shut-offs went up because consumers did not have the money to pay their accumulated bills. Spring shut-offs are fast becoming a common utility practice as utilities face arrears in the tens of millions of dollars.

President Carter recognized the need to deal with the impact of rising energy costs on the elderly and the poor. When he announced his decision to lift price controls for oil companies as a means of spurring domestic production, he proposed a program to assist the needy. He told the American people in July 1979:

> As government controls end, prices will go up on oil already discovered, and unless we tax the oil companies, they will reap huge and undeserved windfall profits. We must impose a windfall tax on the oil companies to capture part of the money for the American people. This tax money will go into an Energy Security Fund, and will be used to protect low-income families from price increases, to build a more efficient mass transportation system, and to put American genius to work solving our long range energy problems.[14]

The White House fact sheet detailing the proposal called low-income assistance "the major purpose" of the excess-profits tax. Under the Carter plan, $24 billion of the expected minimum of $142 billion in trust fund revenues from the excess-profits tax were to be allocated to low-income assistance over a ten-year period, an average of $2.4 billion per year. Such a program contained the promise of real financial assistance to make up for increased energy prices.

The final version of this program, enacted into law as the Crude Oil Windfall Profits Tax of 1980, did not actually require tax revenues to be spent for fuel assistance. But the accounting and reporting scheme in the act seemed to hold great promise for allocating funds to alleviate the frightening situation faced by many of the nation's poor.

Unfortunately, under Reagan's 1982 budget, the congressional appropriation to carry out the act did not match Carter's original intention. Congress has funded LIHEAP at less than $2 billion per year for the past four fiscal years, although it was the intent of the law to supply funding levels in the $3 and $4 billion range. (The figure was raised to $2.4 billion to account for inflation.)

As Senator Heinz explained, "That was the theory. Right now it seems a lot more like theory than practice. Congress looks a lot like Pontius Pilate, assuaging guilt and nagging responsibility with a program—and then washing its hands of the whole thing through steady reductions in funding because the government supposedly can't afford it."[15] Although Heinz singled out Congress, it was intense lobbying by the White House that caused the lower appropriations.

According to a 1982 congressional staff study prepared for the Subcommittee on Investment, Jobs, and Prices of the Joint Economic Committee, *Oil Price Decontrol and the Poor: A Social Policy Failure*, the loss in purchasing power for low-income Americans because of domestic oil decontrol was $9.1 billion, and the loss due to higher oil import costs was $5.6 billion.[16] Thus oil price increases during the 1979–1981 period cost the poor a total of $14.7 billion. In contrast, federal appropriations for energy assistance programs, which offset the loss in purchasing power, amounted to only $4.2 billion during the same period. Accordingly, the report estimates that the loss in purchasing power for the poor which was not offset by energy assistance programs reached $11.1 billion, or 76 percent of their total loss in purchasing power. Various other studies put the *annual* loss in purchasing power of the poor at around $5 billion.

Under the Reagan administration, the Crude Oil Windfall Profits Tax has been reduced by $7 billion over a five-year period. Although LIHEAP has, since its inception, consistently been underfunded by $1 to $2 billion, Reagan's 1984 budget calls for a more drastic 30 percent reduction in energy assistance funds to $1.3 billion. The HHS estimates that 20 million low-income households are eligible for LIHEAP energy assistance funds. Because of inadequate outreach efforts, however, less than 35 percent of the eligible population—6.4 million households—is currently receiving assistance.[17] As information on eligibility reaches more people and as higher gas prices drive more people to seek assistance, there will be fewer benefits for each household.

If natural gas is deregulated, as Reagan has urged, these problems will be exacerbated. Under Reagan the hope for establishing a windfall profits tax on producers of natural gas is slim indeed. According to the *Washington Post*, the top 20 producers of natural gas—led by Mobil, Exxon, Texaco, Gulf, and Shell—control more than 70 percent of our natural gas supplies and stand to gain a $40 billion windfall profit between now and 1990 if decontrol is put in effect without a special tax.[18] As Representative Stokes wryly commented, "It is obvious that the oil companies will be the big winners in the president's legislation and that the consumers will be the losers."[19]

One of the biggest mistakes in the Reagan administration's energy program has been its attempt to terminate the low-income weatherization program. It costs the government roughly $11 per barrel of oil (or its equivalent) to weatherize a low-income home, while it costs the government $50 to $150 per barrel to pay part of a low-income household's utility bill. Further, the weatherization is a one-time cost, while the energy assistance funds are an annually recurring expense.

Jane Brown, director of the Minnesota State Energy Assistance Program, pointed out another economic benefit of weatherization while testifying before the Senate Select Committee on Aging:

> For every $1 returned to circulation in our economy through the conservation of energy, the federal government receives 24 cents each year this $1 remains in our economy. Therefore, for each federal tax dollar used to conserve $1 in energy, an additional $1 in tax revenues is generated in 4.2 years. This results in the federal government receiving complete payback for its investment for energy conservation in 4.2 years without considering the additional payback in reduced assistance needs.[20]

Senator Edward Kennedy (Democrat-Massachusetts) vigorously defended the weatherization program:

> No society—least of all America—can permit those who contributed their best years to the growth and prosperity of the nation to spend their retirement in a constant struggle for food and fuel. The elderly in Canada, for example,

can apply for weatherization assistance by mail, and receive a check to cover one hundred percent of the first five hundred dollars of weatherization work. A US program like Canada's would cost twenty-five billion dollars over ten years. It would save almost two million barrels per day.[21]

Within several years, he could have added, it would also save many times over that amount in LIHEAP payments.

The majority of families across the nation are also feeling the strain of rising energy prices, both directly and indirectly. Fuel adjustments and electric rate hikes are becoming more frequent with larger increases each time; filling up the gas tank buys fewer gallons with more dollars. Indirectly, rising gas prices are regularly boosting the price of food and clothing. High-priced oil has been a major culprit in fanning inflation and hence raising house payments, costs of food and medical assistance, and other essential items.

Although the price of gas has not fluctuated much recently, the days of historically cheap gas and oil supplies are over. Statistics from industry indicate that it now costs ten times more to drill and deliver "frontier" oil or gas than it did from old deposits. Electricity generated by nuclear power is even higher, roughly one hundred times more expensive than energy from old deposits.

It is true that oil in the Mideast and other OPEC nations remains incredibly cheap to produce—still fifty cents to a dollar a barrel. The price of continued dependence upon this cheap source of oil, however, is to live with the ever-present danger of supply cutoffs, whether embargoed for political reasons or disrupted because of wars such as the Iraq-Iran conflict.

What energy course, then, offers the safest, surest, and least costly supply? What path can this nation pursue that minimizes the damage to family budgets, protects us against another bout of inflation fanned by sudden price hikes or energy interruptions, and accomplishes these goals without sacrificing the environment, or public and occupational health and safety?

A number of reports over the past decade have provided an unequivocal answer to that question. It always seems to elicit a surprised reaction when people first learn that conservation by means of improved efficiency remains the quickest, cleanest, surest, and cheapest supply of energy for the United States. The word "conservation" has unfortunately been tainted with the narrow impression of curtailment, as in shutting down factories and rationing gasoline, or, as President Reagan calls it, "sweating in the summer and being cold in the winter." Improving efficiency in fact rarely calls for any sacrifice or significant change of behavior.

As *Energy Future*, a report by the Energy Project of the Harvard Business School, states:

> Conservation may well be the cheapest, safest, most productive energy alternative readily available in large amounts. By comparison [with other energy sources], conservation is a quality energy source. It does not threaten to undermine the international monetary system, nor does it emit carbon dioxide into the atmosphere, nor does it generate problems comparable to nuclear waste.[22]

Productive conservation takes many forms, but the common feature of all such measures is to enable an end-use device, such as a furnace, air conditioner, water heater, refrigerator, lamp, or automobile, to perform with a lower level of energy input. In 1975, the American Institute of Physics (AIP) analyzed the efficiency potential of the many end-use devices that Americans employ and found that, on the average, these devices were operating at extremely low efficiencies. Quadrupling that efficiency is feasible with today's off-the-shelf technology—and at a cost far below 1983s world oil prices of $30 per barrel.[23]

In fact, the AIP study found that just six measures alone could have saved 40 percent of the energy consumed in the US: installing heat pumps; improving refrigerator efficiency by 30 percent; reducing heat losses from buildings by 50 percent through better insulation, improved windows, and reduced infiltration; implementing cogeneration (i.e., utilizing the waste heat of a turbine or engine to produce additional electricity or to process heat) for half of the direct-heat applications in industry; using organic waste in urban refuse for fuel; and improving automobile designs to increase fuel efficiency by 150 percent over 1973 levels.

At the request of the House of Representatives Energy and Commerce Subcommittee on Energy Conservation and Power in 1979, the US Solar Energy Research Institute (SERI) undertook a two-year investigation into the "realistic savings through promotion of efficiency in our buildings, transportation system, and industry, as well as the contribution achievable from renewable energy sources."[24] Drawing on the assessments of a team of America's top efficiency experts, SERI reported to Congress in 1981 that by the end of this century the United States could wring twice as much work out of its existing energy supplies and derive a third of that energy from renewable resources. This plan would avoid the need for construction of any new coal or nuclear power plants after 1985. In addition, the SERI analysis showed that within the decade, these improvements would eliminate the foreign oil imports on which we are dependent, halting the economic hemorrhaging caused by a $40 to $80 billion annual cash flow out of America to foreign oil producers.

The ways to achieve this 50 percent reduction in nonrenewable fuels were very similar to the 1975 AIP assessment. What has become more apparent, however, was the enormity of dollar savings to consumers. The accrued financial savings of investing in efficiency and a modest amount of renewables rather than coal, uranium, oil, and gas amount to *several trillion* dollars in fuel, operating and maintenance costs over the next twenty-year period.

Obviously, public and environmental health and safety gains would be made by foregoing the extraction, processing, transporting, combustion and fissioning, and disposal of billions of tons of noxious and toxic fuels. Cleaner air and water would not have to be purchased by an increase in taxes; they would be achieved while improvements in efficiency were actually reducing the need for ongoing low-income and other subsidies.

Production of weatherized homes and fuel-efficient vehicles does not require bureaucracies that perpetuate themselves with the annual multibillion-dollar budget requests needed to monitor the safety of nuclear power-plant construction and operation. Efficient refrigerators and air conditioners do not generate radioactive wastes that have to be dismantled and entombed for hundreds of years, as do nuclear plants at the end of their working lives. Efficient motors and furnaces do not injure workers through radiation or endanger the environment with core meltdowns. Efficient devices do not pose the ever-present threat of diversion of spent fuel rods from nuclear reactors to nuclear bomb proliferation. Nor do they require more taxpayers' dollars to be allocated for security forces and protection devices to keep weapons-grade plutonium from being extracted from spent fuel rods of nuclear power plants.

Unfortunately, there is no natural constituency promoting improvements in efficiency and Ronald Reagan is not interested. Consumer interest is too diffused over a wide range of economic sectors. In contrast, energy corporations continue to mount highly effective lobbying campaigns to keep public policy focused on nonrenewable energy sources. According to a Battelle Labs study prepared in 1979 for the DOE, nonrenewables have received nearly all of the more than $200 billion in federal energy subsidies for the past fifty years.[25] Efficiency was not even a category that was listed. Despite the incredible advancements recently in identifying numerous cost-effective efficiency improvements, Reagan's FY 1984 budget for DOE requests roughly fifteen times as many dollars for nonrenewables as for efficiency and renewable energy sources. In contrast to 9 percent in Reagan's budget, Carter's 1981 budget allocated 49 percent of the DOE's budget to solar energy, renewables, and conservation.[26]

Two other major roadblocks stop America from becoming energy efficient: institutional barriers and lack of investment capital. Institutional barriers abound at the state and local level. More than half of the households in America are made up of people who rent. They may pay the fuel bills yet have little incentive to sink cash into making their homes more permanent or valuable by weatherizing them. The landlords, on the other hand, realize no savings if they spend the money to make improvements, because most tenants pay the fuel bills. Building contractors purchase nearly half of all new-building appliances and frequently buy the cheapest, most inefficient models to keep initial costs down. A more efficient machine would eventually save the owner several times the initial cost.

Lack of access to reliable information about the best investments in efficiency is a critical problem, not just for families, but for businesses, school districts, nonprofit organizations, and local governments. High energy costs have forced budget cuts in a number of public services that might have been unnecessary if efficiency information had been available.

Ultimately, however, it is the lack of financing capital that is the major impediment to implementing conservation. Weatherizing a home typically costs several thousand dollars, yet the savings would be equivalent to fuel costing between $1 and $30 per barrel, which is considerably cheaper than utility rates at $50 to $75 per barrel for oil and gas, and $100 to $200 per barrel for electricity. Yet, because utilities borrow money in million- and billion-dollar chunks, while families and small businesses borrow money in hundreds and thousands, banks provide utilities with much lower interest rates than they charge to lower-income consumers. Obviously those households who could best benefit from the weatherization loans—the elderly, poor, and unemployed—are also the least likely candidates for even high-interest loans.

By the time Ronald Reagan entered office, a number of programs were under way to encourage energy conservation. Perhaps the single most effective one, achieving the greatest fuel savings, was the government's Automotive Fuel Economy Program, carried out by the NHTSA.[27]

The Energy Policy and Conservation Act of 1975 established fuel economy standards for all cars manufactured after 1977. The act required that by 1985 the corporate average fuel economy (CAFE) for all companies selling cars must be 27.5 miles per gallon (mpg), nearly 100 percent higher than the average of 14 mpg at the time of the 1973 Arab oil embargo. According to the NHTSA Fifth Annual Report to Congress in 1981, this program has benefited consumers by saving the average purchaser of a 1980 car $1,700 in gasoline costs, and will save the average purchaser of a 1985 car an *additional* $1,600 over the lifetime of the vehicle. For the next twenty years, projected fuel economy improvements will save the nation about $1 *trillion* in imported oil—or about $200 per person for each of those years.

The report also documents that it is both technically feasible and economically viable to *quadruple* between 1980 and 1990 the fuel efficiency of vehicles. The higher initial cost of the car would pay for itself in gas savings within fourteen months, and continue to repay the consumer over the life of the vehicle.

In spite of its undeniable benefit to consumers, the Reagan administration cut this program drastically, eliminating all automotive fuel economy research and most technical staff, and revoking the Carter proposal for post-1985 fuel economy standards. President Reagan, supposedly a free market advocate, has decided to rely upon the continued subsidization of the $88 billion Synthetic Fuels Corporation, set up under the 1980 Energy Security Act, to produce 2 million barrels of oil a day from shale or conversion of coal to gasoline. As international energy expert Amory Lovins noted in a memorandum to OMB director David Stockman, it would be quicker and cheaper to save oil by using the same funds to pay anywhere from half to all of the cost of giving people free diesel Volkswagen Rabbits or Honda Civics (or an equivalent American car if Detroit would make one) in return for scrapping their gas guzzlers to get them off the road. This alternative would result in saving four million barrels of oil a day—the present level of foreign oil imports—before a single syn-fuels plant delivered a drop of oil.[28]

But neither Stockman nor Reagan has paid any attention to the economic and safety advantages of conservation. Reagan has accelerated decontrol of oil, pushed for total decontrol of natural gas, and repeatedly tried to gut both the LIHEAP and the low-income weatherization program. At the same time that Reagan proposes tax breaks for nuclear power companies, he has attacked small energy tax credits for homeowners, renters, and small businesses. He tried to shut down the Solar and Conservation Bank, which was set up by Congress to help modest-income families unable to take advantage of tax credits or low-income weatherization funds to obtain long-term, below-market energy loans. It is one of the few federal programs that can directly benefit renters.

The administration's contempt for conservation has been further reflected in a purge of high-ranking DOE directors. Dennis Hayes, director of SERI, and sixty of his staff were fired for publishing the SERI report. Tina Hobson, director of the DOE's highly respected Office of Consumer Affairs, and her staff were relocated, then fired, and the office was essentially shut down. Dr. Maxine Savitz, director of the $140 million Conservation Research and Development branch, was demoted and then fired. No substantive reason was given for the demotion, but the result, as with the other two firings, was to effectively eliminate a high level of expertise and throw the programs into turmoil.

Despite all of his talk about cost-benefit analysis, Reagan has made no attempt to evaluate the most successful of the DOE's programs, in terms of getting the best return on expended tax dollars. The Energy Extension Service, for example, was set up by Congress to help families and small businesses with information on the best buys not only in the new field of solar energy but also in the products and services promoting efficiency. The program was instrumental in getting the public to invest $15 in efficiency systems for every $1 spent in tax money to distribute this information. But this service has been scheduled for termination, along with industrial, commercial, and institutional outreach programs.

The administration foolishly has scuttled plans for setting efficiency standards for appliances or buildings. According to a study in 1983 by the American Council for an Energy Efficient Economy, the promotion over the next two decades of purchases of large home appliances judged most efficient would eliminate the need for building one hundred nuclear power plants.[29]

The President's Economic Recovery Plan, which Congress passed in 1981, provides windfall tax breaks for utilities that construct capital-intensive nuclear power plants. In essence, taxpayers will be subsidizing nearly two-thirds of the capital charges and more than one-third of the construction costs of a nuclear reactor. If these tax subsidies were directly reflected in the delivered price of electricity, consumers would experience a dramatic 50 percent jump in their utility bills.

In addition to being the most expensive energy option available to America, nuclear power also is the one technology most plagued by health and safety problems, and is an ever-present menace to national security. According to the *Nuclear Power Safety Report*, prepared in 1983 by Public Citizen's Critical Mass

Energy Project from data obtained from the Nuclear Regulatory Commission (NRC), nuclear reactors in 1982 sustained 4,500 mishaps.[30] These failures included such equipment breakdowns as pipe ruptures and steam generator leaks; design or fabrication flaws, such as undersized pumps or inadequately lubricated equipment that failed to operate at critical moments; and human errors, such as failing to follow correct procedures or maintenance schedules.

The number of workers at nuclear plants exposed to excessive radiation levels has been steadily climbing. In 1982, 84,322 nuclear plant workers were exposed to more than fifty thousand rems of radiation. (Cleanup of Three Mile Island alone will expose workers to more than forty thousand rems.) This represents a rampant increase in the number of workers exposed, up 113-fold since 1969. During the same period, electricity generated from nuclear plants increased only 25-fold. A third of those workers were exposed to radiation levels three times higher than the maximum level allowed the general public—thereby increasing their chances of chromosomal damage, cancer, and leukemia, as well as the probability of miscarriages and birth defects.

The reason for the increase in workers exposed to radiation is obvious. There is a legal limit on the amount of radiation that workers may be exposed to, but no legal limit on the total number of workers who may be exposed. Hence, as reactors degenerate through mishaps or radiation levels increase as a result of aging, more workers are needed to perform the repairs. An increasing percentage of the hired workers are made up of temporary help. They are called jumpers or sponges, because they jump into hot radiation spots, soak up the maximum level of radiation, and then are laid off, only to move on to other plants.

Plant mishaps, which have been growing over the years in part because of the increasing number (and size) of reactors coming on-line, have been partly responsible for the skyrocketing costs of nuclear-generated electricity. The time that plants are closed to repair mishaps has drastically reduced the amount of nuclear electrical output. Most plants are operating at less than 60 percent of maximum capacity (which is far below the 80 percent figure that nuclear vendors had quoted to sell the plants to utility companies). Because of the mammoth size of the plants, whenever a plant closes down for repairs, it may cost a utility $1 million or more each day to purchase replacement fuel, often high-priced oil.

There was a 140-percent construction-cost increase in new plants during the seven years preceding the partial core meltdown at Three Mile Island (TMI). Two-thirds of this cost increase was due to new safety features to deal with potentially catastrophic accidents. In the aftermath of the TMI accident, the Nuclear Regulatory Commission has been mandating these additional safety features, which, nuclear cost analysts have anticipated, will raise the price of nuclear reactors throughout the 1980s.

A sinister aspect of expanded nuclear production is its threat to national security. According to former nuclear weapons designer Ted Taylor, it takes less than six kilograms of plutonium to fashion a bomb so small that it can fit beneath a bed, and so powerful that it can produce the total explosive power released in World War II.[31] If the Reagan nuclear energy plan succeeds, it will place in transit (to and from nuclear reactors) nuclear material equivalent to hundreds of thousands of nuclear bombs. According to a GAO report issued in 1980, present auditing techniques are incapable of measuring nuclear fuel inventories to within plus or minus 5 to 10 percent.[32] In short, significant diversion or theft for unintended purposes is undetectable.

With the aggressive nuclear exports policy that Reagan is implementing, nuclear experts warn that it will not be long before the number of nations possessing the ability to build nuclear bombs will grow tenfold. With this proliferation of nuclear material, subnational terrorist groups will have a much better chance of obtaining or building a bomb. As Taylor noted in testimony before the House Subcommittee on Oversight and Investigations, making a nuclear bomb is no more difficult a procedure than the method that criminals now routinely use to process morphine base into heroin. Taylor believes that the governments will be no more successful in apprehending terrorists with bombs than they have been in shutting down the heroin trade.

A 1981 study by Amory and Hunter Lovins funded by the Department of Defense looked at the vulnerabilities of the US energy system and singled out nuclear reactors as the worst conceivable energy facility, from a national security perspective.[33] During military conflicts, energy facilities are the first sites that are targeted for destruction. The bombing during World War II of Germany's energy installations shut down its military-industrial complex and brought the European war to an end within six months. Targeting a nuclear reactor, according to the study, would vaporize the core, contaminating for centuries hundreds of square miles—an area forty times greater than if the bomb landed on a nonradioactive target. The same damage could be accomplished with a crude terrorist bomb planted in a truck next to a reactor site.

Despite all the studies documenting the problems of nuclear power and the advantages of conservation, Reagan continues to lobby Congress for legislation that would cut in half the time it takes the NRC to license nuclear reactors. The president would do well to heed the words of Ted Taylor, the former atom bomb maker turned community energy designer:

> Which kind of world do we really want for ourselves, our children, and their children—one with thousands of NRC and IAEA [International Atomic Energy Association] inspectors, or one with thousands of building energy auditors; with thousands of plutonium breeders protected like fortresses, or countless community-scale, low-cost solar electric cells floating on shallow ponds; fuels that can be incorporated into thousands of nuclear weapons, or methanol and methane from plants and organic wastes; secrecy, or open exchange of information that is beneficial for all of us? My answer to such questions is that I would far prefer that we vigorously pursue a world that may seem too good to be true, than continue to drift toward a world that is too dreadful to contemplate.[34]

GLOSSARY OF ACRONYMS

AFDC	Aid to Families with Dependent Children
AIP	American Institute of Physicists
AMA	American Medical Association
ANDA	abbreviated new drug application
BACT	best available control technology
BAT	best available technology
BCT	best conventional technology
BMP	best management practices
CACTUS	Citizens against Chemical Toxins in Underground Storage
CBO	Congressional Budget Office
CDC	Centers for Disease Control
CFA	Consumer Federation of America
CIB	consumer intelligence bulletins
Co	carbon monoxide
COSH	Committee on Occupational Safety and Health
CPI	consumer price index
CPSC	Consumer Product Safety Commission
DBCP	dibromochloropropane
DES	diethylstilbestrol
DOE	Department of Energy
DOT	Department of Transportation
EDB	ethylene dibromide
EDF	Environmental Defense Fund
EO	executive order

EPA	Environmental Protection Agency
EtO	ethylene oxide
ETS	emergency temporary standards
FAA	Federal Aviation Administration
FACA	Federal Advisory Committee Act
FDA	Food and Drug Administration
FOIA	Freedom of Information Act
FORMULA	an organization of parents formed to protect the nutritional quality and safety of infants' formulas
FRAC	Food Research and Action Center
FTC	Federal Trade Commission
FY	Fiscal Year
GAO	General Accounting Office
GRAS	generally recognized as safe
GSA	General Services Administration
HC	hydrocarbon
HEW	(Department of) Health, Education, and Welfare
HHS	(Department of) Health and Human Services
IAEA	International Atomic Energy Association
LIHEAP	Low-Income Home Energy Assistance Program
MS(s)	mechanically separated (species)
MVSS	Motor Vehicle Safety Standard
NAM	National Association of Manufacturers
NAS	National Academy of Sciences
NCLC	National Consumer Law Center
NDA	new drug application
NHTSA	National Highway Traffic Safety Administration
NIH	National Institutes of Health
NIOSH	National Institute of Occupational Safety and Health
No	nitrogen oxide
NRC	Nuclear Regulatory Commission
NRDC	Natural Resources Defense Council
NSPS	new source performance standards
OMB	Office of Management and Budget
OPP	Office of Pesticide Programs
OSHA	Occupational Safety and Health Administration
OTC	over-the-counter (drugs)
PCB	polychlorinated biphenyl
PIK	Payment-in-Kind (Program)
POTW	Publicly Owned Treatment Works
PPB	parts per billion
PPI	patient package inserts
PPM	parts per million
PSD	Prevention of Significant Deterioration
RCRA	Resource Conservation and Recovery Act

RSIP	Regulatory Strategies Implementation Program
SERI	Solar Energy Research Institute
SSI	Supplemental Security Income
TWA	time-weighted average
UFFI	urea formaldehyde foam insulation
USDA	United States Department of Agriculture
WIC	Women, Infants, and Children (Program)

NOTES

INFANT FORMULA

1. Testimony of Shane Roy, MD, Hearing before the Subcommittee on Oversight and Investigations of the House Committee on Interstate and Foreign Commerce, Ninety-sixth Congress, First Session, 4–9, 1979.
2. *Ibid.*, p. 7.
3. *Ibid.*, p. 8.
4. Letters submitted to the FDA, Docket no. 80N-0025, 1981.
5. Hearing before the Subcommittee on Oversight and Investigations of the House Committee on Energy and Commerce, Ninety-seventh Congress, Second Session, 1982.
6. "Infant Formula: Our Children Need Better Protection," Report of the Subcommittee on Oversight and Investigations of the House Committee on Interstate and Foreign Commerce, Committee Print 96-IFC 42, Ninety-sixth Congress, Second Session, 4, 1980.
7. *Ibid.*, p. 2.
8. S. Rep. No. 96-916, 96th Cong., 2d Sess. 4, 1980.
9. Pub. L. 96-359, 94 Stat. 1190, 21 U.S.C. § 350a Supplement IV, 1980.
10. 47 Federal Register 86362, 30 December 1980.
11. Hearing before the Subcommittee on Health and Scientific Research of the Senate Committee on Labor and Human Resources, Ninety-sixth Congress, Second Session 94, 1980.
12. Testimony of Charles F. Hagan, vice-president, American Home Products Corporation, Hearing before the Subcommittee on Over-

sight and Investigations of the House Committee on Energy and Commerce, Ninety-seventh Congress, Second Session 42–68, 1982.

13. *Ibid.*, p. 66.
14. Testimony of Commissioner Arthur Hull Hayes, Jr., Hearing, *ibid.*, p. 11.
15. *Ibid.*, pp. 7, 25.
16. 47 Federal Register 17016, April 20, 1982.
17. 47 Federal Register 17017.
18. Memorandum from Jeffrey Gibbs to Tom Scarlett, FDA chief counsel, 8 March 1982.
19. Memorandum to the Secretary of the Department of Health and Human Services, from Arthur Hull Hayes, Jr., 11 March 1982.
20. Memorandum of Need—Request for Establishment of an Interagency Agreement, "Economic Analysis of Infant Formula Quality Assurance Regulations," Division of Contracts and Grants Management (HFA-520), 27 October 1981.
21. *FORMULA, et al.,* v. *Schweiker, et al.,* Civ. No. 82–3406, D.D.C., 1 December 1982.
22. "Soyalac Infant Formula Is Being 'Silently' Recalled," *Cleveland Plain Dealer,* 4 August 1983, p. A1.
23. HHS press release, 15 September 1983.
24. Letter from Senators Metzenbaum, Kennedy, Randolph, Pell, Riegle, Matsunaga, and Dodd to Senator Orrin G. Hatch, chairman, Senate Committee on Labor and Human Resources, 20 July 1983.

FOOD AND NUTRITION

1. General Accounting Office, "Future of the National Nutritional Intelligence System," 7 November 1978.
2. Dr. Theodore Cooper, "Dietary Goals for the United States," 2nd ed., Select Committee on Nutrition and Human Needs, US Senate, December 1977, pp. 1–2.
3. Congressional Budget Office (CBO), "Major Legislative Changes in Human Resources Programs since January 1981," August 1983, p. 15; CBO, Letter and Tables to Senator Robert C. Byrd, 15 April 1983.
4. Data from Food and Nutrition Service (USDA).
5. Center on Budget and Policy Priorities, "The Administration's New Budget Proposals for Child Nutrition Programs."
6. CBO, "Major Legislative Changes," p. 15; CBO, Letter and Tables to Senator Robert C. Byrd.
7. Telephone conversation with Carolyn Brickey, Food Research and Action Center, 19 August 1983.
8. *Ibid.*
9. National Archives and Records Service, GSA, "The Weekly Compilation of Presidential Documents," 15 June 1982.

10. CBO, "Major Legislative Changes," p. 15.
11. *Ibid.*
12. *Ibid.*
13. Coalition on Women and the Budget, "Inequality of Sacrifice: The Impact of the Reagan Budget on Women," March 1983, p. 2.
14. CBO, "Demographic and Social Trends: Implications for Federal Support of Dependent-Care Services for Children and the Elderly," June 1983, p. 19.
15. *Ibid.*, p. 22.
16. CBO, "Major Legislative Changes," p. x.
17. *Ibid.*, p. xi.
18. Telephone conversation with Bob Greenstein, Center for Budget and Policy Priorities, 15 October 1983.
19. CBO, "Major Legislative Changes, pp. xi–xii.
20. United States Census Bureau, Current Population Report, #140, "Money Income and Poverty Status of Families and Persons in the United States: 1982," July 1983, p. 60.
21. Center on Budget and Policy Priorities, "The Presidential Task Force," 25 August 1983.
22. *Ibid.*
23. Rick Atkinson, "Reagan Defends Meese Stand," *Washington Post*, 14 December 1983.
24. *Ibid.*
25. Spencer Rich, "500,000 Children May Suffer Malnourishment, Study Shows," *Washington Post*, 12 January 1984.
26. Spencer Rich, "Reagan Task Force Finds No Evidence of Great Hunger," *Washington Post*, 10 January 1984
27. Editorial, "Hunger Commission: No Surprises," *Washington Post*, 9 January 1984.
28. Cass Peterson, "Cost Control Panel to Suggest Cuts Up to $7 Billion," *Washington Post*, 16 April 1983, p. A4.
29. *National Anti-Hunger Coalition, et al.*, v. *Executive Committee of the President's Private Sector Survey on Cost Control, et al.*, Civ. No. 82–3592 (DDC, Memo, 26 July 1983), p. 4.
30. Data from Food and Nutrition Service, USDA.
31. *Ibid.*
32. *Ibid.*
33. *Ibid.*
34. Interview with Lynn Parker, Food Research and Action Center, 10 November 1983.
35. "USDA Abandons School Lunch Rule," *Nutrition Action*, November 1981, p. 3.
36. *Ibid.*
37. System Development Corporation, "The National Evaluation of School Nutrition Programs: Final Report," Vol. 1, April 1983, p. 144.
38. Joint Statement of Joseph Brenner, MD, *et al.*, Subcommittee on

Employment, Manpower, and Poverty, Committee on Labor and Public Welfare, US Senate, 11, 12 July 1967, p. 47.

39. United Nations, "Population Bulletin of the United Nations," No. 14–1982, 1983.

40. Fair Budget Action Campaign, "Briefing Manual, Reagan Administration's FY '84 Budget Proposals," February 1983, p. 49.

41. Quoted from *New York Times*, 1 April 1982; from *There He Goes Again: Ronald Reagan's Reign of Error*, Mark Green and Gail Mac-Coll, eds. (New York: Pantheon Books, 1983), p. 92.

42. Fair Budget Action Campaign, p. 49.

43. Nick Kotz, "Hunger in America," Subcommittee on Nutrition, Committee on Agriculture, Nutrition, and Forestry, US Senate, 30 April 1979, pp. 42–55.

44. Memorandum from President Ronald Reagan to Edwin Meese III, on the Task Force on Food, August 1983.

45. CBO, "Major Legislative Changes," p. 15.

46. Cf. CBO, "Major Legislative Changes"; phone conversation with Bob Greenstein, Center for Budget and Policy Priorities, 15 September 1983.

47. *Ibid.*

48. *Ibid.*

49. CBO, "An Analysis of the President's Budgetary Proposals for Fiscal Year 1984"; phone Conversation with Bob Greenstein.

50. *Ibid.*

51. Charles Fishman, "Food Stamp Diet Passes Block Family Test," *Washington Post*, 5 August 1983, p. A7.

52. John Mintz, "Food Stamp Recipients Call Block's Experiment a 'Publicity Stunt,'" *Washington Post*, 5 August 1983.

53. *Ibid.*

54. *Ibid.*

55. Preliminary Report, "Characteristics of Food Stamp Households," Food and Nutrition Service, USDA, July 1982.

56. Gladys L. Baker, *et al.*, "Century of Service: The First 100 Years of the United States Department of Agriculture," Government Printing Office, 1963, pp. 22–23.

57. *Ibid.*, p. 33.

58. *Ibid.*

59. *Ibid.*, p. 79.

60. Food Safety and Inspection Service, "Food News for Consumers," May 1982.

61. Kathleen Hughes, "Return to the Jungle," Center for Study of Responsive Law, 1983, p. 27.

62. *Ibid.*

63. Kathleen Hughes, "Inspected Meat," *New York Times*, 2 April 1983.

64. Cf. *ibid*, Kathleen Hughes, "Return," pp. 30, 45.

65. Press release, Better Government Association, 19 September 1983.

66. Carol Foreman, testimony before the Senate Committee on Agriculture, 11 August 1982, p. 16.

67. *Ibid.*

68. Marian Burros, "Residue of Chemicals in Meat Leads to Debate on Hazards," *New York Times.*

69. *Ibid.*

70. Telephone conversation with Thomas Smith, Public Voice for Food and Health Policy, 16 September 1983.

71. Marian Burros, "Residue."

72. Thomas B. Smith, "A Market Basket of Food Hazards: Critical Gaps in Government Protection," Public Voice for Food and Health Policy, April 1983, p. 44.

73. *Ibid.*, p. 43.

74. *Ibid.*, p. 41.

75. *Ibid.*, p. 47.

76. Marian Burros, "Residue."

77. *Ibid.*

78. Thomas Smith, "A Market Basket," p. 54.

79. Kathleen Hughes, "Return," p. 61.

80. Thomas Smith, "Market Basket," p. 50.

81. Telephone conversation with Thomas Smith.

82. *Ibid.*

83. Kathleen Hughes, "Return," p. v.

84. William B. Schultz, "What's Wrong with 'Just a Little Bit' of Cancer?" *Public Citizen,* Summer 1983, p. 15.

85. *Ibid.*

86. *Ibid.*

87. *Ibid.*

88. *Ibid.*

89. *Ibid.*

90. *Advertising Age,* 6 September 1979.

91. Carol Foreman, testimony before the Senate Committee on Appropriations, 16 July 1980, p. 254.

92. Interview with Carol Foreman, 17 June 1983.

93. Phone conversation with Greg Moyer, Center for Science in the Public Interest, 16 November 1983.

94. *Ibid.*

95. Public Affairs Office, American Dietetic Association, 16 November 1983.

96. Interview with Michael Jacobson, Center for Science in the Public Interest, 19 August 1983.

97. Greg Moyer, "Trashing Nutrition at USDA," *Nutrition Action,* July–August 1982, p. 8.

98. "USDA Reneges on Promise to Provide Free Guidance on Low-Fat Diets," *Nutrition Action,* May 1983, p. 5.

99. Greg Moyer, "Trashing Nutrition," p. 7.
100. *Ibid.*
101. *Ibid.*, p. 6.
102. Interview with Carol Foreman, 17 June 1983.
103. 44 Federal Register, 40016–40041, 5 July 1979.
104. Federation of American Societies for Experimental Biology, "Evaluation of the Health Aspects of Sodium Chloride and Potassium Chloride as Food Ingredients," 1979, p. 36.
105. Statement by Center for Science in the Public Interest, House Subcommittee on Health and the Environment, Committee on Energy and Commerce, 25 September 1981, p. 337.
106. Cf. Victor Cohn, "FDA Reports Progress Against Too-Salt Diet," *Washington Post,* 10 March 1982, p. A10; *FDA Talk Paper: Salt and Potassium Chloride,* 17 August 1979.
107. Dr. Arthur H. Hayes, testimony before House Subcommittee on Health and the Environment, Committee on Energy and Commerce, 25 September 1981, p. 198.
108. Center for Science in the Public Interest, Statement before Subcommittee on Health and the Environment, *op. cit.,* p. 328.
109. Statement of Congressman Neal Smith (Iowa), Subcommittee on Health and the Environment, pp. 168–69.
110. Statement of Congressman Albert Gore, Jr. (Tennessee), Subcommittee on Health and the Environment, p. 172.
111. Testimony of Congressman Henry A. Waxman (California), Subcommittee on Health and the Environment, p. 175.
112. Statement of Dr. Arthur H. Hayes, Subcommittee on Health and the Environment, p. 185.
113. Testimony of Congressman Henry A. Waxman (California), Subcommittee on Health and the Environment, p. 186.
114. Testimony of Congressman James H. Scheuer (New York), Subcommittee on Health and the Environment, p. 194.
115. Statement of William E. Dickinson, president of the Salt Institute, Subcommittee on Health and the Environment, p. 206.
116. *Center for Science in the Public Interest, et al.,* v. *Arthur Hull Hayes, Jr., Commissioner, Food and Drug Administration, et al.,* Civ. No. 83–0801 (D.D.C., Memorandum, 22 July 1983), p. 10.
117. Food and Drug Administration, "FDA Consumer," April 1983.
118. 47 Federal Register 28214, 28215–28223, 29 June 1982.
119. 41 Federal Register 17535, 27 April 1976.
120. *Community Nutrition Institute* v. *Butz,* 420 F. Supp. 751, D.D.C., 1976.
121. 43 Federal Register 26416, 20 June 1978.
122. Letter from Carol Tucker Foreman, USDA assistant secretary for Food and Consumer Services, to Rosemary Mucklow, executive director, Pacific Coast Meat Association, 30 May 1979.

123. 47 Federal Register 28214, 29 June 1982.
124. *Community Nutrition Institute, et al.,* v. *Block* (D.D.C., 1 December 1982).
125. GAO Report to the Congress: "Federal Regulation of Meat and Poultry Products—Increased Consumer Protection and Efficiencies Needed," 4 May 1983.
126. Presidential proclamation announcing National Consumers' Week, 21 January 1982.
127. Interview with Ellen Haas, Public Voice for Food and Nutrition, 24 June 1983.
128. Jeffrey H. Birnbaum, "Some Farmers Like It, But Critics Call PIK a Major Miscalculation," *Wall Street Journal,* 19 July 1983.
129. CBO, "Major Legislative Changes," *op. cit.,* pp. 34, 39–40.
130. Thomas J. Moore, "PIK: The Costliest Farm Subsidy Plan Yet," *Chicago Sun-Times,* 29 May 1983, p. 4.

DRUGS

1. *Burlington Free Press,* 16 June 1982, p. 9A.
2. *Labeling of Salicylate-Containing Products, Advance Notice of Proposed Rulemaking,* 47 Federal Register 57886, 28 December 1982.
3. *Ibid.*
4. *Public Citizen Health Research Group* v. *Hayes,* Civil Action No. 82–1346, D.D.C., 16 May 1982.
5. Press release, Department of Health and Human Services, 4 June 1982.
6. *Wall Street Journal,* 6 June 1983, p. 1.
7. Interview with Sidney M. Wolfe, MD, director, Public Citizen Health Research Group.
8. "Tamper-Resistant Packaging Is Feasible for Drug Items, US-Industry Panel Says," *Wall Street Journal,* 8 October 1982.
9. *Tamper-Resistant Packaging Requirements for Certain Over-the-Counter Human Drug and Cosmetic Products,* 47 Federal Register 50442, 5 November 1982.
10. Kaufman, *et al., Over-the-Counter Pills That Don't Work* (New York: Pantheon Books, 1983), p. xiv.
11. *Ibid.,* p. xiv.
12. 1962 Amendments to the Federal Food, Drug, and Cosmetic Act, 21 U.S.C. §§ 321(p), 355.
13. 37 Federal Register 85, 5 January 1972; 37 Federal Register 9464, 11 May 1972.
14. *Cutler* v. *Kennedy,* 475 F. Supp. 838 D.D.C., 1979.
15. *Cutler* v. *Hayes,* 549 F. Supp. 1341, D.D.C., 1982.
16. Report of the General Accounting Office, "FDA's Approach to Reviewing Over-the-Counter Drugs Is Reasonable, but Progress Is Slow," 26 April 1982, p. 7.

17. Affidavit of Joy M. Dowling, evaluator for General Accounting Office, filed in *Cutler* v. *Hayes, supra.*

18. Federal Food, Drug, and Cosmetic Act, 21 U.S.C. §§ 321(p), 355.

19. *Ibid.*, §§ 355(d).

20. *Ibid.*

21. "FDA Wasn't Told of British Oraflex-Related Deaths," *Washington Post*, 22 September 1982, p. A20.

22. Food and Drug Administration, Statistical Review and Evaluation of NDA No. 18–250, 13 August 1981.

23. Interview with Sidney M. Wolfe, MD, director, Public Citizen Health Research Group.

24. "FDA Wasn't Told."

25. Eli Lilly and Company, Six-Month Report to FDA for the Quarter Ending 30 July 1982.

26. Letter from Pharmaceutical Division, Eli Lilly and Company, 29 June 1982.

27. Letter from Sidney M. Wolfe, MD, director, Public Citizen Health Research Group, to Richard Schweiker, secretary, Department of Health and Human Services, 22 July 1982. Most of these adverse reactions were minor and involved skin sensitivity.

28. "FDA Wasn't Told."

29. Report by Public Citizen Health Research Group, "Decreased FDA Law Enforcement during 1981," 28 July 1982; letter from Sidney M. Wolfe, MD, director, Public Citizen Health Research Group, to John D. Dingell, chairman, House Committee on Energy and Commerce.

30. Figures are for 1978–81, Pharmaceutical Manufacturers' Association newsletter, 24: 3, 25 January 1982.

31. *Ibid.*, for example, the FDA took an average of 21 months in 1980 and 23.3 months in 1981.

32. 45 Federal Register 60773, 12 September 1980; letter from Alexander Grant, associate commissioner for Consumer Affairs, Food and Drug Administration, to Sidney M. Wolfe, MD, director, Public Citizen Health Research Group, 25 September 1980.

33. Drug Abuse Warning Network, *1980 DAWN Annual Report.* DEA Contract Nos. 81–3, US Drug Enforcement Administration, 1981.

34. "Prescription Drugs Used Improperly, FDA Chief Says," *Washington Post*, 30 July 1983.

35. New Drug and Antibiotic Regulations (proposed rule), 47 Federal Register 46622, 19 October 1982.

36. The FDA frequently denies members of the public access to raw data on the grounds that they contain secret trade information. The Public Citizen Health Research Group, however, has succeeded, on a number of occasions, in obtaining access to raw data through the Freedom of Information Act, 5 U.S.C. § 552. If drug companies are not required to submit raw data to the FDA, then members of

the public would forever be denied the opportunity to review it.

37. Sidney M. Wolfe, M.D., "Survey of FDA (Office of New Drug Evaluation) Medical Officerson Proposed Revisions to New Drug Approval Process," December 16, 1982.

38. 425 U.S. 748, 1976.

39. *Competition in the Drug Industry*, Hearings before the Subcommittee on Oversight and Investigations of the House Committee on Energy and Commerce, Ninety-seventh Congress, First Session, 5, 1981; American Association of Retired Persons News Bulletin, XXIII: 2, March 1982 p. 8.

40. Schultz, "*United States* v. *Generix:* A Preview," 37 F.D.C.L.J. 337, 1982.

41. "Post-1962 ANDA Reg. Proposal in the Works Would Build in Fifteen-Year Gap between Pioneer Approval Date and Generic Eligibility for ANDA," F.D.C. Reports, 8 March 1982, p. 6.

42. Office of Technology Assessment, "Patent-Term Extension and the Pharmaceutical Industry," 1981.

43. "An Unwanted Patent Stretch," *New York Times* (editorial), 7 August 1982.

44. "Who Did Best and Worst Among the 500?" *Fortune*, 2 May 1983, p. 226; "Corporate Scoreboard," *Business Week*, 16 May 1983, p. 55.

PRODUCT SAFETY

1. David R. Pittle, "Regulatory Trends at the National Consumer Product Safety Commission," *Consumerism: A New Force in Society* (Lexington, MA: D.C. Heath, 1976).

2. Wendy Swallow, "Consumer Product Agency Is Battling for Its Independence and Its Life," *National Journal*, 27 June 1981, p. 1163.

3. Ann Lower, Ann Averyt, David Greenberg, "On the Safe Track: Deaths and Injuries, Before and After the Consumer Product Safety Commission," Consumer Federation of America, 15 September 1983.

4. Statement of Henry Waxman, Consumer Product Safety Amendments of 1983, *Congressional Record*, House of Representatives, 20 June 1983, H4111.

5. Statement of Henry Waxman, Consumer Product Safety Amendments of 1983, *Congressional Record*, H4760, 29 June 1983.

6. Jean Cobb, "Recalling Consumer Safety," Common Cause, May–June 1983, p. 29.

7. Wendy Swallow, "Consumer Product Agency," p. 1163.

8. Henry Waxman, 20 June 1983.

9. Consumer Product Safety Amendments of 1983, *Congressional Record*, House of Representatives, H4758 29 June 1983.

10. Molly Sinclair, "Inside the Consumer Product Safety Commission," *Washington Post*, 10 March 1983.

11. Henry Waxman, 20 June 1983.

12. "Warning: Reaganomics Is Still Harmful to Consumers," National Consumers League, January 1983, p. 12.
13. Interview with David Pittle, former commissioner of CPSC, 14 September 1983.
14. Wendy Swallow, p. 1164.
15. Jean Cobb, "Recalling Consumer Safety," p. 30.
16. *Ibid.*
17. "Warning: Reagonomics Is Harmful to Consumers," National Consumers League *et al.*, January 1982, p. 27.
18. Jean Cobb, "Recalling Consumer Safety," p. 30.
19. Margaret G. Warner, "Rise of Consumer Agency's Chief: A Tale of Ambition in Washington," *Wall Street Journal*, 6 July 1982.
20. Ronald Brownstein and Nina Easton, *Reagan's Ruling Class* (Washington, DC: The Presidential Accountability Group, 1982), p. 682.
21. Margaret G. Warner, "Rise of Consumer Agency's Chief."
22. Caroline Mayer, "Consumer Product Safety Chairman Perks Along," *Wall Street Journal*, 8 October 1981.
23. Margaret G. Warner, "Rise of Consumer Agency's Chief."
24. Caroline Mayer, "Consumer Product Safety Commission Director Quits, Slams Chairman," *Washington Post*, 23 October 1981.
25. *Gulf South Insulation, et al.*, v. *Consumer Product Safety Commission*, Nos. 82–4218, 82–4136, 82–4311, 82–4135, US Court of Appeals, Fifth Circuit, 7 April 1983.
26. 47 Federal Register, No. 64, Part IV, 2 April 1982.
27. Jeanne Sadler, "US Won't Ask High Court to Reinstate Ban on Use of UFFI," *Wall Street Journal*, 26 August 1983.
28. *Ibid.*
29. *Athlane Industries, Inc.* v. *CPSC*, 707.72d 1485 (D.C. Cir., 1983)
30. Molly Sinclair, "Court Rules Out Fines by Consumer Product Safety Commission," *Washington Post*, 14 May 1983.
31. P.L. 92-573; Consumer Product Safety Act, E6(b), 15 U.S.C. E2055(b).
32. *GTE Sylvania, Inc.*, v. *Consumers Union of the United States*, 445 U.S. 375, 1980.
33. Response to Public Citizen Health Research Group, 6 May 1982; Freedom of Information Request, 8 June 1983.
34. P.L. 92-573; 1981 amendments.
35. Michael Hinds, "Consumer Product Agency: Small but Busy," *New York Times*, 30 April 1983, p. 17.
36. *Ibid.*
37. *Ibid.*
38. Interview with David Pittle.
39. Interview with CPSC enforcement staffperson, 29 November 1983.
40. "1982 Annual Report," US Consumer Product Safety Commission, pp. 5–13.
41. CPSC Re-authorization Hearings, June 1983.

THE HEALTH AND SAFETY OF WORKERS

1. Patricia Theiler, "Slacking Off on Worker Safety," *Common Cause* magazine, May/June 1983, p. 20.
2. Philip J. Simon, *Reagan in the Workplace, Unraveling the Health and Safety Net* (Washington, DC: Center for Study of Responsive Law, 1983), p. 71.
3. Testimony of Tom Larson, Hearing before the Committee on Government Operations, House of Representatives, 21 June 1982, p. 45.
4. *Ibid.*, p. 46.
5. R. Brownstein and N. Easton, *Reagan's Ruling Class* (Washington, D.C.: Presidential Accountability Group, 1982), p. 236.
6. *Ibid.*, p. 237.
7. Simon, *Reagan in the Workplace*, p. 3.
8. Hearing before a Subcommittee of the Committee on Appropriations, House of Representatives, 16 March 1983, p. 803.
9. Stephen G. Crapnell, "Unions Step Up Their Attacks on OSHA," *Occupational Hazards*, October 1982.
10. Bertram Cottine, speech before a Public Citizen Forum, 31 August 1983.
11. R. Brownstein and N. Easton, *Reagan's Ruling Class*, p. 238.
12. Bertram Cottine, *op. cit.*
13. K. Sawyer and Pete Earley, "OSHA Befriends Industry, but Draws New Fire," *Washington Post*, 5 July 1983.
14. P.L. 91–596.
15. *Ibid.*
16. *New York Times*, 19 February 1978.
17. 28 November 1981.
18. Testimony of Stephen M. Hessl, MD, Hearing before the Committee on Government Operations, House of Representatives, 21 June 1982, p. 28.
19. Joanne Grozuczak, *Poisons on the Job: The Reagan Administration and American Workers* (San Francisco: Sierra Club, Natural Heritage, report no. 4, October 1982).
20. Philip J. Simon, *Reagan in the Workplace*, p. 4.
21. R. Brownstein and N. Easton, *Reagan's Ruling Class*, p. 239.
22. Statement of Thorne Auchter before the Subcommittee on Administrative Law and Governmental Relations of the House Committee on the Judiciary, 16 June 1983, pp. 1–2.
23. Letter to T. Timothy Ryan, Jr., US Department of Labor, from Christopher DeMuth, Administrator for Regulatory Affairs, OMB, 16 August 1982.
24. K. Sawyer and Pete Earley, "OSHA Befriends Industry."
25. "Inside OSHA," *Washington Post*, 18 March 1983.

26. Cass Peterson, "OSHA May Drop Standard Setting Efforts," *Washington Post,* 21 September 1983.
27. Philip J. Simon, *Reagan in the Workplace,* p. 53.
28. "Cotton Dust" (Washington, DC: US Department of Labor, OSHA, 1980), Worker Health Alert, #3065, p. 2.
29. Testimony of Lori Abrams, Public Citizen's Health Research Group, "Proposed Revisions in the Cotton Dust Standard," 23 September 1983, p. 1.
30. "Cotton Dust," p. 3.
31. *American Textile Manufacturers Association, et al.,* v. *Raymond Donovan, Secretary of Labor, et al.,* No. 79–1429, June 17, 1981.
32. Abrams, p. 2.
33. Joanne Grozuczak, *Poisons on the Job,* p. 8.
34. Ruth Ruttenberg, "Compliance with the OSHA Cotton Dust Rule," Office of Technology Assessment, March 1983.
35. Telephone interview with Eric Frumin, 25 October 1983.
36. Joanne Grozuczak, *Poisons on the Job,* p. 8.
37. *United Steelworkers of America, AFL-CIO-CLC* v. *Marshall,* no. 79–1048 US Court of Appeals, 13 August 1980.
38. Joanne Grozuczak, *Poisons on the Job,* p. 9.
39. Hearings before a Subcommittee of the Committee on Appropriations, House of Representatives, 16 March 1983, p. 751.
40. Letter to Thorne Auchter from Sidney M. Wolfe, MD, 13 August 1981, p. 3.
41. S. Wolfe, B. Freese, and E. Bargmann, Health Research Group Report on EtO, 24 November 1982.
42. *Ibid.*
43. *Ibid.*
44. Hearings before a Subcommittee of the Committee on Appropriations, p. 726.
45. *Ibid.*
46. Court of Appeals, *PCHRG, et al.,* v. *Thorne Auchter, Assistant Secretary of Labor, OSHA, et al.,* D.C. Civil Action No. 81-02343, 15 March 1983, p. 6.
47. Hearings appropriations.
48. Memoranda between R. Leonard Vance, Director, Health Standards Programs, OSHA, and Peter F. Infante, Director, Office of Carcinogen Identification and Classification, concerning reproductive risk assessment for EtO, dated 23 August, 25 August, and 16 September 1983; Howard Kurtz "OSHA Official Blocked Efforts to Restrict Chemical," *Washington Post,* 11 November 1983.
49. *American Petroleum Institute, et al.,* v. *OSHA, et al.,* US Court of Appeals, Fifth Circuit, 5 October 1978.
50. Felicity Barringer, "OSHA Announces Intent to Propose Stiffer Benzene Standards," *Washington Post,* 1 April 1983.

51. Letter to Thorne Auchter from Sidney M. Wolfe and Barbara Freese, 14 April 1983.

52. Petition Requesting a Reduced Exposure Level for Benzene through an Emergency Temporary Standard Issued under the Authority of the Occupational Safety and Health Act, 4 April 1983.

53. Letter from Thorne Auchter to Sidney M. Wolfe, 1 July 1983, p. 7.

54. Personal conversation with Sidney M. Wolfe, MD, director of Public Citizen's Health Research Group, May 1983.

55. Transcript, "First Camera," NBC News, 25 September 1983, p. 25.

56. Harvey Lipman, "Letting America's Workers Die," City Paper, 30 September 1983, p. 1.

57. Transcript, "First Camera," p. 26.

58. Philip Shabecoff, "EPA Bars Use of Pesticide but Safety Rules are Blocked," New York Times, 1 October 1983, pp. 1, 12.

59. Harvey Lipman, "Letting America's Workers Die."

60. Cass Peterson, "OSHA Ignored Cancer Risk," Washington Post, 15 September 1983.

61. Cass Peterson, "OSHA May Drop Standard Setting Efforts," pp. 1, 8.

62. Hearings before a Subcommittee of the Committee on Appropriations, p. 726.

63. Ibid., p. 729.

64. Harvey Lipman, "Letting America's Workers Die," p. 6.

65. Ibid., p. 1.

66. Transcript, "First Camera," p. 38.

67. Cass Peterson, "OSHA Ignored Cancer Risk," op. cit.

68. Felicity Barringer, "Budget Office Deals Another Blow to the Controls Proposed for EDB," Washington Post, 31 October 1983.

69. Ibid., pp. 26–27.

70. Statement of Steve Wodka before the Manpower and Housing Subcommittee, House Committee on Government Operations, 28 June 1983.

71. Statement of Steve Wodka before OSHA Hearing on Proposed Chemical Hazard Communication Standard, 15 June 1982.

72. Hearings before the Manpower and Housing Subcommittee, House Committee on Government Operations, 28 June 1983, p. 135.

73. Joann S. Lublin, "Emergency Rule on Exposure to Asbestos Is under Serious Consideration by OSHA," Wall Street Journal, 26 August 1983, p. 2.

74. "Emergency Ruling Set by Job Agency on Asbestos Peril," New York Times, 3 November 1983.

75. Joanne Grozuczak, Poisons on the Job, p. 16.

76. Michael Wines, "Auchter's Record at OSHA Leaves Labor Outraged, Business Satisfied," National Journal, 1 October 1983, p. 2008.

77. Barbara Freese and Sidney M. Wolfe, MD, "Decreased Law Enforcement at OSHA: FY 1982," 8 November 1982.

78. "OSHA Enforcement under the Reagan Administration: An Update," AFL-CIO Report, May 1983.
79. Michael Wines, "Auchter's Record."
80. *Ibid.*, p. 2009.
81. *Ibid.*, p. 2008.
82. OSHA news release, "Individual Establishment Safety Inspection Targeting Plan Announced by OSHA," 23 September 1981.
83. "OSHA Enforcement," p. 2.
84. "OSHA Enforcement," p. 3.
85. *Ibid.*
86. "OSHA Enforcement," *op. cit.*
87. K. Sawyer and Pete Earley, "OSHA Befriends Industry."
88. "OSHA Enforcement."
89. Philip J. Simon, *Reagan in the Workplace*, p. 32.
90. *Ibid.*, p. 9.
91. *Ibid.*, p. 34.
92. *Ibid.*, p. 47.
93. *Ibid.*, p. 66.
94. *Ibid.*
95. *Ibid.*, p. 67.
96. "OSHA Enforcement," p. 1.
97. Wodka testimony, 23 June 1983.
98. Philip J. Simon, *Reagan in the Workplace*, p. 72.
99. *Ibid.*, pp. 73–74.
100. *Ibid.*
101. OSHA news release, 12 July 1982.
102. *Ibid.*, 1 February 1982.
103. *Ibid.*, 12 July 1982.
104. Philip J. Simon, *Reagan in the Workplace*, p. 7.
105. *Ibid.*
106. Thorne Auchter, An Address before the American Occupational Health Conference, Toronto, Ontario, 28 April 1982, p. 12.
107. George Miller, "OSHA Sure Is Backsliding," *Washington Post*, 30 January 1982.
108. "OSHA Calling Card," *New York Times*, 5 October 1982.
109. Hearings before a Subcommittee of the Committee on Appropriations, p. 679.
110. Interview with Philip J. Simon, 27 November 1983.
111. Hearings before the Subcommittee on Investigations and Oversight of the Committee on Science and Technology, House of Representatives, Ninety-seventh Congress, 16 July 1981, p. 72.
112. Joann S. Lublin, "Worker Access to Health and Safety Records Would Be Narrowed under OSHA," *Wall Street Journal*, 5 March 1982.
113. Auchter address. See note 106.

114. Ben A. Franklin, "Novel Pressures in Toxic Labels Case," *New York Times*, 23 March 1982.
115. Michael Wines, "Auchter's Record," p. 2012.
116. Hearings on Appropriations, p. 830.
117. Michael Wines, p. 2012.
118. Cass Peterson, "Chemical Industry Is Now Supporting Administration Proposal for Labeling," *Washington Post*, 23 September 1983.
119. Michael Wines, p. 2012.
120. Cass Peterson, "Chemical Industry."
121. Charles Piller, "Business Applauds Proposal," *In These Times*, 11–24 August 1982, p. 9.
122. Cass Peterson, "Chemical Industry."
123. Felicity Barringer, "Workers Get Access to Health Hazard Information," *Washington Post*, 22 November 1983.
124. *Public Citizen, Inc., et al.*, v. *Thorne G. Auchter*, United States Court of Appeals for the Third Circuit, 22 November 1983.
125. Felicity Barringer, "Workers Get Access."
126. P.L. 91–596.
127. Thorne Auchter, An Address, p. 3.
128. Philip J. Simon, *Reagan in the Workplace*, p. 14.
129. Pete Earley, "Exodus in Progress at Safety Agency Unit," *Washington Post*, 2 April 1982.
130. Harvey Lipman, "Letting America's Workers Die," p. 6.
131. Pete Earley, "Exodus."
132. Philip S. Simon, *Reagan in the Workplace*, p. 15.
133. Hearings before the Subcommittee on Investigations and Oversight, p. 1.
134. R. Brownstein and N. Easton, *Reagan's Ruling Class*.
135. Interview with Sidney M. Wolfe, MD, 31 October 1983.

ENVIRONMENTAL PROTECTION

1. Michael de Courcy Hinds, "Capable Administrator, Anne McGill Gorsuch," *New York Times*, 21 December 1982.
2. Cf. Philip Shabecoff, "EPA and Aide Reach Settlement Averting Hearing on Harassment," *New York Times*, 15 February 1983; interview with Hugh Kaufman, 27 March 1983.
3. Dale Russakoff, "EPA Woes Dramatize the Struggle over Pollution Policy," *Washington Post*, 6 March 1983, p. A4.
4. "Texts of Letters on the Resignation," *New York Times*, 10 March 1983.
5. Dale Russakoff and Mary Thornton, "For Ruckelshaus, EPA Job Is More Than Filling Vacant Offices," *Washington Post*, 27 March 1983, p. A5.
6. "White House Is Portrayed as Eager to Aid Congressional Probes of EPA Operations," *Wall Street Journal*.

7. "Shuffling EPA Inadequate, Environmentalists Say," *Washington Post*, 29 March 1983.

8. National Wildlife Federation, *The Full Story behind the EPA Budget Cuts*, 4 February 1983, p. 7.

9. Harris Survey, "Substantial Majorities Indicate Support for Clean Air and Clean Water Acts," 11 June 1981.

10. David Hoffman, "Fresh Start at EPA May End 2 Years of White House Neglect," *Washington Post*, 27 February 1983, p. A2.

11. National Wildlife Federation, *The Full Story*, p. 10.

12. William Drayton, SAVE EPA, "Reagan-Gorsuch EPA Cut Up to 50%, Further 1,000 Staff Cut Also Proposed," 7 December 1982.

13. Robert Boyle, "An American Tragedy," *Sports Illustrated*, 21 September 1982, p. 82.

14. *Ibid.*

15. Mary Thornton, "OMB Pressured EPA, Ex-Aide Says," *Washington Post*, 28 September 1983.

16. Lawrence Mosher, "EPA Reversing Course," *National Journal*, 25 April 1981, p. 743.

17. Jonathan Lash, Natural Resources Defense Council, Statement before the Senate Committee on Appropriations, Subcommittee on HUD and Independent Agencies, May 1983, p. 2.

18. Patrick Leahy, "Report on EPA Enforcement Budget," 8 April 1983, p. 22.

19. Congressional Budget Office, "The Environmental Protection Agency: Overview of the Proposed 1984 Budget," April 1983, p. 3.

20. Leahy, "Report on EPA Enforcement Budget."

21. Stewart Udall, Natural Resources Defense Council Letter.

22. Timothy Wirth, *Congressional Record*, 2 June 1983, H3469; James Scheuer, *Congressional Record*, 2 June 1983 H3471.

23. Lawrence Mosher, "Will EPA's Budget Cuts Make It More Efficient or Less Effective?" *National Journal*, 15 August 1981, p. 1468.

24. Cass Petersen, "EPA Scientists, Budget Officers Wrangle over Grants Program," *Washington Post*, 1 March 1983.

25. Cf. Dale Russakoff, "EPA Woes Dramatize Struggle over Pollution Policy," *Washington Post*, 6 March 1983; "Purported Hit List Targeted Wide Ranging EPA Employee Dismissals," *Inside EPA*, 4 March 1983, p. 2; Eliot Marshal, "EPA's Troubles Reach a Crescendo," *Science*, 25 March 1983, p. 1404.

26. Marshal, "EPA's Troubles Reach a Crescendo."

27. R. Jeffrey Smith, "White House Names New EPA Chief," *Science*, 4 January 1983, p. 36.

28. Howard Kurtz, "EPA Officials Testify about Pressure," *Washington Post*, 19 March 1983.

29. *Ibid.*

30. David Burnham, "1965 Memos Show Dow's Concerns about Dioxin," *New York Times*, 19 April 1983.

31. *Ibid.*
32. General Accounting Office, *Potential Impact of Reducing the Environmental Protection Agency's Budget,* 30 December 1982, p. 12.
33. Congressional Budget Office, "EPA 1984 Budget," p. 6.
34. Eleanor Randolph, "30% Cut in EPA Aid to States Planned, Severe Impact Feared," *Los Angeles Times,* 12 December 1982.
35. Leahy, "Report on EPA Enforcement Budget," p. 3.
36. General Accounting Office, *Potential Impact,* p. 10.
37. *Ibid.,* p. 10.
38. Philip Shabecoff, "Environmental Agency: Deep and Persisting Woes," *New York Times,* 6 March 1983.
39. House Energy-Commerce Committee, Subcommittee on Oversight Investigations, memo, "Update on Administration Enforcement of Key Environmental Statutes," 8 October 1982, p. 2.
40. Cf. David Hawkins, Natural Resources Defense Council, "A Review of Air Pollution Control Actions under the Reagan Administration as of July 1982," p. 25; "A Conversation with Chris Rice," 2 August 1983.
41. Leahy, "Report on EPA Enforcement Budget," pp. 1–10.
42. Cf. Philip Shabecoff, "EPA Said to Lift Penalty for Lead Offense," *New York Times,* 13 April 1982; Nicholas Wade, "Government by Nudge and Wink," *New York Times,* 14 June 1982.
43. Robert Hershey, "EPA Assailed on Rule for Lead in Gasoline," *New York Times,* 26 May 1982.
44. Mosher, "EPA's Budget Cuts," p. 1466.
45. Interview with Anthony Roisman, 28 July 1983.
46. Sandra Sugawara, "EPA Enforcement Team Is Off or Running," *Washington Post,* 23 June 1982.
47. Jonathan Lash, "The Real Scandal at EPA," Presentation to the American Bar Association, 4 March 1983, pp. 5–6.
48. *Ibid.,* pp. 4–5.
49. Cass Peterson, "Carolinians Fighting Toxic Dump, Find No Ally in US Rules," *Washington Post,* 31 March 1983, p. A8.
50. *Ibid.*
51. *Ibid.*
52. Interview with Anthony Roisman, 28 July 1983.
53. *Ibid.*
54. Khristine Hall, Environmental Defense Fund, Testimony before House Committees, 22 July 1983, pp. 13–14.
55. Environmental Defense Fund, Comments on the Interim Hazardous Waste Land Disposal Regulations, 23 November 1982, p. 15.
56. Peter Skinner, P.E., New York State Law Department Environmental Protection Bureau, Testimony before the California State Assembly, 2 February 1982, pp. 5–10.
57. Interview with William Sanjour, 29 June 1983.

58. Interview with Hugh Kaufman, 27 March 1983.
59. Peter Skinner, Environmental Protection Bureau, p. 12.
60. EPA, *Environmental News*, "EPA Pledges Groundwater Protection," 13 June 1982.
61. Environment Defense Fund, "Comments," pp. 63–67.
62. Interview with William Sanjour, 29 June 1983.
63. Environmental Defense Fund, "Comments," pp. 63–67.
64. Cass Peterson, "Carolinians Fighting Toxic Dump."
65. General Accounting Office, "Interim Report on Inspection, Enforcement, and Permitting Activities at Hazardous Waste Facilities," 21 September 1983.
66. Cass Peterson, "Waste Sites May Threaten Health, Group Tells EPA," *Washington Post*, 10 June 1983.
67. Khristine Hall, Environmental Defense Fund, p. 17.
68. *Ibid.*, pp. 17–18.
69. General Accounting Office, "Interim Report," p. 15.
70. *Ibid.*, p. 12.
71. Office of Technology Assessment, Technologies and Management Strategies for Hazardous Waste Control, pp. 17–18.
72. William Sanjour, Testimony before the House Committee on Science and Technology, Subcommittee on Natural Resources, Agriculture Research, and Environment, 30 November 1982.
73. Lawrence Mosher, "Who's Afraid of Hazardous Waste Dumps? Not Us, Says the Reagan Administration," *National Journal*, 29 May 1982, p. 956.
74. *Ibid.*
75. Natural Resources Defense Council, *et al.*, *Hitting Home: The Effects of the Reagan Environmental Policies on Communities across America*, October 1982, p. 9.
76. *Ibid.*
77. Interview with Anthony Roisman, 28 July 1983.
78. "Two EPA Officials Testify Burford-EPA Sought to Slow Superfund Program," *Inside EPA*, 15 April 1983.
79. Philip Shabecoff, "Environmental Agency: Deep and Persisting Woes."
80. Interview with Hugh Kaufman, 27 June 1983.
81. Cf. Friends of the Earth, Natural Resources Defense Council, Wilderness Society, Sierra Club, National Audubon Society, Environmental Policy Center, Environmental Action, Defenders of Wildlife, Solar Lobby, *Indictment: The Case against the Reagan Environmental Record*, March 1982, p. 6; Lash, "The Real Scandal at EPA."
82. Interview with Hugh Kaufman, 27 June 1983.
83. Cf. Charles Babcock, "Months after EPA Settlement, Ohio Cleanup Has Yet to Begin," *Washington Post*, 26 February 1983; Stephen

Kinzer, "Cleanup Delayed at Ohio Waste Site Where Chemicals Leak into Ground," *New York Times*, 4 March 1983; telephone conversation with Jack Garretson, 11 July 1983.

84. Tracy Freedom and David Weir, "Polluting the Most Vulnerable," *The Nation*, 14 May 1983, p. 600.

85. Mary Thornton, "Lawsuit Is Filed for Cleanup of Stringfellow Pit," *Washington Post*, 22 April 1983.

86. Cf. Dale Russakoff, "EPA Woes"; interview with Hugh Kaufman, 27 June 1983.

87. Interview with Hugh Kaufman, 27 June 1983.

88. Cf. Ralph Blumenthal and Raymond Bonner, "Leader in Toxic Dumps Accused of Illegal Acts," *New York Times*, 21 March 1983; N. R. Kleinfeld, "$7 Million Settlement for Cleaning Up Hazardous Waste Dump Draws Fire," *New York Times*, 3 March 1983; Mary Thornton, "Firm under Cloud Got EPA Contract, *Washington Post*, 22 February 1983; Interview with Hugh Kaufman, 27 June 1983.

89. Cf. Cass Peterson and Howard Jurtz, "EPA Speeds Friend's Permit," *Washington Post*, 19 Feb. 1983; Ralph Blumenthal, "Waste Hauler's Business Acts Faulted," *New York Times*, 24 March 1983, p. B12.

90. "EPA to Expand Cleanup List by 133 Dumps," *Wall Street Journal*, 2 September 1983.

91. Cf. *ibid.;* Cass Peterson, "Lawmakers Prod Reagan with Son of Superfund," *Washington Post*, 10 February 1984, p. A17.

92. Phillip Shabecoff, "Dioxin Strategy Adopted by EPA," *New York Times*, 15 December 1983.

93. Telephone conversation with Chris Rice, 5 July 1983.

94. David Hawkins, "A Review of Air Pollution Control Actions," p. 14.

95. Cf. National Clean Air Coalition, *The Clean Air Act*, pp. 68–75; Sandra Sugawara and Philip Hilts, "Clean Air Act Rewrite Tangled in Thicket of Conflicting Interests," *Washington Post*, 2 August 1982.

96. Cf. National Clean Air Coalition, *The Clean Air Act*, pp. 39–45; David Doniger, Natural Resources Defense Council, "Comments on the Environmental Protection Agency's Emissions Trading Policy Statement," 6 July 1982; David Hawkins, "A Review of Air Pollution Control Actions," pp. 16–20.

97. David Hawkins, *ibid.*

98. Friends of the Earth, *et al.*, *Indictment*, p. 4.

99. Sandra Sugawara and Philip J. Hilts, "Clean Air Act Rewrite."

100. EPA Memo quoted in David Doniger's testimony, Subcommittee on Investigations and Oversight of House Committee on Science and Technology, 6 May 1982, p. 4.

101. Telephone conversation with David Doniger, Natural Resources Defense Council, 7 October 1983.

102. Natural Resources Defense Council, *et al.*, *Hitting Home*, p. 7.

103. *Ibid.*, pp. 23–24.

104. Telephone conversation with Harrison Wellford, 24 September 1983.
105. *Ibid.*
106. Dale Russakoff, "Man-Made Air Pollution Blamed for Acid Rain," *Washington Post,* 9 June 1983.
107. Philip Shabecoff, "Scientists Give EPA Chief Varying Views on Acid Rain Problem," *New York Times,* 21 July 1983.
108. Philip Shabecoff, "Ruckelshaus Puts Off Plan to Curb Acid Rain," *New York Times,* 23 October 1983.
109. Thomas Jorling, "Common Sense Wisdom," *Amicus Journal,* Spring 1982, p. 34.
110. Clean Water Action Project, "Fact Sheets on Major Amendments to Clean Water Act," September 1982.
111. Cf. "EPA Proposes Controversial Antidegradation Policy in Water Quality Regs," *Inside EPA,* 15 October 1982; James Banks and Frances Dubrowski, Natural Resources Defense Council, "Clean Water: Act III," *Amicus Journal,* Spring 1982, pp. 28–30; Jack Lorenz and Daniel Weiss, Izak Walton League, "Keeping Water Clean," *New York Times,* 18 April 1983.
112. James Banks and Frances Dubrowski, "Clean Water," p. 34.
113. Robert Flacke, "Cleaner Water in Spite of Reagan's EPA," letter to *New York Times,* 4 October 1982.
114. Dale Russakoff, "Sorting Out Fees and Friends," *Washington Post,* 9 February 1983.
115. Cass Peterson, "EPA to Keep Water-Quality Goals Strong," *Washington Post,* 1 November 1983.
116. Cf. Frances Dubrowski, Natural Resources Defense Council, testimony before the Senate Subcommittee on Environmental Pollution, 4 April 1983, pp. 1–3; Clean Water Action Project, "Uniform Industrial Pretreatment Program Is Necessary," June 1983.
117. Telephone conversation with Fran Dubrowski, 17 September 1983.
118. Cf. interview with Daniel Weiss, 26 July 1983; "EPA, Chafee Negotiate over Nonpoint Controls, beyond BAT Rules in CWA," *Inside EPA,* 24 June 1983, p. 3.
119. Council on Environmental Quality, "Contamination of Ground Water by Toxic Organic Chemicals," January 1981, p. 25.
120. *Ibid.,* p. 30.
121. John Wilke, "EPA Chief Resists Prodding on Water," *Washington Post,* 30 June 1983.
122. Dr. Irving Selikoff, Testimony before House Committee on Science and Technology, 28 July 1983, pp. 17–18.
123. Agency memo, June 1981, p. 15, cited by Maureen Hinkle, policy analyst, National Audubon Society, testimony before the House Agriculture Committee, Subcommittee on Department Oversight Research and Foreign Agriculture, 6 April 1983, p. 5.
124. *Ibid.,* 21 October 1982.

125. *Ibid.*
126. Natural Resources Defense Council, *et al., Hitting Home,* pp. 40–42.
127. Pete Earley, "EPA Adds Restrictions to Use of Pesticides Data," *Washington Post,* 27 May 1983.
128. Cass Peterson, "EPA Pesticide Standard-Setting Challenged in Suit," *Washington Post,* 27 May 1983.
129. Ward Sinclair, "Streamlining at EPA," *Washington Post,* 31 January 1983.
130. *Ibid.*
131. Subcommittee on Department Operations, House Committee on Agriculture, "EPA Pesticide Regulatory Program Study," 17 December 1982, p. 193.
132. *Ibid.,* p. 211.
133. Ward Sinclair, "Streamlining."
134. *Ibid.*
135. Cf. *ibid.;* Keith Schneider, "Hard Times," *Amicus Journal,* Fall 1982.
136. Barton Gellman, "35 Pesticides Face Suspension over Test Data," *Washington Post,* 12 July 1983.
137. Barton Gellman, "Faking It: The Case against Industrial Bio-Test Laboratories," *Amicus Journal,* Spring 1983.
138. "EPA Pesticide Regulatory Program."
139. Interview with Maureen Hinkle, 30 June 1983.
140. Ward Sinclair, "The Return of DBCP, a Classic Tale of Pesticide Registration," *Washington Post,* 1 February 1983.
141. Natural Resources Defense Council, *et al., Hitting Home,* pp. 25–26.
142. Ward Sinclair, "The Return of DBCP."
143. Dale Russakoff, "EPA Places Ban on Major Uses of Toxaphene," *Washington Post,* 19 October 1982.
144. *Ibid.*
145. Jack Anderson, "US Officials Drag Feet on Pesticide Ban," *Washington Post,* 11 January 1983.
146. *Ibid.*
147. *Ibid.*
148. Philip Shabecoff, "EPA Bans Use of Pesticide, but Safety Rules Are Blocked," *New York Times,* 1 October 1983.
149. Andy Pasztor, "US Crackdown on EDB Pesticide Aims to Avoid Disrupting Grain-Product Sales," *Wall Street Journal,* 6 February 1984.
150. Michael Wines, "Scandals at EPA May Have Done in Reagan's Move to Ease Cancer Control," *National Journal,* 18 June 1983, p. 1266.
151. *Ibid.*
152. "Ruckelshaus Says Only President Can Repair Reagan Environmental Image," *Inside EPA,* 22 July 1983, p. 1.

153. "Transcript of Reagan News Parley on Nomination of Ruckelshaus to EPA," *New York Times*, 22 March 1983.

154. *Ibid.*

155. Hedrick Smith, "Movement to Center," *New York Times*, 22 March 1983.

156. Philip Shabecoff, "Ruckleshaus Says Administration Misread Mandate on Environment," *New York Times*, 28 April 1983.

157. Philip Shabecoff, "Ruckleshaus Said to Have Wanted Air Rules Eased," *New York Times*, 28 April 1983.

158. *Ibid.*

159. William Ruckleshaus, speech to National Academy of Sciences, 22 June 1983.

160. "EPA Latest Cost-Benefit Guide Hikes Value of Life by $4.5 Million," *Inside EPA*, 24 June 1983.

161. Cf. Cass Peterson, " 'No Hit Lists' at EPA, Vows Ruckleshaus," *Washington Post*, 5 May 1983; Lawrence Mosher, "Ruckelshaus' First Mark on EPA—Another $165.5 Million for Its Budget," *National Journal*, 25 June 1983.

162. John Wilke, "EPA Chief Resists, Prodding on Water."

163. "OMB Blocks EPA Testimony on Nonpoint Pollution Controls, Citing Costs," *Inside EPA*, 22 July 1983, p. 6.

164. "Ruckleshaus Says Only President Can Repair Environmental Image," p. 5.

165. Cass Peterson, "OMB Letter Calls EPA Too Cautious," *Washington Post*, 19 November 1983.

166. Cf. Philip Shabecoff, "New EPA Chief Seeks More Funds," *New York Times*, 5 December 1983; Save EPA, "Reagan 1985 EPA Budget Gives EPA 1974 Resources," 31 January 1984.

167. *Ibid.*

168. *Ibid.*

TRANSPORTATION SAFETY

1. "Miraculously Saved by an Air Bag," pamphlet by the Automotive Occupant Protection Association, Arlington, Virginia, 1981.

2. "Automobile Occupant Crash Protection, Progress Report No. 3," NHTSA, DOT, July 1980, p. 65.

3. Haddon, Sachman, and Klein, *Accident Research* (New York: Harper and Row, 1964), p. 553.

4. Summary, "The Cost of Automobile Safety Regulations," NHTSA, DOT, March 1982, p. 1.

5. "Planning for Safety Priorities, 1983 Safety Priorities Plan," NHTSA, DOT, May 1983, p. 40.

6. Larry Givens, "Speaking Personally," *Automotive Engineering*, July 1981, p. 5.

7. 42 Federal Register 34289, 15 July 1977.
8. 46 Federal Register, 29 October 1981.
9. Statement by Raymond Peck, administrator, NHTSA, at the news conference announcing rescission of standard 208, 23 October 1981.
10. Statement by Congressman Timothy Wirth, chairman, Subcommittee on Telecommunications, Consumer Protection and Finance, Energy and Commerce Committee, House of Representatives, on the rescission of standard 208, 23 October 1981.
11. "Necessity for Air Bags and Seat Belts," remarks of Senator John Danforth, *Congressional Record*, 5 August 1982, pp. S1000–1001.
12. Alan Parachini, "Air Bags Still Stalled in Controversy," *Los Angeles Times*, 17 July 1983, Pt. VI, p. 1.
13. *State Farm Mutual Automobile Insurance Company* v. *Department of Transportation*, No. 81–2220 (D.C. Cir., June 1, 1982) (Mikva, J.). Included were medical groups such as the American Public Health Association, the American Trauma Society, the American Academy of Pediatrics, the Epilepsy Foundation, the National Spinal Cord Injury Foundation; other major insurance companies included Allstate, Nationwide, Travelers, the Hartford Insurance Group, the National Association of Independent Insurers, the American Insurance Association, and others; the International Association of Chiefs of Police; the National Association of Emergency Medical Technicians; the United Auto Workers; and public interest groups, including Ralph Nader, the Center for Auto Safety, the Disability Rights Center, Public Citizen, Mothers Against Drunk Driving.
14. Comments of William Nordhaus, John Master professor of economics, Yale University, on Notice of Proposed Rulemaking on Federal Motor Vehicle Safety Standard 208—Occupant Crash Protection, NHTSA Docket No. 74–14, Notice 22, 26 May 1981.
15. *Motor Vehicle Manufacturers Association* v. *State Farm Mutual Automobile Insurance Company*, U.S. (1983), 77 L Ed 2d rre, 103 S.Ct. 2856, 51 USLW 4935.
16. John E. Peterson, "Court Says US Erred on Air Bags," *Detroit News*, 24 June 1983, p. 1A.
17. Letter to Secretary of Transportation Elizabeth Dole from Roger B. Smith, chairman of the board, General Motors Corporation, 29 August 1983.
18. Department of Transportation and Related Agencies Appropriations Bill, 1984, Report No. 98–179, Committee on Appropriations, US Senate, 14 July 1983.
19. "A One Man Campaign for Air-Bag Legislation," *Business Week*, 3 October 1983, p. 45.
20. Opening Statement by Chairman John C. Danforth, Surface Transportation Subcommittee Oversight Hearings, US Senate, 13 September 1983.
21. Douglas B. Feaver, "Dole Touts Air Bags as US Fights Them,"

Washington Post, 10 April 1983; Robert D. Hershey, Jr., "Elizabeth H. Dole, Transportation Secretary, a Political and Bureaucratic Force," *New York Times*, 22 August 1983.

22. "Federal Cars to Get Air Bags," DOT press release, 14 March 1983.

23. Bill Peterson, "Reagan Is Finally Picking Up Support in the Boardrooms," *Washington Post*, 19 May 1980, p. A2.

24. John E. Peterson, "Despite Supreme Court Ruling, Airbag Fight Will Continue," *Ward's Auto World*, August 1983, p. 45.

25. 48 F.R., 46822 (29 October 1983); Transcript from Press Conference on Automatic Restraints, Held by Secretary Elizabeth Hanford Dole, 18 October 1983, Washington, DC.

26. "Wirth Accuses DOT of Delay on Automatic Crash Protection," press release by Representative Timothy Wirth, Washington, DC, 18 October 1983.

27. "Danforth: Administration's Auto Safety Decision 'A Lethal Stall,'" press release by Senator John Danforth, Washington DC, 18 October 1983.

28. "A Retrospective Analysis of the General Motors Air Cushion Restraint System Marketing Effort, 1974 to 1976," National Analysts, a Division of Booz, Allen and Hamilton, July 1983.

29. National Coalition to Reduce Car Crash Injuries, 1211 Connecticut Avenue, NW, Suite 802, Washington, DC 20036; attention: Mr. Charles Bruse.

30. "Report on Traffic Accidents and Injuries, 1981," the National Accident Sampling System, NHTSA, DOT, March 1983.

31. *Ibid.*

32. "Automatic Crash Protection Standards," Hearings before the Subcommittee on Telecommunications, Consumer Protection and Finance, Energy and Commerce Committee, House of Representatives, 27 and 30 April 1981, p. 208.

33. *"Automotive Fuel Economy Program,"* Fifth Annual Report to the Congress, US DOT, NHTSA, January 1981.

34. *Washington Post*, 23 November 1976.

35. Edward N. Cole, president of General Motors from 1967 to 1974, in a letter to William Haddon, Jr., MD, president of the Insurance Institute for Highway Safety, 20 January 1977.

36. Paper presented by Joan Claybrook, president, Public Citizen, before the American Bar Association Annual Meeting, Administrative Law Section Panel, 1 August 1983; remarks by Joan Claybrook, Motor Vehicle Occupant Restraint Policy, National Academy of Sciences Conference on Risk Assessment, 1 June 1981.

37. Interview with Jerome Sonosky, Hogan and Hartson, counsel to Mercedes-Benz, 8 September 1983.

38. Letter to administrator, NHTSA, from W. R. F. Bodack, president, Mercedes-Benz of North America, Inc., 28 January 1983.

39. "Crashes That Need Not Kill," film produced by the Insurance

Institute for Highway Safety, Watergate 600, third floor, Washington, DC 20037, 1976.

40. "One Man Dies, Six Injured When Car, Bus Collide, *Washington Post*, 17 September 1983.

41. "Crashes That Need Not Kill."

42. "Crash Claims Life of Second Teen," *Beacon News*, Aurora, Illinois, 4 August 1983.

43. National Accident Sampling System, NHTSA, DOT; "Planning for Safety Priorities, 1983 Safety Priorities Plan," April 1983; "The Economic Cost to Society of Motor Vehicle Accidents," January 1983; "Fatal Accident Reporting System," 1981, National Center for Statistics and Analysis; Preliminary Report, "the Cost of Automobile Safety Regulations," March 1982.

44. "The Economic Cost to Society."

45. Shella Anne Feeney, "Drunk Driving Accident Causes Financial Trauma for Young Family," *Seattle Times*, 23 December 1982.

46. Gladys Kaufman and Barbara Bilge, "Effects of Automobile Accidents upon American Families," prepared for NHTSA, DOT under contract No. DTNH 22-80-C-07695, August 1982.

47. Lorrie R. Rubin, "Children in Automobile Accidents, the Effects on the Family," prepared for NHTSA, DOT, August 1982.

48. "The Economic Cost to Society."

49. "Lewis Favors Moratorium on Auto Rules," *Washington Star*, 11 February 1981.

50. "Actions to Help the US Auto Industry," office of the press secretary, the White House, 6 April 1981.

51. Jane Seaberry, "Auto Industry Relief Plan Outlined by White House," *Washington Post*, 7 April 1981.

52. Louis Mleczko, "US Hit on Auto Policy, Critics Assail Easing of Rules," *Detroit News*, 8 April 1981.

53. Preliminary report, "The Cost of Automobile Safety Regulations," NHTSA, DOT, March 1982.

54. "Planning for Safety Priorities, 1983 Safety Priorities Plan," NHTSA, DOT, May 1983, p. 40.

55. "Motor Vehicle Safety Issues," hearings before the Subcommittee on Telecommunications, Consumer Protection and Finance, Committee on Energy and Commerce, US House of Representatives, Ninety-seventh Congress, First Session, 4 June and 29 July 1981, pp. 68 and 84.

56. Interview with Clarence Ditlow, director, Center for Auto Safety, Twelfth Floor, Dupont Circle Building, 1346 Connecticut Avenue, NW, Washington, DC 20036, 10 August 1983.

57. Statement by Philip Caldwell, president, Ford Motor Company, 16 January 1979.

58. Statement by Raymond Peck, administrator designate, NHTSA, during remarks at the farewell party for Dr. Rhoades Stephenson,

former director of Research and Development, NHTSA, February 1981.

59. Interview with Henry Ford II, chairman of the board, Ford Motor Company, on "Meet the Press," NBC, 30 October 1977.

60. Subcommittee on Telecommunications, Consumer Protection, and Finance, Committee on Energy and Commerce, House of Representatives, 23 March 1982.

61. United States Department of Transportation Launches New Highway Safety Efforts, press release, 14 April 1982.

62. "International Seat Belt and Child Restraint Use Laws, a Study of Occupant Restraint Use Requirements and Their Impact in Foreign Countries," American Seat Belt Council, April 1981.

63. "Estimates of Shoulder Seat Belt Use According to 1979–1982 Surveys, Transport of Canada Road Safety Office, January 1983.

64. "Automobile Occupant Crash Protection."

65. Letter to Raymond Peck, administrator, NHTSA, from William Lehman, chairman, Subcommittee on Transportation Appropriations US House of Representatives, 30 April 1983.

66. House Appropriations Subcommittee Report, Federal Register, 19 August 1982.

67. 44 Federal Register 70204, 6 December 1979.

68. 47 Federal Register 30084, 12 July 1982.

69. "Planning for Safety Priorities, 1983 Safety Priorities Plan," NHTSA, DOT, April 1983, p. 37.

70. Ibid., p. 39.

71. Office of Program Evaluation, NHTSA, DOT, "An Evaluation of Federal Motor Vehicle Safety Standards for Passenger Car Steering Assemblies, Standard 203—Impact Protection for the Driver—and Standard 204—Rearward Column Displacement," NHTSA, DOT Office of Program Evaluation, January 1981, p. 36.

72. Michael Brownlee, et al., "Implications of the New Car Assessment Program for Small Car Safety," Small Car Safety in the 1980s, NHTSA, DOT, December 1980, pp. 117–29.

73. 46 F.R. 48260, 1 October 1981.

74. "Planning for Safety" Priorities, p. 40.

75. Ibid., p. 159.

76. Ibid., p. 160.

77. Joan Claybrook, Jacqueline Gillan, Anne Strainchamps, "Reagan on the Road, the Crash of the US Auto Safety Program," Public Citizen, Washington, DC, September 1982, pp. 1–28.

78. "55 Miles Per Hour Speed Limit: Mid-Year Report," NHTSA, DOT, July 1980; "Reagan on the Road," pp. 45–50.

79. "A Report to the Congress on the Effect of Motorcycle Helmet Use Law Repeal—a Case for Helmet Use," NHTSA, DOT, April 1980; "Planning for Safety Priorities, p. 59; National Center for Statistics and Analyses, NHTSA, DOT, Mrs. Grace Hazard.

80. "Report to the Congress on Motorcycle Helmet Use."

81. J. W. McQuaid, ed., "Plea to Motorcyclists: Wear Your Helmets," *New Hampshire Sunday News*, Manchester, NH, August 1983.

82. Study prepared by Local 3313 of the American Federation of Government Employees, *Transport Specialist*, February 1983.

83. Department of Transportation Appropriations Bill, p. 55.

84. "Reagan on the Road," pp. 51–61.

85. "Small Car Safety Technology," hearings before the Subcommittee on Transportation, Aviation and Materials, and the Subcommittee on Oversight and Investigations, Committee on Science and Technology, US House of Representatives, 30 November and 2 December 1982.

86. 47 Federal Register 30084, 12 July 1982.

87. *Public Citizen, et al.*, v. *NHTSA*, Complaint for Declaratory and Injunctive Relief, Civil Action No. 83–1720, (complaint filed 15 June 1983).

88. *Public Citizen, et al.*, v. *NHTSA*, Civil Action No. 83–1720 (Stip. settlement filed 12 October 1983).

89. 48 Federal Register 26, 7 February 1983, pp. 5690–5701.

90. 46 Federal Register 7025 (22 February 1981); see also "Crash Rating Program Proposed by NHTSA," Insurance Institute for Highway Safety, *Status Report*, 16: 2.

91. Paul Magnusson, "US Isn't Hiding Recalls of Autos, Safety Official Says," *Detroit Free Press*, 12 August 1981, p. D5.

92. David Burnham, "Brake Tests on GM's '80 X-Cars Suggest Wider Recall Is Needed," *New York Times*, 5 January 1983, p. 1.

93. "Department of Transportation Makes Initial Finding of Defect in 1980 X-Body cars," Press Release, Department of Transportation, 14 January 1983.

94. Jack Anderson, "NHTSA's Recall of GM's X-Cars Fatally Delayed," *Washington Post*, 2 July 1983.

95. "GM to Start Sending Notification Letters on X-Body Recall," US Department of Transportation Press Release, 30 March 1983.

96. "Department of Transportation's Investigation of Rear Brake and Lockup Problems in 1980 X-Body Cars Should Have Been More Timely," Comptroller General of the US, 5 August 1983, pp. V 48, RCED-83-195.

97. Richard Severno, "Brake Dispute Touches Many Lives," *New York Times*, 15 August 1983.

98. *The United States of America* v. *General Motors Corporation*, complaint for Declaratory and Injunctive Relief and for Civil Penalties, Civil Action 83-2220, 3 August 1983; "DOT Seeks Recall and Penalty of $4 Million in Suit Against General Motors," DOT press release, 3 August 1983.

99. Warren Brown, "GM X-Car Brake Case Reveals Regulatory System Breakdown," *Washington Post*, 5 September 1983, p. 1.

100. Meeting, Aviation Executive Conference, FAA, 30 June 1981.
101. James Hedlund, Robert Arnold, Exio Cerrelli, and Susan Partyka, NHTSA, Paul Hoxie and David Skinner, Transportation Systems Center, "An Assessment of the 1982 Traffic Fatality Decrease," Department of Transportation, Washington, DC, October 1983.

ENERGY

1. *Out in the Cold* (Washington, DC: National Consumer Law Center, 1983).
2. US Senate, Special Committee on Aging, "Energy and the Aged: The Widening Gap" (Washington, DC, 19 February 1982).
3. *Ibid.*, (9 April 1982) p. 201.
4. *Ibid.*, p. 74.
5. US Senate, "Energy Equity and the Elderly in the 80's," 28 October 1980, p. 88.
6. Department of Energy 1984 Budget Highlights, US Department of Energy, Washington, DC, 1983.
7. Memo by Congresswoman Claudine Schneider to Secretary of Defense Casper Weinberger, March 1981.
8. US Senate, Statement of Senator William Cohen, p. 5.
9. *Ibid.* Statement of Jack Ossofsky, executive director, National Council on Aging, p. 73,
10. Northeast-Midwest Institute, *Regional Energy Economics* (Washington, DC, 1982).
11. See note 1.
12. "Energy Debts: The Coming Crisis for the Poor" (Washington, DC: National Consumer Law Center, 1983).
13. Statement by Representative Lewis Stokes, Congressional Record, 8 March 1983, p. 892.
14. Statement by President Carter on the Crude Oil Windfall Profits Tax (Washington, DC, July 1979).
15. US Senate, Statement by Senator John Heinz.
16. US Congress, Joint Economic Committee, Subcommittee on Investment, Jobs, and Prices, *Oil Price Decontrol and the Poor: A Social Policy Failure* (Washington, DC, 1982).
17. See note 1.
18. Ed Petrini, "The Broken Promise" (Washington, DC: National Consumer Law Center, 1982).
19. See footnote 13.
20. US Senate, Special Committee on Aging, "Energy and the Aged" (Washington, DC, 9 April 1981).
21. US Senate, Statement by Senator Edward Kennedy, p. 3.
22. Robert Stobaugh and Daniel Yergin, eds., *Energy Future* (New York: Random House, 1980).

23. Marc Ross and Robert Williams, *Efficient Use of Energy* (New York: American Institute of Physics Conference Proceedings, 1975).

24. Solar Energy Research Institute for the US House of Representatives, Committee on Energy and Commerce, Subcommittee on Energy Conservation and Power, *Building a Sustainable Future*, (Washington, DC, 1981).

25. B. W. Cone, *et al.*, *An Analysis of Federal Incentives Used to Stimulate Energy Production*, Battelle Pacific Northwest Laboratory report to US Department of Energy (Washington, DC: February 1980).

26. Summary of Reagan FY 1984 Energy Budget Request News Release, Subcommittee on Energy Conservation and Power, Committee on Energy and Commerce, US House of Representatives, 4 February 1983.

27. Fifth Annual Report to Congress, Annual Automotive Fuel Economy Program, National Highway Traffic Safety Administration (Washington, DC, 14 January 1981).

28. Amory Lovins, "Funds for Fuel Efficient Vehicles," Congressional Record (Washington, DC, 21 May 1981), p. E2512.

29. Howard Geller, *Energy Efficient Appliances* (Washington, DC: American Council for an Energy Efficient Economy, 1983).

30. Public Citizen's Critical Mass Energy Project, *1982 Nuclear Power Safety Report* (Washington, DC, 1983).

31. US House of Representatives, Committee of the Interior and Insular Affairs, Subcommittee on Oversight and Investigations, Testimony of Theodore Taylor (Washington, DC, 23 October 1981).

32. General Accounting Office, "Nuclear Fuel Reprocessing and Problems of General Accounting Office, Safeguarding against the Spread of Nuclear Weapons," EMD-80-38 (Washington, DC, 18 March 1980).

33. Amory and Hunter Lovings, *Brittle Power: Energy Security for National Security* (Andover, MA: Brick House, 1981).

34. See note 30.

INDEX

ABOUT THE AUTHOR

Public Citizen is a nonprofit citizens' research, lobbying, and litigation organization based in Washington, DC. Since its founding by Ralph Nader in 1971, Public Citizen has fought for consumer rights in the marketplace, for safe products, for a healthy environment and workplace, for clean and safe energy sources, and for corporate and government accountability.

Public Citizen is active in every public policy forum: Congress, the courts, government agencies, and the news media. Support funding comes from the sale of publications and from small individual contributions from citizens throughout the country. Public Citizen fights for citizens through five affiliated groups:

- Congress Watch monitors legislation on Capitol Hill and lobbies for the public interest;
- The Health Research Group fights for protection against unsafe foods, drugs, and workplaces, and for greater consumer control over health decisions;
- The Litigation Group brings precedent-setting lawsuits on behalf of citizens against the government and large corporations to enforce rights and ensure justice under the law;
- The Tax Reform Research Group advocates progressive tax reform and monitors the Internal Revenue Service;

- The Critical Mass Energy Project works for safe, efficient, and affordable energy.

Joan Claybrook has been president of Public Citizen since 1982. During Jimmy Carter's presidency, she served as administrator of the National Highway Traffic Safety Administration. From 1970 to 1977, in association with Ralph Nader, she founded and directed Public Citizen's Congress Watch. For ten years before that, she worked for the Social Security Administration and the Department of Transportation.